Phantom Islands of the Atlantic

Also by Donald S. Johnson:

Charting the Sea of Darkness: The Four Voyages of Henry Hudson
Cruising Guide to the Coast of Maine

PHANTOM ISLANDS
of the ATLANTIC

DONALD S. JOHNSON

GOOSE LANE

Published by Goose Lane Editions, 1994.

Illustrations by Donald S. Johnson.
Interior design by Brenda Berry.
Edited by Laurel Boone.
Printed in Canada by Gagné Printing.

10   9   8   7   6   5   4   3   2

Canadian Cataloguing in Publication Data

Johnson, Donald S., 1932-
   Phantom islands of the Atlantic
   Includes bibliographical references and index.
   ISBN 0-86492-149-7

1. Geographical myths.   2. Legends.   I. Title.

GR940.J64 1994   398'.42   C94-950194-8

Goose Lane Editions
469 King Street
Fredericton, New Brunswick
CANADA E3B 1E5

Contents

For Ewan

Acknowledgements

I AM GRATEFUL TO THE FOLLOWING publishers for permission to quote from their books: Harvard University Press (C.H. Oldfather, trans., *Diodorus Siculus*); Liverpool University Press (Kenneth Baxter Wolf, *Conquerors and Chroniclers of Early Medieval Sp*ain); Oxford University Press (Felipe Fernàndez-Armesto, *Columbus*); Princeton University Press (F. Rosenthal, *The Muqaddimah*); and State University of New York Press (Taris Khalidi, *Islamic Historiography*). I am also grateful to the Hudson's Bay Company Archives for permission to quote from archival material, and to the Newberry Library, Chicago, for kind assistance and for permission to use maps in their collection.

I also wish to thank Yolande Theunissen of the Osher and Smith Cartographic Collections, University of Southern Maine, Portland, Maine, for her help in locating the map of the New World by R. Petri adapted for this book (*Fig. 11-6*) in the Osher and Smith Collections, and for drawing my attention to additional maps found in the Osher and Smith Collections and various other collections, also adapted here.

Preface

I DON'T THINK ANYONE CAN TRULY comprehend just how vast the North Atlantic Ocean is without spending six or seven weeks sailing it in a small boat. One's total world is encompassed within the thin line of the horizon extending in a full circle. It is a monochromatic world — blue sky, blue water — until land is finally reached; then, the green of vegetation and the orange of tile roofs seem so vivid they virtually assault the senses. Five times now I have crossed the Atlantic with my son, Ewan, in our 27-foot schooner. I know the ocean's perils and the fear it engenders, as well as the joys of good sailing, accurate landfalls and new acquaintances.

While working on my previous book, *Charting the Sea of Darkness: The Four Voyages of Henry Hudson*, I spent considerable time reconstructing the historic events, as they were cartographically expressed, that led to his voyages and discoveries. With minor variations, maps of the western reaches of the Atlantic progressed in a relatively logical manner; each expedition to the New World brought forth new information which was incorporated into the maps. Gradually, outlines of North America became more accurate and the empty spaces were filled in. But I noticed also that many islands on these maps seemingly had a life of their own; they emerged without any apparent cause and continually shifted around as though trying to find a place to anchor permanently. They never did — slowly, they disappeared altogether. I became intrigued by these "phantom" islands and started to gather information on them.

My fascination with the islands that never were and my own experiences as a mariner re-discovering personally what had been learned about the Atlantic over a period of centuries led to this book — *Phantom Islands of the Atlantic*.

Readers will not recognize the names of many of these islands; this is precisely why I chose to bring them out of obscurity. The legends that created these islands are as exciting a part of the story as their cartographic record, and they need to be retold lest they, like their pictorial counterpart, fall into oblivion. Not all the nonexistent islands are explored here. According to Al-Idrîsî, a twelfth-century Arab geographer, the Atlantic contained 27,000 islands; even for the sake of completeness, I don't think I, or anyone else for that matter, could sustain a reader's interest *that* long.

The chapter "Mapping the Unknown Seas," a summary of the development of geographical knowledge of the Atlantic, may seem at times to contain gaps and discontinuities, discrepancies, contradictions and apparent regressions in knowledge. However, that is exactly how the learning occurred. As an example of the erratic nature of this process, consider that at the time Christopher Columbus made his historic attempt to reach the Orient by sailing west across the Atlantic, and so to corroborate the theory that the earth is a globe, the earth's place in the universe had not yet been resolved. It wasn't until the mid-sixteenth century that the geocentric schema proposed by Aristotle was replaced with the heliocentric theory of Copernicus; yet that was not a deterrent to Columbus.

As *Phantom Islands* progressed, I became increasingly aware of the number of times I refer to Columbus, that "Admiral of the Ocean Sea." At first, I wanted variation. "After all," I told myself, "this is *not* a book on Christopher Columbus." But I reconsidered. Of all the mariners who played a part in the great Age of Discovery, people are best acquainted with Columbus. His personal life, theories, accomplishments and even failures are all well known, especially after the recent quincentennial celebration of his 1492 voyage. The geographical knowledge in his time serves as a handy benchmark for the discoveries of other voyagers.

I have redrawn all the maps used as illustrations throughout the book from reproductions in various atlases of cartography. Frequently, the replicas in books are of poor quality, second- or even third-generation prints. By converting the maps to line art, I have enhanced the clarity considerably. I have also stripped away all unnecessary detail, thus focusing attention on the relevant information. Unfortunately, line reduction also obliterates the great beauty and full account of history contained in these maps. For further enjoyment and enlightenment, seek out colour photographs of these maps and charts.

I have not attempted to regularize ancient and medieval spellings of place names except in my own writing. Variant spellings appear as they stand in quotations from works by other authors.

Almost all the maps and charts from the time period covered by this book (roughly the thirteenth through the sixteenth centuries) carry captions in Latin; as well, pertinent sections of some texts contain quotations as they were originally written in Latin. I cannot claim that the translations in *Phantom Islands* are the result of my remembering my ancient high school Latin. They are due to the invaluable aid of Liz Peare, who kindly deciphered the countless fragments of manuscripts I gave her. I am particularly grateful to Charles Peirce for his insights into the Saint Brendan story. He was the first to recognize that the history of the Catholic Church in its early years in North Africa, expressed graphically in the floor mosaics of basilicas, used the same symbolic language found in the *Navigatio* of Saint Brendan, and that they both came from a single, common source — the *Book of Revelation* in the New Testament.

At this point it is customary for the author to absolve those who have worked with him for any responsibility for the errors and problems that may be found in the book, and to claim them solely as his own. I don't know when this practice started, but in 1627 Captain John Smith followed it in the preface to his *Sea Grammar*. I will let Captain Smith speak for me:

Honest Readers,

If my desire to doe good hath transported mee beyond myselfe, I entreat you to excuse mee, and take for requitall this rude bundle of many ages observations; although they be not so punctually compiled as I could wish, and it may bee you expect. At this present I cannot much amend them; if any will bestow that paines, I shall thinke him my friend, and honour his endevuors. In the interim accept them as they are, and ponder errours in the balance of good will.

> *Your friend,*
> *John Smith*

Donald S. Johnson
Perry, Maine
March, 1994

Modern map of the North Atlantic Ocean based on the Mercator projection

Introduction

IN THE GLORIOUS AGE OF DISCOVERY, the known world was small and imperfectly understood. The first sailors to venture out across the Atlantic had before them an uncharted wilderness, one that far exceeded in its dangers and its terrors that of any overland travel route; here there were no signposts to guide their way, no precedents to rely upon. Once out of sight of land they were completely on their own, at the mercy of violent storms, while unpredictable winds and currents altered their course. Records of earlier voyages were few and often ambiguous; maps were rare and scant in detail.

Voyages of exploration were sporadic, but when sailors returned from their long voyages, their wondrous tales of strange new lands extended the bounds of the world. Gradually, new lands and islands appeared on maps, filling the heretofore empty spaces. But the cartographer had to be careful about what he showed, lest his observations, no matter how accurate, be considered contrary to Christian dogma.

In the trackless, open ocean where navigation was imprecise, sailors found verifying or refuting geographic features difficult. Cartographers often copied and recopied errors, which remained on maps or charts for centuries. The inability to determine longitude caused some nonexistent islands to appear on early maps, while other geographic fallacies were created by cartographers in their attempts to reconcile widely disparate accounts of discoveries.

Some maps depict entirely mythical islands — islands with names such as Heather-Bleather, Tir-n'an-og, Gog and Magog, Drogeo, Podanda, and Neome. Other nonexistent islands can be attributed to delusion — mirages brought about by atmospheric temperature variation. On the other hand, there are islands remaining on maps today that were once thought to be enchanted and hold special magic power, such as Bermuda, the Isle of Devils, and Bimini, with its fountain of life. But what stimulates the curiosity and excites the imagination are those islands which at one time were thought to exist, but which were eventually removed from maps for lack of verification.

Was the Isle of Demons merely a fable created by pious Christians? Did the sixth-century Irish monk, Saint Brendan, actually travel to distant islands in the Atlantic?

It was not caprice that compelled the medieval cartographer to place these islands on his maps. He did not use them simply to fill the void of a vast sea — a remedy for *horror vacuui*. Embellishments with sea monsters, strange beasts and ships took care of the empty spaces. Discoveries rapidly changed the world order set forth by Aristotle, and cartographers shaped an ancient cosmography into a new, orderly geography based on direct observation, not on a philosophical construct.

Today, fourteenth- and fifteenth-century maps are viewed as the product of the unenlightened Middle Ages, interesting only as footnotes to history. Their geography is not taken seriously but is considered a display of the gross errors that were supplanted by "true" geographic knowledge. Or medieval maps are valued merely for their decorative beauty. But these maps served a far greater function than as visual additions to the narrative tales of explorers. Cartographers tried in every way possible to assure the greatest topographic accuracy. Not only did mariners depend upon maps to prevent their running aground on uncharted shoals or succumbing to other perils of the sea, but the wealth of nations was at stake.

The greatest impetus for voyages of exploration was commerce. In order for the mariner to repeatedly make the same landfall at his port of trade and be able to return to where he started from, he had to have correct charts and maps. Newly discovered lands increased the power of the explorer's sovereign and yielded wealth through trade, or, more directly, through plunder. Islands in the Atlantic were also seen as convenient stepping stones to the Far East and its treasures.

It would be convenient to start a history of geographical exploration of the Atlantic with the very first voyages, and in a neat, chronological order work up through the centuries to present evidence of an increased understanding of the Sea of Darkness, or the Great Green Sea of Gloom, as Arab geographers called it. Unfortunately, this is not possible. The body of knowledge about the Atlantic grew from many simultaneous lines of investigation, sometimes overlapping, sometimes containing large gaps, and even on occasion contradicting one another. But through the centuries one goal remained constant and undiminished in strength — to bring order out of chaos.

Chapter I

Mapping the Unknown Seas

*"The world of reality wears a rich garb that was woven
for it by the world of tradition ages ago."* (C.B. Firestone)

IN THE WESTERN WORLD, THE STUDY OF GEOGRAPHY followed two different paths. Authors of Greek antiquity provided an empirical understanding of the astronomical and mathematical aspects of the geography of the earth. Meanwhile, philosophers pursued their inquiry into the cosmography of the earth. Aristotle used reason and logic to produce a *philosophical* description of the earth, one that in large part remained the accepted view for the next seventeen centuries. But with the development and expanding influence of Christianity, much of this learning was lost. The Church Fathers, in their interpretations of scripture, rejected the knowledge of the ancients and stimulated a rethinking of geographical problems. Individuals like Lactantius found it impossible to accept the concepts of Aristotle, for by necessity they included a belief in an antipodean region that was contrary to Christian dogma. However, some Latin writers of the Roman era, and, later, Muslim historiographers of the eighth through the tenth centuries, maintained the fund of geographical knowledge, and to it they added their own experience.

Until voyages of exploration became more frequent, producing new observations, much of what was known about islands in the Atlantic had been handed down as folklore. Inherited from the past were the fables and legends of Greece and Rome, along with tales from Celtic and Norse mythology. These blended with information brought back by occassional mariners, who, in expanding their trade routes, ventured a bit farther than any before them, or by chance came upon an unknown island when tempestuous weather blew their vessel off course. Gradually, this mixture of legend, speculation and travellers' tales began to be replaced by a new kind of geographic knowledge, one that was the result of direct observation. In the Age of Discovery, islands previously known only through tradition began to be rediscovered and included in history and cartography. At this point, when the geography of tradition gave way to a geography of observation, the phantom islands reached their highest form of cartographic expression.

Until the fifteenth century, history was considered a branch of rhetoric, a discipline in which exaggerated language was used to persuade or influence others. Cicero proclaimed that "rhetors were permitted to falsify somewhat in their histories, in order to make their point more forcibly." The twenty-one centuries of history in this chapter have been condensed and events have been selected in a way that must be regarded as subjective, but there is no intent to deliberately alter history. There is no ultimate authority for what I have put down save my own judgement.

Geographical Knowledge of the Ancients

Mathematical Geography

Scientific investigation into the general form and features of the universe virtually goes back to the beginnings of western civilization. Since Greek antiquity, philosophers have speculated on the physical, mathematical and astronomical aspects of the earth's geography. Anaximander of Miletus (c. 610-540 BC) believed that the earth was disc-shaped, immovable, and rested upon the waters; it was located in the centre of the universe, and around it passed the paths of the sun and moon. The earth could not fall because, "being in the centre, equidistant from all points, there was no more reason why it should move in one direction than in the other, and it would be impossible to move in opposite directions at once."

As early as the sixth century BC, Pythagoras recognized that the earth was not a flat plane, but a globe. Though Pythagoras was correct, he based his hypothesis of the sphericity of the earth on philosophical grounds, much like those used by Anaximander, rather than on any empirical evidence. To Pythagoras, the earth was a sphere "because the sphere was the most perfect form; it was the centre of the universe, because that was the place of honour; it was motionless, because motion was less dignified than rest." Nonetheless, once this cosmological concept was expressed and adapted by Plato in his *Phaedo*, it was never seriously doubted thereafter.

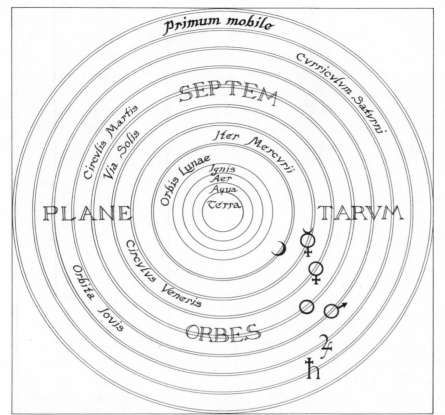

Fig. 1-1.
Spheres of the universe. In Aristotle's theoretical construct of the universe, the earth was completely enclosed by the sphere of water. This did not match what was observed in reality, creating a problem that cosmographers of the Middle Ages tried to reconcile.

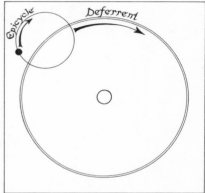

Aristotle (382-336 BC), too, believed in the sphericity of the earth. But rather than basing his belief on speculation and theory, he looked for physical proof. In his treatise *De Caelo*, Aristotle described the properties of the heavenly bodies and summarized the necessity for assuming the earth to be a sphere. He observed "the unvarying circularity of the earth's shadow at eclipses of the moon, and the proportionate change in the altitude of stars resulting from changes in the observer's latitude." Pliny, Cleomedes and other philosophers of natural history also provided proofs.

Aristotle placed the earth at the centre of the universe and surrounded it with spheres of the remaining three elements — water, air and fire. These, in turn, were enclosed by the spheres of the planets: Lunae (Moon), Mercurii (Mercury), Veneris (Venus), Solis (Sun), Martis (Mars), Jovis (Jupiter) and Saturni (Saturn). Each planet was attached to a rotating sphere whose equator inclined in a different plane to the others. Beyond this was a sphere containing the fixed stars. All these spheres were controlled by the outermost sphere, called *Primum mobile*, itself controlled by "divine power."

But this arrangement could not explain all the observed motions of the planets, and in the second century AD, the astronomer Claudius Ptolemaeus (known as Ptolemy) tried to reconcile the discrepancies by introducing a variation into the system. He devised an arrangement wherein the planet rotated in a small circle around a centre, which itself moved in a circle around the earth. The major orbit of the sphere was called the deferrent and the smaller circle at its circumference was called the epicycle. This cosmology, with only small modifications, remained the accepted concept of the universe until the middle of the sixteenth century.

Then, in 1543, Copernicus made a revolutionary departure from the established system. He proposed a heliocentric universe, one with a stationary sun, rather than the earth, at its centre, and with the planets making circular orbits around the sun. In this arrangement, he explained, a year represented one complete circuit of the earth around the sun, while the spinning of the earth on its axis accounted for the alternating pattern of night and day.

Great as these changes were, the basic structure of the cosmological pattern remained unchanged from the time of Aristotle. The universe was still conceived as a finite whole, constructed of a limited number of spheres moving in circles and bound by the outermost, the *Primum mobile*.

Once the globular form of the earth had become unassailable doctrine, successors to Aristotle set about to determine the earth's circumference. Eratosthenes, who flourished in the middle of the third century BC, was an astronomer and mathematician at the library of Alexandria. To determine the circumference of the earth, he measured the meridian altitude of the sun from two different geographic points of latitude on the same day and at the same meridian of longitude. The points he used for these observations were Syene and the gnomon at Alexandria. The linear distance between these two points was known. Eratosthenes then calculated the angle subtended at the centre of the earth, and arrived at a circumference of either 250,000 or 252,000 stadia — the stadium being an ancient Greek measure of length equal to 125 paces, or 182.7 metres (600 feet). This translates into a circumference of 39,375 or 42,336 kilometres (24,452 or 26,291 miles), a surprisingly accurate calculation deviating from the true circumference of the earth, 40,000 kilometres (roughly 25,000 miles), by only 2%-5%.

That there are two different sets of figures is due to uncertainty about whether Eratosthenes used the Olympic foot or the Attic foot to convert stadia into feet. Some scholars of metrology claim that he devised a standard geographical measure, the stadium, composed of feet equal to one-half the Egyptian ell — but there were also two kinds of Egyptian ells, the royal and the common. And there are those who believe that Eratosthenes used a system based on the Egyptian schonus, which contained 16,000 small ells. Whatever standard of measure that Eratosthenes used, he came up with a circumference that was certainly much more accurate than the figure of 400,000 stadia claimed by Aristotle or 300,000 stadia declared by Archimedes.

Hipparchus of Rhodes (c. 167-127 BC), one of the greatest of Greek astronomers and the founder of trigonometry, accepted the calculations of Eratosthenes, as did Strabo in his *Geographia*, Pliny the Elder in *Historia Naturalis*, and other philosophers. But these calculations did not go unchallenged. Posidonius of Rhodes (c. 131-51 BC) devoted several years of his life to scientific research in the western Mediterranean provinces and in North Africa. He made his own estimate of the circumference of the earth by using the difference in altitude of the sun at Canopus in Rhodes and at Alexandria. According to the astronomer and author Cleomedes (c. AD 150-200), Posidonius arrived at a figure of 240,000 stadia — a result remarkably close to the 250,000 stadia of Eratosthenes.

But Strabo reported the Posidonius findings as 180,000 stadia, not 240,000 stadia. It has been suggested that the difference in numbers was due to a subsequent re-evaluation of the distance between Rhodes and Alexandria. Based on a distance of 5000 stadia between the two sites, and a calculated arc of ¹⁄₄₈th part of a

Fig. 1-2.
Measuring the circumference of the earth. The gnomon at Alexandria (C) and Syene (D), on the same meridian of longitude, were observed on the same day and at the same time. There was no shadow at point D, for at its location, the declination of the sun was the same as the latitude at point D. At point C, the angle of the shadow (CFE) cast from the obelisk was 7.2°. For all practical purposes the distance between the sun and the earth may be considered infinite; thus, line ADB and line AFE are parallel. Angle CFE, 7.2°, is then the same as angle CBD. 360° (a circle — in this case the circumference of the earth) divided by 7.2 = 50. The measured distance between points C and D, 800 km (500 mi), is thus ¹⁄₅₀ of the circle. The total circumference of the earth, then, is 800 x 50 = 40,000 km (25,000 mi).

circle, then the circumference would be 240,000 stadia (5000 x 48 = 240,000). Based on a distance of 3750 stadia, the circumference would be 180,000 stadia. The latter figure, in spite of being wrong, became accepted as the true measure of the world — a world 28% smaller in circumference than what Eratosthenes calculated. The work of Eratosthenes had its followers, and so did the writings of Posidonius. This created two main traditions of mathematical geography, which were both handed down through the centuries.

The most notable person to accept the Posidonius figures was Claudius Ptolemaeus, popularly known as Ptolemy. The greatest of all geographers and cartographers of classical antiquity, he created a body of knowledge about astronomy and geography of unrivalled extent.

Little is known of the events of Ptolemy's life other than that he lived during the second half of the second century AD and resided in Alexandria, or close by. Yet that in itself says much, for Alexandria was the ancient seat of enlightenment. The most gifted scholars were to be found in its institutions, and its library contained the wisdom of the ages.

Alexandria was situated along the trade routes where goods from the Far East were brought, bartered and further transported to Europe. It became one of the richest cities in the world. Since it was a meeting place of travellers arriving by overland caravans as well as by sea, Ptolemy had ready access to the latest information from distant lands. This he collected, and he produced an atlas of twenty-seven maps showing all that was known of the inhabited world. It consisted of one "master map" of the entire world, plus twenty-six detailed, regional maps. Accompanying the atlas were eight books containing a catalogue of the latitude and longitude for 8000 geographic localities, plus extensive treatises on the techniques of cartography, astronomy and mathematics. In his most extensive work, *Geographia*, Ptolemy stated:

> One must contemplate the extent of the entire earth, as well as its shape and its position under the heavens, in order that one may rightly state what are the peculiarities and proportions of the part of which one is dealing, and under what parallel [latitude] of the celestial sphere it is located . . . the length of its days and nights, the stars which are fixed overhead, the stars which move above the horizon, and the stars which never rise above the horizon at all. . . . *It is the great and exquisite accomplishment of mathematics to show all these things to the human intelligence.*[1]

As late as the fifteenth century, Ptolemy's work dominated all geographic

Fig. 1-3.
World map of Claudius Ptolemaeus (Ptolemy), from his *Geographia*. Successive editions of the atlas were expanded and modified by the incorporation of new geographical information. This map comes from a 1490 Rome edition. In the second century, Ptolemy knew only two of the Canary Islands, which he called the Fortunate Islands; here the number has been increased to six.

thought; his methods of cartography and concepts of geography were thoroughly studied. According to Ptolemy, "The known world extended in a continuous landmass from the western extremities of Europe to the easternmost limit of Asia, and between the two points lay an intervening ocean." Since he accepted that the earth's circumference was only 180,000 stadia, his estimate of the size of the ocean was correspondingly small.

One of the most important cosmological works of the fifteenth century was *Imago Mundi* by Pierre d'Ailly, a reforming cardinal of Touraine. D'Ailly drew from many sources and helped perpetuate the concept of an extended landmass covering most of the globe, leaving relatively little space for the ocean. Since Pierre d'Ailly was a follower of Ptolemy, he too chose to use the erroneous interpretation of Posidonius's calculations.

Far from being of merely academic interest to mathematicians, this miscalculation of the circumference of the earth had very great and direct consequences in the early exploration of the Atlantic. Christopher Columbus formulated many of his geographical theories from d'Ailly's *Imago Mundi* and Ptolemy's *Geographia*; accepting the figures of these authorities, Columbus came to believe the ocean to be smaller than it actually is. His reliance on these sources also explains why, on his first voyage, he believed he had finally reached the fabled land of Cipangu (Japan). Columbus was not the only explorer to navigate using the Posidonius calculations of a smaller earth; Magellan, too, set out in the same misguided belief.

In fairness to Columbus and Magellan, it should be noted that Strabo's *Geographia*, which reported the correct figures of Eratosthenes, wasn't translated from the Greek until 1469. Though the mathematical geography went back almost eighteen centuries, it wasn't available for study in the vernacular until the very lifetime of Columbus. But Strabo was no champion of Eratosthenes's geographical concepts. Strabo said:

> [Eratosthenes] says that if the extent of the Atlantic Ocean were not an obstacle, we might easily pass by sea from Iberia to India, still keeping in the same parallel [latitude], the remaining portion of which parallel . . . occupies more than a third of the whole circle. . . . But it is quite possible that in the temperate zone there may be two or even more habitable earths [lands], especially near the circle of latitude which is drawn through Athens and the Atlantic Ocean.[2]

Rather than discrediting Eratosthenes by mockery, as he intended, Strabo only reinforced the ideas of a narrow Atlantic and a small world.

Theoretical Geography

Also of concern to the ancient Greek writers was the general distribution of land and water over the earth's surface. In his great and comprehensive work, *Meteorologica,* Aristotle described the geography of the known world — its lands, seas, mountains and rivers. It was a small world, bounded by lands familiar from colonization, conquest and trade. Centred around the Mediterranean, the limits extended to India in the east and the Pillars of Hercules (Strait of Gibraltar) in the west. Encircling the known lands was a narrow stream of water — the River Oceanus.

In *Phaedo*, Plato explained that all the waters pierced the earth to a sea called Tartarus at the centre, and that all the rivers, lakes and oceans were drawn into this "primary and original mass" of water. The constant oscillation and surging of this underground sea kept the rivers and lakes replenished, "but all

Fig. 1-4.

Map of the geography of the known world as perceived by Aristotle and reconstructed from his descriptions in *Meteorologica*. The three coordinates used to frame the map are a typical Greek plan: Summer Sunset — Summer Dawn, Equinoctial Sunset — Equinoctial Dawn and Winter Sunset — Winter Dawn. Though the map bears a good resemblance to present-day maps, Aristotle shifted some of the features to enhance the symmetry.

(Redrawn from Lee, Aristotle's Meteorologica.*)*

Fig. 1-5.

Plotting of the same region as the map above, using modern geographical coordinates of latitude and longitude.

of them pass round again in a circle to the original source from which they flowed." Aristotle could not accept Plato's theory, pointing out that, according to the incline of the sea of Tartarus, at times its surge would have to force water to flow uphill — which is impossible.

In Aristotle's formulation of the world there were only two habitable zones. He described them as drum-shaped bands which girdled the globe. One band, in the northern hemisphere, was bound on its southern edge by the tropic of Cancer (23°28′ N lat.) and on its northern edge by the Arctic Circle (66°32′ N lat.). The other band, in the southern hemisphere, had as its northern edge the tropic of Capricorn (23°28′ S lat.) and its southern edge the Antarctic Circle (66°32′ S lat.). "Habitation ceases on one side because of the cold, and on the other because of the heat." According to Aristotle, if it weren't for the ocean, the habitable zone of the world would extend right around the globe in two broad bands.

Fig. 1-6.
The T-O map, of which this is representative, is found in manuscripts of the ninth through the thirteenth centuries. The three known continents, Europe, Africa and Asia, are enclosed in a circle and surrounded by the Ocean Stream. These maps functioned more as diagrammatic representations of the earth than as attempts to depict its geography.

These zones were later extended and further subdivided by geographers. Ptolemy delineated fourteen climate zones, with seven zones extending from each side of the equinoctial to the Arctic and Antarctic circles. So strongly did the concept of these zones affect the thinking about the habitable regions of the earth that, fully eighteen centuries later, Columbus's crew feared to enter the tropical zones. They believed their blood would boil on account of the heat, or, failing that, their skin would turn black and remain so permanently, like the skin of the natives of the region.

The Greek world had an ordered architecture in which masses of land were distributed over the surface of the earth in a balanced fashion and all the waters were interconnected and in constant flow. This symmetry necessitated the principle that whatever was in the north — land, water, winds — would also be found in the south. Aristotle said: "Since, then, there must be a region which bears to the other pole the same relation as that which we inhabit bears to our pole, it is clear that this region will be analogous to ours in the disposition of winds, as well as in other respects."

Aristotle's notion of the world was based on philosophy and logic, rather than on knowledge of distant regions gained from travel and discovery. His philosophical construct became the unshakable basis throughout the centuries in the search for the Northwest and Northeast passages to Cathay,

Fig. 1-7.
Map of the world by Aurelius Macrobius. This map is contained in his essays on metaphysical and cosmographical topics, *Interpretatio in Somnium Scipionis.* The geographical theories of Macrobius may have been borrowed from Homer's description of the ocean currents.

which would balance the Southeast Passage around the Cape of Good Hope and the Southwest Passage around Cape Horn.

The tradition of theoretical geography continued well into the fourteenth century. A commonly used world map was the T-O type map, so called because a T, placed within an O, divided the continents from the water. Obviously the knowledge of geography was far more advanced than what was shown on these maps, but the philosophers were more concerned with the abstract plan of the *Orbis terrarum* than they were with the practical details of mapmaking.

Macrobius, who wrote during the late Roman Empire, composed a number of essays on metaphysical and cosmological topics. In *Interpretatio in Somnium Scipionis,* he included a map showing the general distribution of land and water on the globe. Based on Aristotelian geography, it shows an equatorial ocean connected with the encircling ocean. This further emphasized the notion of balance and symmetry by creating a southern continent — the Antipodes — that mirrored in all respects the landmass of Europe, North Africa and Asia in the northern hemisphere. Both his commentaries and his map were used as the basis for maps for another ten centuries.

Observed Geography

Explorations beyond the familiar waters of the Mediterranean were few and mostly confined to coastal navigation. The limitless reaches of the Atlantic were "regarded with awe and wonder, seeming to bound the world as with a chaos, into which conjecture would not penetrate, and enterprise feared to adventure."[3] There, the mariner was beset by every tempest of nature, while hidden rocks and uncharted reefs, with seeming malice, destroyed his frail vessel. Grotesque and dangerous monsters lay in wait: the giant squid might crush ships and men by entwining them with its powerful tentacles, or, in an enraged fit, the Kraken (from Scandinavian tales) would smash them with its thrashing spikes and shining horns. Arab geographers assured the navigator that along the coast of Africa he would enter an inpenetrable green swamp filled with fiendish beasts, or encounter a sea of mud rising from the sunken island of Atlantis.[4]

But tentative travels along the coasts gradually expanded to longer passages farther offshore, and mariners ventured into the Sea of Darkness. Their voyages were not generated solely as an intellectual desire for exploration, or as romantic excursions into the realm of the unknown. Nor were they conceived primarily as a means to claim new land and hence increase the power of their sovereign. The greatest incentive was to find new, faster routes to distant lands for the purpose of trade.

Phoenician sailors, in steadily longer commercial voyages, extended their routes from the easternmost part of the Mediterranean Sea northward into the Aegean Sea and westward along the north coast of Africa. They traded Phoenicia's products — ivory carvings, silverwork, glass and fabrics — for the ores, smelted metal and slaves of other countries. Shortly after the Trojan War (1200 BC), Phoenician navigators were exploring beyond the Pillars of Hercules. By 750 BC Phoenicians had founded cities on Cyprus and Sardinia at Numidia and Tripolis on the north coast of Africa, and on the southern shores of Iberia. In 600 BC the

Phoenicians aided Necho II of Corinth in his project to cut a canal between the Nile River and the Red Sea; in doing so, they were the first mariners to completely circumnavigate Africa. By the third century BC, Phoenicians had a well-established maritime trade along the northwest coast of Africa. To the north, they sailed along the coast of Spain and France as far as the Scilly Islands off the Cornish coast of England, where they traded pottery and salt for tin. In his *Geographia*, Strabo mentions the Cassiterides (the Tin Islands, that is, the Scillys), and how the inhabitants there traded their metals to the Phoenicians. The Phoenicians' navigational ability and sailing experience may even have led them into the open waters of the Atlantic to the Canary and Madeira archipelagos, or possibly even to the Azores.

Writing in the first century BC, the Greek historian Diodorus Siculus recounts the seafaring exploits of the Phoenicians and the wealth they amassed. One time, he says, while exploring the African coast outside the Pillars of Hercules, Phoenician traders were blown far out into the ocean by a great storm. After many days at sea they were finally carried safely to a distant island. In addition to giving them blessed deliverance from the fate of a watery grave, they noted, the island possessed many natural gifts:

> The land is fruitful, much of it being mountainous and not a little being a level plain of surpassing beauty. . . . The mountainous part of this island is covered with fruit-trees of every variety, and springs of sweet water flow in great number. . . . [It] is well supplied with every manner of beast and wild animal, and the sea which washes its shore contains a multitude of fish. . . . And speaking generally, the climate of this island is so altogether mild that it produces in abundance the fruits of the trees and the other seasonal fruits for the larger part of the year, so that it would appear that the island, because of its exceptional felicity, were a dwelling place of a race of gods and not of men.[5]

This island had not previously been discovered, Diodorus says, "because of its distance from the entire inhabited world."

Whether the island the Phoenicians discovered was one of the Canary Islands or Madeira is uncertain; arguments can be made in support of either. What does matter are the many centuries during which mariners sailed to ocean islands off the west coast of Africa.

Diodorus Siculus goes on to say that the Phoenicians kept their knowledge secret from the rest of the world so that in an emergency — "an incalculable turn of fortune, or some total disaster" — the inhabitants of Carthage would have a ready place to seek refuge, one unknown to their conquerors. Perhaps so, but more likely they wished to keep their discovery to themselves in order to maintain a monopoly of trade with the island. It was not kept secret, however. Through the writings of Diodorus and other historians of antiquity, as well as the constantly increasing number of voyages for trade and exploration, information about the islands in the central part of the Atlantic Ocean grew continuously.

No maps or nautical charts remain from the time of these Phoenician voyages, nor is the means known by which they navigated. Certainly, the Phoenicians had maps, charts and navigational instruments — otherwise it would have been impossible for them, in two thousand years of sailing, to make trips to distant lands and return safely.

Not all of these early expeditions into the Atlantic were shrouded in anonymity; the travels of some individuals were so extraordinary that they were recorded by historians and preserved in treatises on geography. Exploits of Himilco, a Carthaginian navigator, are told in *Ora Maritima* by Festus Avienus, a fourth-century Latin writer. In Avienus's account, Himilco made a four-month-long voyage to the tin country in the northeastern Atlantic in 500 BC. On the way, he found himself in a strange place:

> No breeze drives the ship forward, so dead is the sluggish wind of the idle sea. He [Himilco] also adds that there is much seaweed among the waves, and that it often holds the ships back like bushes. Nevertheless, he says that the sea has no great depth, and that the surface of the earth is barely covered by a little water. The monsters of the sea move continually hither and thither, and the wild beasts swim among the sluggish and slowly creeping ships.[6]

It appears from this description that Himilco sailed as far west as the Azores, or even beyond, on his way to Brittany. During the summer months the large Azores-Bermuda high pressure system becomes firmly established, centred in the region of the Azores. As a result, winds there are extremely light, with prolonged periods of calm. Southeast of the Azores, a huge mass of floating seaweed is caught in the centre of a clockwise gyre of currents. Himilco's description very well matches the conditions in this sea of floating weed — the Sargasso Sea.

However, *Ora Maritima* gives only the vaguest suggestion of how far west Himilco may actually have travelled:

> Farther to the west from these Pillars [Gibraltar] there is a boundless sea. . . . None have sailed ships over these waters, because propelling winds are lacking . . . likewise because darkness screens the light of day with a sort of cloaking, and because fog always conceals the sea.[7]

Pytheas of Massalia (Marseilles) made an even more extensive journey in about 333 BC. Strabo, Diodorus and Pliny all describe how Pytheas departed from Gades (Cadiz) and coasted northern Europe as far as Britain, where he visited Belerium (Cornwall). It is not the length of the journey (in itself a notable achievement), but the descriptions Pytheas provided that make it so important. He related his observations of the sea, land and sky; the change in crops as he travelled farther north; the varying methods of threshing grain; and how in Britain mead was produced by fermenting honey.

His account of Thule (Iceland) is most significant of all, for Pytheas was the first to portray it. He told how "beyond Britain there was neither earth, air, or sea, but a mixture of all three — something like the element that held the universe together." It "had the consistency of jellyfish, and rendered navigation impossible."

This "sluggish sea," as the Romans later named it, has been interpreted to mean a mixture of water and broken or slush ice and fog. There is another possibility. The mixture of three elements — earth, air and sea — may refer not to ice and fog but to volcanic ash in the air and pumice floating in the water. This would be consistent with the intense volcanic activity of Iceland. At times volcanic ash from Iceland has blown all the way to the Orkney Islands, 300 miles away, causing fishermen there to exclaim that black snow was falling. This combination would also account for the rather strange analogy to "the element that held the universe together," which would be Ignis (Fire), Aer (Air) and Aqua (Water).[8]

After Pytheas circumnavigated Britain, his route becomes less certain. Probably he entered the North Sea and sailed as far as Denmark before returning to Cadiz. The information gained from his expedition about the islands and coasts of outer Europe became the foundation for western geography for all the writers of later antiquity.

Continual voyages by the Romans to their provinces in Gaul and Britain increased familiarity with the geography of the northern European coasts and the adjacent waters and islands. Then, in the sixth century, the Roman Empire collapsed, and a new power emerged — Christianity. Most of what had been learned since ancient Greek times slipped into oblivion. About all that remained was the realization that the Atlantic was not a circumfluent river — Aristotle's River Oceanus — but a vast open sea.

Ecclesiastic Influence

Developing Christian doctrine rejected much of the intellectual and artistic legacy of Greece and Rome along with its paganism. This rejection included geographic information. In its early years of struggle to propagate the Christian religion, the Church felt that time was much better spent in contemplation of the true faith than in investigating natural science.

Although men of classical learning knew that the earth is spherical, this concept was not so readily accepted by the Catholic hierarchy. Many distinguished leaders of the Church condemned it, and especially its corollary — the existence of the antipodes, a region of people with "opposite-facing feet." Among these leaders were Paulus Orosius, a fifth-century defender of early Christian orthodoxy, and Saint John Chrysostom (347-407), a renowned preacher and the archbishop of Constantinople. Lactantius (c. 240-320), a Christian convert, strongly opposed the concept of the antipodes. In his *Divinae Institutiones*, written as a response to attacks on Christianity by its opponents, Lactantius exclaimed:

> Is there anyone so foolish as to believe that there are men with the soles of their feet above their heads? Or plants and trees that grow *downwards*? Or, indeed, rain, snow and hail that falls to earth *upwards*? . . . I really do not know what to say about these matters except that at times I think people discuss them as a kind of philosophical joke; and then again on occasions it is possible that sensible and learned men maintain that these lies can be upheld as truth, as though to use their intelligence for wrongful purposes [that is, to distort the truth].[9]

This question had already been answered two centuries earlier by Pliny, who said, "In regard to the problem of why those on the opposite side to us do not fall, we must ask in return whether those on the opposite side do not wonder that we do not fall."

The problem the Church had with the antipodes was that if antipodean peoples existed in the south, separated from the north by uninhabitable torrid zones, they obviously could not be derived from the race of Adam. To accept that they existed would be heresy.

Not all members of the Church disposed of the learning of the ancients so completely. Some were able to accept the spherical form of the earth but could not go so far as to agree with the concept of the antipodes; others, such as Martianus Capella, a late fourth- and early fifth-century humanist, scholar and poet, and Saint Augustine (354-430) kept the concepts of Aristotle alive.

Geographical Knowledge in the Middle Ages

One of the greatest encyclopedists and excerptors of late antiquity was Saint Isidore (Isidorus Hispalensis, 570-636), a bishop of Seville who wrote many books on history, natural science and theology. His greatest work, called *Etymologiae Sive Originum Libri XX*, contained twenty books on the seven liberal arts, medicine, law, the Church and other topics. It was a compilation of information drawn from both classical sources and the Bible. Much of Isidore's material also came from the fifth-century work of Paulus Orosius. Under the heading of *De Oceanus*, Isidore writes, "The philosophers say that beyond the ocean there is not any land, and that the sea is only limited by dense cloudy air, just as the land situated in the lower regions of the world." The spheres of the universe defined by Aristotle are here unchanged. In other sections of the work, however, Isidore incorporates the steadily increasing information on Atlantic islands brought back by voyagers. He not only describes the Fortunatae Insulae, known to Ptolemy, but mentions two additional groups — Hesperidum Insulae and the Gorgades. The Hesperides

Fig. 1-8.
Map of the world drawn by Isidore of Seville for his *Etymologiae Sive Originum Libri XX*. Isidore presents a concept of the world, handed down from pagan times, in a typical T-O form. But in keeping with his own Christian background the map is oriented with east at the top, and on the three continents are the names of the three sons of Noah — Shem, Ham and Japhet — among whom Noah had divided the earth.

were the Madeira islands, and the Gorgades were either the Azores or the islands of Cape Verde.

Accompanying the text was a map of the world Isidore himself had drawn. In the original manuscript and in subsequent versions, it was reproduced in the form of a woodcut. Much later, in 1472, when *Etymologiae* was printed using the new process developed by Gutenburg, this map became the first printed map of the world.

Another eminent historian was the Irish monk, Dicuil, whose works date from 814 to 825. Dicuil belonged to that era of migrant Irish monks — *Scotti peregrinantes* — who left their monasteries during the eighth and ninth centuries for the continent, where they founded new centres of learning. However, Dicuil didn't go to a monastery, but to the court of Charles the Great.

In the second half of the eighth century the Frankish kingdom included much of present-day France, Burgundy and Austrasia (the eastern Frankish Empire). Under the rule of Charles the Great (768-814), popularly called Charlemagne, this kingdom was expanded to include the kingdom of Lombardy and most of continental Europe all the way to the frontier of Spain. On Christmas Day, 800, Pope Leo III crowned Charlemagne not only absolute ruler of the Frankish Empire, but emperor of the entire western part of the old Roman Empire. Determined to make his court the "intellectual, as well as political and administrative centre of the realm," Charlemagne attracted to it the greatest scholars and teachers from all lands. He established a court library and filled it with the works of both religious and secular writers.

At the court of Charlemagne, Dicuil wrote his major treatise, *Liber de Mensura Orbis Terrae* (On Measuring the Earth). Like his predecessor, Isidore (whom Dicuil quotes), the erudite Dicuil drew his material from as many as thirty Greco-Roman sources, some of them twenty to thirty volumes long. About Thule, he quoted from Pliny the Younger, who wrote extensively about Pytheas of Massalia. Pytheas claimed Thule was a six-day sail north of Britain, and that it lay on the Arctic Circle at about 67°00′ N latitude. Daylight lasted for six months as the sun passed through the tropic of Cancer (23°30′ N) during the summer solstice.

These estimates about the position of Thule are credible. The 270 nautical miles from its nearest neighbour, the Färoe Islands, or even the 420 nautical miles from the Hebrides, could be covered in a voyage of six days under favourable winds. The northernmost part of Iceland is just barely on the Arctic Circle (66°32′ N). The true midnight sun, which never sets below the horizon, is visible from the island of Grímsey, or from the mountains near Raufarhöfn on the northeast coast. But that the sun stayed above the horizon for six months was an error on the part of Pliny, who confused conditions at the Arctic Circle with conditions at the North Pole. Cleomedes, also writing about Pytheas, reduced the period of perpetual light to thirty days.

The first settlers on Iceland were not the Vikings but Irish hermits in search of solitude — a desert in the ocean — where they could live their lives as anchorites and serve only God. Dicuil says that they lived in the Färoes for about a hundred years until occupation by the Norsemen forced them to move to more distant lands. They arrived in Iceland on February 1, 795, and stayed until August 1. During this time they observed that the setting sun "not only at the solstice, but for many days in the year, seemed merely to hide itself behind a little mound (*quasi trans parvulum tumulum*), so that there was no darkness to hide a man from doing what he liked, even from picking lice out of his clothes." They thought that "if they had been on the top of a mountain they never would have lost sight of the sun at all." Dicuil correctly perceived that the same thing, only in reverse, must occur during the winter solstice, when for a few days (not for six months or even thirty days) it would be dark most of the time, with only a brief period of dusk.

According to Dicuil's knowledge, other Irish hermits made voyages from the Färoes to Iceland, and their presence in Iceland before the Norsemen is confirmed in the Icelandic sagas of *Landnámabók* (Book of Settlements) and *Íslendingabók* (Book of Iceland). Ari the Learned, a thirteenth-century Icelandic chronicler, says that when Norsemen arrived in Iceland in the ninth century they found Christians, called "Papa" (i.e., priests), already there, "but then they departed because they did not wish to live with the heathens, and left behind Irish books and bells and croziers, from which one could know that they were Irishmen." Once again the peaceful seclusion of the hermits was shattered, and they fled elsewhere or perhaps were killed.

Not all of Dicuil's depiction of the northern Atlantic was second-hand. He personally travelled to the islands around Ireland and Britain. "Among these I have lived in some, and have visited others; some I have only glimpsed, while others I have read about." Perhaps this explains why he writes so convincingly of the navigations of others. In more southerly waters, however, his knowledge was less certain, and Dicuil reverts to a simple report of the mythical islands maintained by tradition: the Fortunate Islands, the Hesperides and the Gorgades. Quoting other writers about the islands that lie in the sea west of Africa, Dicuil says:

The Gorgodes are farther from Africa than the Fortunatae, and the Hesperides farther than the Gorgodes. Since in the *Cosmography* the river Malva is said to rise near the Fortunatae islands, from this it is reckoned to be close to Africa. The Gorgodes are distant a two days' journey by ship from the continent, as Isidorus says in the 14th book of his *Etymologiae.*[10]

But Dicuil's was one of only a few voices in the Middle Ages that kept the knowledge of the ancients and the memory of the Atlantic archipelagos alive. Besides the domination of the Catholic Church, there was another reason why scientific information, such as the size of the earth, was virtually lost to western Europe. All this material was written in Greek, and very few men in medieval times, even among the most learned, could read the language. It wasn't until the Byzantine scholar Emanuel Chrysoloras (1355-1415) translated Ptolemy's work into Latin that Ptolemy's importance and immense influence spread in the western world. From the time of its first printing in 1472, Ptolemy's *Geographia* was the standard authority for the next hundred and fifty years.

Chapter II

Geographical Knowledge of the Muslims

THOUGH THE LIGHT OF SCIENTIFIC and geographic knowledge was eclipsed in Europe during the Middle Ages, elsewhere it continued to shine brightly. Geographers and historians of the Muslim world incorporated the teachings of classical authors, particularly Aristotle and Ptolemy, into their treatises. Through Syriac translations and translations directly into Arabic from Greek, the ideas of the ancients were examined and discussed and the succession of knowledge maintained. Muslim thinkers were not hampered by a conflict of ideologies. Their theology coexisted peacefully with Greek science and philosophy, as well as with Christian and Judaic beliefs; to them all knowledge was a "continuity of divine inspiration among the prophet's progeny."

Mohammedan historians assimilated the scientific information from the Greco-Roman world into the fund of knowledge gained from Arabic travellers. Al-Mas'ûdî (first half of the tenth century), Al-Idrîsî (middle of the twelfth century) and Ibn Khaldûn, with his monumental work, *Muqaddimah* (c. 1375), were among the greatest of these writers.

The Greek concept of a world which consisted of symmetrical landmasses surrounded by an encircling ocean was adopted by the Arabs, as was the theory of climate zones and the practice of using Ptolemy's parallels (latitudes) to mark the boundaries of these zones. Ptolemy's books on astronomy (*Almagest*) and geography (*Geographia*) served as the basis for most of the Arabic texts — usually called *Kitâb sûrat al-ard* (Book of the Description of the Earth). As might be expected, emphasis in the Arabic works was on the lands and seas to the east, the region of trade routes between the Arab world and Asia.

Between the seventh and ninth centuries, Arab merchants had established links with China by overland caravans and ships. To the south, they knew the African coast as far as Zanzibar; to the north, they reached the heart of Russia. But they were not unfamiliar with the Western (Atlantic) Ocean, having made explorations in that direction, though on a much more limited basis.

Tales tell of Arab mariners sailing westward sometime in the tenth century and reaching the Canary Islands, or possibly even the Azores.

From the seventh through the twelfth centuries, the most prominent mathematicians and astronomers were Arabs. As early as the eighth century, the Muslim astronomer Msha'allah described how to determine latitude from the meridian altitude and declination of the sun. The city of Toledo, even after its conquest by the kings of Castile in 1085, remained the western centre of Islamic science. Az-Zarqalî of Toledo developed a new type of astrolabe, used for measuring the angular arc of celestial bodies above the horizon, in 1080. He also wrote commentaries on the astronomical tables, produced at an earlier time by Jewish and Muslim scholars, for finding the meridian altitude of planets and stars.

Arab astronomers set up observatories and produced geographic coordinates for many cities and other points. They calculated latitude in two different ways: one involved measuring the altitude of the sun, the other used the Pole Star, Polaris. They also devised rules for determining longitude by observing lunar eclipses, a method first suggested by Hipparchus. But the infrequency of eclipses and the inaccuracy of predicting when they would occur or their duration made this method difficult; longitude was generally determined by estimating distances reported by travellers. Even so, Arab geographers were able to correct Ptolemy's gross over-estimation of the length of the Mediterranean. These advances prepared the way for mariners to navigate with a greater degree of reliability when sailing beyond sight of land.

Al-Mas'ûdî

In the tenth century, "the renaissance of Islam took place, like the renaissance of Europe." Arab geographers greatly expanded the knowledge of regional, descriptive, astronomical and mathematical geography, largely by travelling themselves to distant, little-known lands.

Al-Mas'ûdî was a historian, anthropologist, philosopher and scientist of encyclopedic knowledge. He travelled extensively, and in a period of thirty-four years (915-949) he explored Syria, Palestine, Amman, Mesopotamia (Iraq), Persia (Iran), the southern coast of the Caspian Sea, India, Zanzibar, the African coast, Abyssinia (Ethiopia), Egypt, Sudan, Central Asia and Asia

Minor. It is quite likely that he also made several voyages to the China Sea. Mas'ûdî says that he made these trips "not just for the sake of adventure, but to acquire first-hand knowledge by personal observation." Mas'ûdî's ideas on cosmography, cosmology and physical geography came extensively from Aristotle and Ptolemy, though he drew from Muslim scientists as well. Great as these authorities were, Mas'ûdî did not accept them unquestioningly. He used his own reasoning, coupled with his observations and experience, to look for proof before deciding to either accept or reject their notions.

In all, he wrote thirty-six books on history, geography and astronomy. Most of them are lost, and only two have survived in complete form: *Murûj al-Dhahab wa-Ma'âdin al-Jawahir* (Meadows of Gold and Mines of Precious Stones) and *Kitâb al-Tanbîh wa'l-Isshrâf* (Book of Warning and Review).

The universe described by Mas'ûdî in his books was derived from that of Ptolemy. Mas'ûdî says that "the earth is round [globular] and rests in the middle of nine concentric spheres." Each sphere contains the circular orbit of a planet. He goes on to say that the elements of water, air and fire surround the earth and are contained within the first seven spheres. The earth has two parts — the habitable and the uninhabitable — and the habitable region is further divided into seven latitudinal zones. All of man's physical, mental and cultural attributes are controlled by these zones, elements and spheres, which are arranged in the universe according to their potency. Earth, the factor that exercises the greatest influence, occupies the centre of the universe. "The order of this universe is a sign of God's creative wisdom."

Mas'ûdî' describes the Western Ocean as that "Green Sea of Gloom of unknown extent or depth, without cultivated or inhabited lands, and impossible of navigation — an impenetrable green swamp, filled with monsters."

After measuring the habitable portion of the earth, which is from the Fortunate Isles (al-Djazâ'ir al-khâlidât) — six populated islands situated in the Atlantic Ocean (Uquiyânus al-gharbî) — until the farthest populated part of China, they [the knowledgable ones] found that the distance was 12 hours of revolution of the earth; that is, 180° away. They found that when the sun was going down at the extreme limit of China, it was just beginning to rise on the Fortunate Islands, and when it set there, it was just beginning to rise in China. This represents half of the circumference of the earth.[1]

Of particular interest is the reference to the six populated Fortunate Islands.

In spite of trepidations about entering the Green Sea of Gloom, Arabic voyagers or other venturers before them had already explored six of the seven Canary Islands, the most distant of which lies 240 miles off the west coast of Africa.

Hudûd al-'Âlam (AD 982)

Like Mas'ûdî, the anonymous author of *Hudûd al-'Âlam*, called in English *The Regions of the World: A Persian Geography*, cites Aristotle and Ptolemy, and he used other unnamed Muslim sources as well. Whether he derived any of his geographical information from his own personal travels is unknown. In the preface, he says:

> We have brought to light every land of the world of which we have found information in the books of our predecessors, and in the memories of our sages, with particulars of that land as regards its greatness or smallness, its deficiency or abundance of amenities, wealth, and populatiions, and its cultivation of the lack of the same; also, the disposition of every land with regard to mountains, rivers, seas and deserts, and all the products coming forth from it.[2]

According to the author, the habitable zones of the earth occupy one-ninth of its total surface. Within this area are "all the cities of the world, the different kingdoms, the seas, the mountains and the rivers, and all the places possessing animals and fishes." In the most easterly part of the habitable region is the capital of China, known as Khumda, and it borders the shore of the Eastern Ocean, called the Green Sea. In the most westerly part of the habitable region are the lands called Sûs-the-Distant, which border on the Western Ocean.

The author quotes Aristotle: "This sea surrounds the earth like the horizon, and ships cannot work in this sea . . . and nobody has crossed it, and it is unknown where it ends." He notes that in all aspects — taste (salinity), colour and smell — the waters of the Eastern Ocean are the same as those of the Western Ocean. He concludes that the two oceans are one, "which surrounds the earth on the East *and* West and passes by the two poles," thereby confirming Aristotle's notion of an encircling ocean. He comments on how

Ptolemy 2nd c. AD	Mas'ûdi d. 956	Hudûd al-'Âlam 982	Al-Idrîsî 1154	Ibn Khaldûn 1377	Contemporary
	Surrounding Sea	al-Bahr al-Muhit (Aristotle's Surrounding Sea)	Surrounding Sea	Lablayah (Oceanos) Surrounding Sea	
Western Ocean	Green Sea Uqiyanus al-gharbi	Western Ocean	Green Sea	Green Sea	Atlantic Ocean
Eastern Ocean		Green Sea darya-yi Sabz		Black Sea	Pacific Ocean
		Rum Sea darya-yi Rumiyan			Mediterranean Sea
	Bahr Hind	The Great Sea Bahr al-A'zam			Indian Ocean
	Bahr as-Sin				China Sea
		Sea of Khãzars darya-yi Khazaran			Caspian Sea
		Bontos Sea			Black Sea
		Sea of Khwarazm			Aral Sea
Fortunate Islands (Islands of the Blest)	al-Djaza'ir al-khalidat	al-Khaliya	al-Khalidat The Eternal Islands	al-Khalidat The Eternal Islands	Canary Islands
		Ghadira	al-Ghanam Island of Sheep		Madeira
			Djaziraro't-Toyour (Raka) Isle of Birds		Azores (Corvo)

mariners can sail north and south along the inhabited zone of the west, but cannot cross the Western Ocean in ships. But he also realizes that since the earth is a sphere, the ocean must pass from east *to* west, for he goes on to say, "On account of this ocean no one knows anything about what there is in that other [invisible] half."

The author gives a detailed description of each of the Seven Seas of the world, its boundaries and gulfs, and the lands and peoples that border it. The first of the Seven Seas is the Green Sea, that is, the Eastern Ocean [Pacific]. The second is the other sea, the Western Ocean [Atlantic]: "Its extension, so far as it is known, is from the extreme limit of the countries of the Sûdân, the Maghrib [collective name for Morocco, Algeria and Tunisia], and Sûs-the-Distant, up to the *Rûmi* Strait [Gibraltar] . . . and up to *Tûlî* [Iceland]." In the northern part of the Western Ocean lie "twelve islands called *Britâniya*, of which some are cultivated and some desolate. They are the storehouse of goods from Byzantium and Spain." In the Western Ocean, he continues, there

Fig. 2-1.
Chart of comparative knowledge among Muslim geographers of islands in the Atlantic. The influence of Aristotle and Ptolemy is pervasive throughout the centuries. Aristotle's River Oceanus — the Surrounding Sea — remains unaltered as a concept for eighteen centuries.

are twenty-five islands. Tûlî is the twenty-fifth island and through it passes the line that is parallel to the equator and marks the northernmost limit [Arctic Circle] of the habitable world. Ptolemy placed it at 63°00′ N.

About the Fortunate Islands, the author says:

> Of them, six lying off the Land of the Sûdân are called *Al-Jazâ'ir al-Khâliya*, and possess gold mines. Once a year people from the region of the Sûdân and the towns of Sûs-the-Distant go to fetch gold from the mines, but nobody can settle down there on account of the intensity of the heat.[3]

These gold mines drew people from a large geographic area. Sûs-the-Distant are the lands on the west coast of Africa which border the Atlantic; to their east is the region of the Sûdân which occupies a major part of north-central Africa. This information about the gold mines is presented for the first time in the *Hudûd al-'Âlam* and is not found in any of the author's sources. If he is correct, it would mean that by the late tenth century, voyages to the Canary Islands were planned and regular events, not just accidents caused by capricious weather.

The author mentions another island in the Western Ocean called Ghadîra, which lies "at the point where the Sea of Rûm (*daryâ-yi Rûmiyâ*) joins the Western Ocean. . . . The mouth of the strait enters into the Rûm Sea." This accurate description of Madeira's location west of the Strait of Gibraltar makes it the first mention in geographical literature of the island of Madeira.

Al-Idrîsî

Of all the Muslim geographers, Abdullah Mohammed al-Idrîsî (commonly called Idrîsî) is the best known outside the Arab world. He was born in Ceuta about 1099 and was a student at the University of Cordova. Like the other Arab geographers, Idrîsî travelled widely to Asia Minor, Morocco, and even France and England. At the request of Roger II, the Norman King of Sicily, Idrîsî joined his court and remained there for the rest of his life.

The court of King Roger, like that of Charlemagne, was a gathering place for intellectuals and scholars of all countries. During the crusades, Palermo was a meeting place for crusaders, pilgrims and merchants from all nations. Roger himself was greatly interested in geography and collected Arabic treatises on distant lands. He summoned Idrîsî to collaborate on the production of a new and comprehensive geographical work.

They selected special observers to travel to all countries and gather information, including the latitude and longitude of towns and the distances between them. This surveillance, when brought back, was correlated with what was known from the writings of other Arab geographers and with the work of Ptolemy. After fifteen years of effort, the two-volume *Kitâb Al-Rojâri* (*The Book of Roger*) was completed. It contained a small, circular map of the world, which followed the classical division into the seven parallel climate zones, plus seventy detail maps of the regions of the earth. In addition to the book, Idrîsî created a celestial sphere and a map engraved on a large silver tablet (about 3.5 x 1.5 metres). Unfortunately, the tablet was smashed in a skirmish in 1160, but *The Book of Roger*, with its maps, remained the most comprehensive geographical treatise written in the twelfth century.

In the two hundred years since the time of Mas'ûdî, the dread of venturing into the Great Green Sea of Gloom remained unchanged. Idrîsî affirms that:

> The ocean encircles the ultimate bounds of the inhabited earth, and all beyond it is unknown. No one has been able to verify anything concerning it, on account of its difficult and perilous navigation, its great obscurity, its profound depth and frequent tempests; through fear of its mighty fishes and its haughty winds; yet there are many islands in it, some peopled, others uninhabited. There is no mariner who dares to enter its deep waters; or if any have done so, they have merely kept along its coasts, fearful of departing from them.[4]

In spite of the ocean's terrors, mariners ventured beyond the coasts, for Idrîsî's information on the Atlantic islands is more extensive than that of earlier writers. Of the many islands to the west of Europe and Africa in the Dark Sea, he names and describes seventeen of the twenty-five enumerated by Ptolemy.

Idrîsî relates the adventures of eleventh-century Muslim wanderers from Lisbon whose ship was blown off course by an easterly wind. Eventually, they reached an island (presumably one of the Canaries) where there were people who spoke Arabic. When a favourable wind from the west arose, they returned home.

Early Anglo-Saxon map ~ 992-994

Edrisi ~ 1154 (first part of 7th climate)

Fig. 2-2.
Islands of the Atlantic off the coast of northern Europe that were known by Idrîsî:
1 Khalie (Empty Isles);
2 Ghazîrat Birlânda (Ireland); 3 Kharâb (Desert);
4 Gals or Vals (Wales);
5 Ghazîrat Angiltâra (England); 6 Ghazîrat Squosia (Scotland);
7 Al-bahral muslimash-shamâlîl; 8 Ghazîrat Islânda (Iceland); 9 Ghazîrat Dânâmarkha (Denmark).

In other accounts these wanderers are sometimes referred to as the eight demented, or eight deluded, folk. To purposely sail into the boundless Green Sea of Gloom was considered a sure sign of insanity. If a mariner did so and actually returned, this proved his derangement and his civil rights were immediately withdrawn. In any case, the story about the eight wanderers is an isolated and unconfirmed example of travel to the Canary Islands.

On his map, Idrîsî shows a long string of islands in the Western Ocean reaching north from the equator to Brittany (see *Fig. 2-3*). Unfortunately, none of them are labelled. It could be argued that the first six islands, spread over three entire climate zones between the equator and the Strait of Gibraltar, represent the six known Canary Islands, forced into this north-south alignment by the physical constraints of the circular map with its narrow band of the Surrounding Ocean. The same linear arrangement of islands appears on fourteenth-century maps such as the Laurentian portolano (1351), and, a full century later, on the Bartolomeo Pareto map (1455), since it was still impossible to determine longitude.

However, Arab geographers and astronomers were much too accurate in their latitude calculations to mistakenly spread the Canary Islands so widely over the ocean. I believe another identification is more likely. The first two islands are the Canary Islands, properly shown in the first climate zone and carried forward from Ptolemy's map as the Fortunate Islands or Islands of the Blest. The sixth island, shown opposite the entrance to the Mediterranean, would be al-Ghanam (Island of Sheep), Madeira.

The three intermediate islands in the chain may be the first cartographic representation of the Azores. After describing the Canary Islands, Idrîsî refers to an island in the Western Sea named Râka, which is the Isle of the Birds, Djazîrato't-Toyour. "It is reported that a species of birds resembling eagles is found there, red and armed with fangs; they hunt marine animals upon which they feed, and never leave these parts." Mas'ûdî, too, mentions the island of Râka, and says, "The King of France sent a ship to find the Isle of Râka, but it never returned."

William Babcock, who has written extensively on legendary islands of the Atlantic, supposes these birds to be cormorants –– sea-crows (*corvi marinis*)

— from which later maps derive the name Corvo for one of the Azores, although he admits that cormorants do not exactly fit Idrîsî's description. I think that Babcock comes close, but, rather than the cormorant, the bird referred to is the goshawk (*Açor*), a species of hawk that closely resembles an eagle and abounds in the Azores, and from which the entire archipelago gets its name. During the period of rediscovery of the Azores under Prince Henry the Navigator, these birds were supposedly responsible for guiding the sailors to these distant islands. If the isle of Râka is indeed one of the Azores, then the discovery of these islands occurred as early as the tenth century.

Idrîsî's description of other islands in the Atlantic appear to have more to do with fanciful legends than with reality. Distinct from the Canary Islands were the Isle of Female Devils, the Isle of Illusion, the Island of Two Sorcerers, and the Isle of Lamentation (Gazîrat al-Mustashkin), which was inhabited and fertile, with tilled fields, but controlled by a terrible dragon. This story may be a borrowing from Greek mythology, where a dragon guarded the golden apples of the Hesperides. On the Island of Two Heathen Brothers, two pirates lived until they were turned into rocks, and the inhabitants of the Island of Kalhan had the bodies of men and the heads of animals.

Some of these islands resemble the islands of Irish legend, and the Arabs may have incorporated parts of the Celtic tradition into their own legends. An exchange of ideas and reciprocal influences between the two cultures certainly took place. In 844, Norman Vikings invaded Spain and attacked and occupied Seville. The Arabs called the Vikings "Magus." According to one historian, friendly relations were established between the Sultan of Spain and the invaders. A later writer (c. 1235) adds that the Sultan of Spain even sent an ambassador to the land of the Magus. Certain adventures of Sinbad the Sailor, from *Tales of the Arabian Nights*, are almost identical to those of Saint Brendan. But whether the Irish borrowed these myths from the Arabs, or vice versa, or if they both obtained them from an earlier common source is a matter of conjecture.

The *Kitab al-Istibar* (Book of Observations), written by an anonymous author and dated 1192, says:

> At the latitude of Tangier, in the Grand Sea, there are situated islands named "The Fortunate Islands." These are spread in the sea, not far away from the west coast [of Africa], the Barbary Coast. That is what the inhabitants of the Maghrib say.[5]

The author of this book was inspired by an earlier writer, d'Al-Bakri (1067). Probably planned voyages to the Canaries were being made by the Maghrebins some time in the twelfth century, but they did not explore beyond them.

Ibn Khaldûn

In 1381, Ibn Khaldûn finished his monumental seven-volume *History* (*Kitâb al-'Ibar*), of which the first volume, *Muqaddimah*, was an introduction. It contained the usual Ptolemaic description of the world, along with material incorporated from Idrîsî's *The Book of Roger*. Like Arab geographers preceding him, Ibn Khaldûn combined the strength of personal observation with the continuity of tradition to make his work authoritative and current.

As a model for his descriptive geography of the best-known countries, rivers and seas, Ibn Khaldûn followed the schema used by Idrîsî. He declares that the first zone, which contains the Canary Islands, was used by Ptolemy as the westernmost longitude of the known world. There are a number of Eternal Islands (the Canaries), and they lie in the Surrounding Sea; three of the largest and best known are cultivated. Ibn Khaldûn says that knowledge about these islands comes from Christian ships which reached them in the middle of the fourteenth century. The Christians fought with the inhabitants, plundered the land and captured some of the people, whom they sold into slavery in Morocco. Once the captives learned Arabic, they were able to convey the following information about their island:

> They said that they tilled the soil with horns. Iron was lacking in their country. Their bread was made of barley. Their animals were goats. They fought with stones, which they hurled backwards. Their worship consisted of prostrations before the rising sun. They knew no (revealed) religion and had not been reached by any missionary activity.[6]

But, Ibn Khaldûn adds, it is not possible to intentionally sail there by navigation. The only way the islands can be reached is by chance. He acknowledges that, for the Mediterranean, there are "compass charts" (portolanos) which show the countries bordering its shores "and [give] their positions along the coast." These charts also have the various winds and their paths on them.

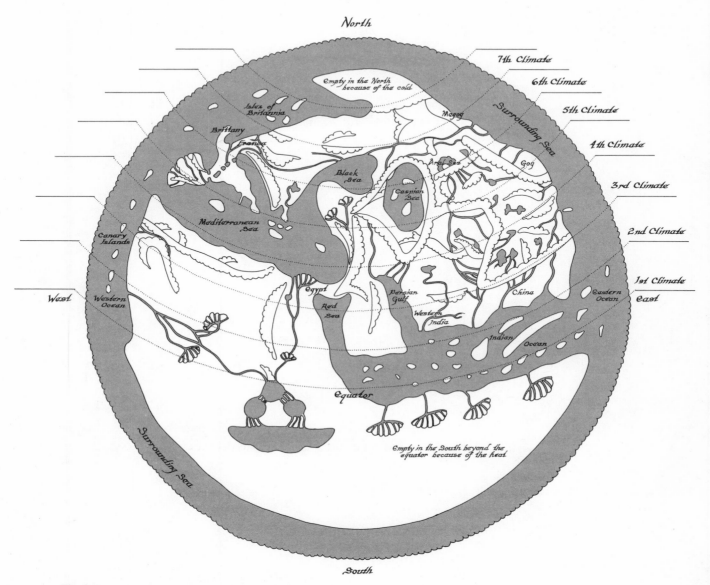

North

7th Climate
6th Climate
5th Climate
Surrounding Sea
4th Climate
3rd Climate
2nd Climate
1st Climate
East

Empty in the North
because of the cold

Magog
Isles of
Britannia
Aral Sea
Gog
Brittany
France
Caspian
Sea
Black
Sea
Mediterranean
Sea
Canary
Islands
China
West
Western
Ocean
Egypt
Persian
Gulf
Eastern
Ocean
Red
Sea
Western
India
Indian   Ocean
Equator

Surrounding Sea

Empty in the South beyond the
equator because of the heat

South

Fig. 2-3.
Map of the world adapted from the *Muqaddimah* (Introduction) to Ibn Khaldûn's
monumental work, *The History of the World*. Completed in 1381, it represents the extent
of Muslim geographical knowledge at that time. For the most part, this map was derived
from an earlier one (1154) by the famed Arab geographer al-Idrîsî. The basic construction is
Ptolemaic, with an arrangement of horizontal divisions into seven parallel climate zones.
These are divided by vertical lines into ten east-west sections for each zone. I have
deleted most of the eighty Arabic place names and annotations[7] and rotated the map
180° in order to place north at the top of the page.

"Nothing of the sort exists for the Surrounding Sea. Therefore, ships do not enter it, because were they to lose sight of the shore, they would hardly be able to find their way back to it."

England, Ibn Khaldûn reports, "is a large, far-flung island which contains a number of cities and is the seat of a magnificent realm"; it lies in the northernmost (seventh) zone. But he mentions no other islands in the Atlantic, even though by the time the *Muqaddimah* was written all seven of the Canary Islands, the complete Madeira archipelago and most of the islands of the Azores were already known.

Chapter III

Filling in the Empty Spaces

AS THE MIDDLE AGES WANED, the geographical knowledge of antiquity once again became known in Europe. From its Greek origins it had been transposed into the Muslim world, there to be studied and extended by its geographers. At the end of the twelfth century and the beginning of the thirteenth century, this knowledge was reintroduced to western Europe by translations from the Arabic treatises and from Greek into Latin.

Among the most important of these translators was Gerard of Cremona (d. 1187), a prodigious writer who produced seventy-four works, including translations of Ptolemy's *Geographia* and the first three books of Aristotle's *Meteorologica*. William of Auvergne, Bishop of Paris from 1228 to 1249, not only translated, but also questioned Aristotle's theories. His work, *De Universo*, contains much of the work of Aristotle as it was found in the works of Arabic authors. Among other translators were Michael Scot (d. 1236), a Scotsman who served as court astrologer to the Emperor Frederick II of Sicily, and Robert Grosseteste (d. 1253), Bishop of Lincoln. *The Book of Roger* by Idrîsî needed no translation, for it was originally written in both Arabic and Latin.

This intellectual revival renewed western European interest in geographical exploration and expanded the knowledge of the physical world. Distant islands, which had remained hidden from view because of the terrors of the ocean, now began to be revealed. Chronicles of visits replaced recollections of occassional chance encounters. By 1350, almost all the Atlantic islands were known to the historians and geographers of western Europe, though their information was vague, often confused, and lacking in precise detail.

An anonymous Spanish Franciscan, writing in the middle of the fourteenth century, was the first European to describe the Canary Islands, Madeiras and Azores. Like the Muslim geographers that preceded him, the friar drew heavily on his own experiences. He claims to have "personally visited every part of the known world," but undoubtedly he added to his own first-hand information material gathered from other sources to produce *The Book of the Knowledge of all the Kingdoms, Countries and Lordships that there are in the World [etc.]*. The Spanish Franciscan relates his visit to the islands known by Ptolemy as the Fortunate Islands, and to the Arabs as the Kalidat; their distance from Cape Boyador, he avers, is 110 miles. In all, he visited all of the Canaries except Palma, all of the Azores except Graciosa and all the islands of the Madeira archipelago. He concludes by saying, "Altogether, the islands in the Atlantic total twenty-five in number," a computation directly traceable through the books of the Arab geographers to Ptolemy.

But before advances in exploration could take place, there had to be major innovations in navigation. Ship design and construction that fit the needs of Mediterranean and coastal sailing had to change to meet the challenge of the open ocean. New calculations in astronomy were needed, and improvements were required in instruments to allow the navigator to determine his position at sea. Only through the development and integration of all these fields could long voyages into the Sea of Darkness become possible.

Boats well-suited for cargo trade in the Mediterranean were inappropriate for conditions on the vast, open ocean, where the ability to sail long distances and return, often against prevailing winds, was more important. The caravel, a ship about seventy feet in length, was produced to fit these needs. It became the standard vessel for Prince Henry's discoverers and the type used by Columbus in his explorations. The caravel had three masts: the foremast, carrying a square foresail and topsail, stepped through the high forecastle at the bow; a mainmast, amidship, with square mainsail and topsail; and aft, on the raised sterncastle, the mizzenmast, with a lateen-rigged sail. Some ships carried a square spritsail hung from the long, steeply pitched bowsprit. With the exception of the lateen sail, all these were athwartship sails, that is, they hung from a yard set at right angles to the longitudinal axis of the boat. The increased number of sails over the simple rig of the Mediterranean vessel created a boat with greater manoeuvrability, one that was faster, easier to sail and required fewer crew.

The caravel, however, was unable to sail close to the wind. Under ideal conditions, the closest the caravel could sail on the wind was five points (56° 15′), but, for the most part, in order to make any real forward progress it had to have the wind on its beam or aft of it. This left it very much dependent on the direction from which the wind was blowing — a direction not always favourable for the intended course. The lateen sail at the stern, set fore-

and-aft, had several advantages over the square sails. It was more efficient in sailing close to the wind, and it could be used to help push the boat around when tacking (changing course). Also, when riding at anchor, the lateen sail kept the boat headed into the wind, where it would sit most comfortably. When the boat ran before the wind, the lateen sail was kept furled to prevent its stealing the wind from the other sails. The bark, or barque, common throughout the sixteenth century, was similarly rigged, but it was larger. In both the vessels, sails were made of linen and the rope rigging of hemp.

Once explorers reached their destination, in order to explore the shallow bays, inlets and rivers, they needed a smaller boat, a pinnace, shallop or longboat. Towing this small boat was a poor plan, for invariably towed boats sank or were damaged or torn free in heavy seas. Also, towing a small boat reduced the speed of the main ship, which was never very great to begin with. Deck space was always at a premium, so the ship's boat was frequently prefabricated and stowed in the hold until land was reached. The boat would then be assembled and used to sound the depths of a bay or river before the main ship entered.

The Problem of Determining Position at Sea

To make open ocean voyages, the navigator was confronted with an entirely new problem: he had to know his exact position at sea, and, its corollary, be able to return whence he started in order to bring back information about his discoveries. Up until the beginning of the sixteenth century, navigators had scant need to fix their precise position by longitude and latitude. Voyages were short and principally followed the coast; ships were rarely out of sight of land for more than a few hours' time. Commerce was well established along routes that seldom varied. The mariner could rely largely upon visual memory for fixing the ship's position, while careful assessment of the contours, colours, scents and textures of the land, sea and seabed all enabled him to move about the coasts with confidence. To prompt his memory, he used a rutter — a book of sailing directions — as well as a lead line to determine the depth of the water and the type of sea-bottom, a compass, and a sand-glass to measure time.

As voyaging increased into the uncharted regions, the mariner brought back his findings to be retained in written records and represented on maps. To create accurate maps, cartographers needed much more than recounted tales and estimated distances. It became apparent that a grid system dividing the earth into coordinates of latitude and longitude was necessary.

Advances in Astronomy

Dividing the globe by equally spaced circumferential vertical lines was a logical construct. Hipparchus had marked off the earth's surface into 260 parts — the "degrees" of modern geography. Ptolemy followed this plan, subdividing each of the degrees into *partes minutae primae* ("minutes") and *partes minutae secundae* ("seconds"). He spaced the meridians of longitude fifteen degrees apart, one space representing one of the twenty-four hours for a full revolution of the earth, making 360 degrees.

Certain obvious reference points for latitude were used by mariners from the earliest times. The equator, the polar points and the swing of the sun from its most northerly declination of 23°28′ (tropic of Cancer) at the summer solstice through to its opposite, equal declination (tropic of Capricorn) in the southern hemisphere at the winter solstice remained constant. To the end of the fifteenth century, the celestial body most often used to determine latitude was Polaris, the North Star, for this was the easiest to use and required no tables of declination.

At first, only the meridian altitude of Polaris was used — that point when it reached its zenith in the sky. This altitude was compared with the known meridian altitude of Polaris at a reference point such as Lisbon. The navigator noted the number of degrees by which his position differed from the reference station, and this enabled him to determine how far north or south he had to travel. Later, navigators were able to make use of Polaris at any time of the night without having to wait for it to reach its zenith.

One degree of latitude equals sixty nautical miles, but distances at sea were usually expressed in leagues rather than miles.[1] Portuguese navigators estimated one degree of latitude at 16.66 leagues, which was later changed to 17.5 leagues, making a single league equal to 3.43 nautical miles. English mariners computed 20 leagues to the degree. In the English measure, this made one league equivalent to three nautical miles.

Once the navigator reached a desired latitude, which he determined by sightings of a celestial body (sun or Polaris), he maintained his course on that latitude by sailing due east or west. This is known as "latitude sailing" or "running down your easting (or westing)." This method required no elaborate tables of declination or complex mathematical calculations; all that was needed was to keep that celestial body at the same declination. Latitude sailing enabled the mariner to reach his objective without having to know the longitude — it was only necessary to keep sailing at the same latitude until the destination was reached. This method does have a built-in error over a period of time, but in the course of a three-week passage the error is negligible. Latitude sailing was the primary means of correcting the vessel's position as it moved across the ocean. It was just as important to the Norsemen in determining the amount of northing or southing needed on their voyages between Norway and the settlements in Iceland and Greenland as it was to the Arabs plying their trade routes across the Indian Ocean. Christopher Columbus practised latitude sailing on his 1492-93 voyage, as did Vasco da Gama when he rounded Cape of Good Hope and reached Calicut, India, in 1498.

A favourite landfall on the western side of the Atlantic for French navigators such as Jacques Cartier was Cape Bonavista, Newfoundland. If the navigator departed from Saint-Malo, France, at 48°39′N and continually sailed west, he would certainly arrive at Cape Bonavista at the latitude of 48°42′N, a difference of only three nautical miles. It was vital for him to constantly keep track of the latitude by celestial observations, for he could not maintain an easterly course by relying on his compass, due to magnetic variation.

As early as the eighth or ninth century the Arabian geographer Msha'allah described how to determine latitude from the meridian altitude of the sun and its declination. By the late fifteenth century, the daily declination of the sun had been recorded on simplified solar tables derived from those of the noted Jewish astronomer Zacuto of Salamanca (1473-1478), so mariners could determine their latitude position from the sun as well as from the stars.

The Riddle of Longitude

Establishing *longitude* at sea was much more difficult than finding latitude and continued to elude navigators even as late as the beginning of the seventeenth century. Samuel de Champlain believed that "God did not intend that man should ever be able to determine longitude at sea." And Sebastian Cabot confided on his deathbed that divine revelation enabled him to calculate longitude, but that he was not allowed to share this knowledge. In 1530, the Flemish mathematician and cartographer, Gemma Frisius, successfully worked out a method of determining longitude based on time, but it wasn't until an accurate timepiece, the chronometer, was constructed in 1761 that his theory could be put into practice. Only then could longitude be determined and the art of navigation finally become a science.

Initial attempts to determine longitude followed the same approach as for latitude, namely, using astronomical observations. Hipparchus was the first to suggest finding longitude by comparing times at two places during a lunar eclipse. The problem with this method was the infrequency of lunar eclipses and the inaccuracy of predicting them. Columbus tried this method during his 1494 voyage, but he was unable to achieve an accuracy any closer than 18°00′ of longitude; at the latitude of the Canary Islands (28°00′ N), this produced an error of 1200 nautical miles. One hundred years later, William Baffin, most noted for his exploration of far northern waters, attempted to fix his positions of longitude by the meridian passage of the moon. That he was unable to accomplish this is not surprising, for it was not until the latter part of the eighteenth century that lunar tables of sufficient exactness for constant use were published.

Another method utilized the satellites of Jupiter. Galileo, the first to observe the four principal satellites of Jupiter, quickly realized that using occultations and eclipses of these satellites could be a means of finding longitude at sea. This method had the advantage over using lunar eclipses because of the greater number of celestial bodies and the greater frequency of occurrences; but, like using lunar eclipses, the method suffered from lack of accurate published almanac data and the difficulties of observation from a moving boat at sea.

Finding longitude by occultations of stars or planets by the moon's disc was also attempted. But the complexity of the mathematical calculations was far beyond the ability of most navigators, and they also needed to know the exact time of observation. Another lunar method for finding longitude involved finding the local time of the moon's transit and comparing it with the time of transit at a prime meridian, but this, too, depended on an accuracy of telling time that was then impossible.

Even after the navigator knew how to calculate longitude, there was still the problem of *where* to place the first line of longitude — the prime meridian. This line is fundamental to both navigation and cartography. Today, the meridian of 0° longitude is universally accepted by convention to be through Greenwich, England. However, well into the seventeenth century, the placement of this one critical line varied from nation to nation and from mapmaker to mapmaker.

The starting point for measuring meridians of longitude had no natural position such as the equator provided for parallels of latitude. The earliest maps used Alexandria, that great seat of ancient learning, as the prime meridian; others used important geographic points such as Rhodes, Carthage, the

Pillars of Hercules, or Rome. Ptolemy used the Insulae Fortunatae for the prime meridian, since they were at the boundary of the known world. Arab geographers naturally used a prime meridian more in keeping with their world. They selected a line that was midway between the farthest east and farthest west and that passed through a mythical city called Arin, situated on the equator. This meridian was subsequently assumed to be 10°00′ east of Baghdad. Until the beginning of the seventeenth century, the most commonly found prime meridians on charts were:

A. Canary Islands — based on their historic precedence of being the most westerly land known.

B. Canary Islands — but specifically through Pico de Teide of the island of Tenerife, for this lofty volcanic mountain peak, rising 12,180 feet above the sea, was visible a long way off.

C. Azores — particularly through the island of São Miguel (St. Michaels). Gerardus Mercator favoured this for his maps, since he thought the true and magnetic meridian (the meridian with no variation) were one and the same only in the Azores.

D. West Africa (westernmost part) — selected as a meridian when it became obvious that the reasons for selecting A, B and C were faulty.

E. Azores — using Ilha da Pico, at 7,613 feet the highest mountain in the Azores. This was favoured by some of the Dutch mapmakers.

F. Cape Verde Islands — used primarily by the Portuguese.

To get around this source of confusion, mapmakers frequently included two, three or even more scales of longitude starting at different points. It is little wonder that mariners had such great difficulty in reporting the position of the Atlantic islands they discovered, and that cartographers were faced with such a dilemma in correctly showing them on their maps. Worldwide acceptance of Greenwich as the datum point for measurement of longitude did not occur until 1884.

Improved Instruments

In order to determine latitude by celestial observations, very little is needed in the way of instruments. All that is required is a means of measuring the altitude of a celestial body above the horizon at its point of meridian passage, that is, when it reaches its highest point (zenith) in the sky. This altitude is compared with tables of declination for the celestial body on that particular day. For example, suppose the altitude of the sun is observed to be 50°26′34″. This figure is subtracted from 89°59′60″ (90°00′); the difference is 49°33′26″. Almanac tables show the sun's declination (geoXgraphical position north or south of the equator) on that day. The declination is added to 49°33′26″ to give the latitude. If the declination in this example was 3°41′34″, the total would be 53°15′00″ — the latitude of Galway Bay, Ireland.[2]

In the northern hemisphere, tnd latitude from Polaris is even easier. Since Polaris is very near the north celestial pole, the height of Polaris is almost equal to the observer's latitude. In the night sky, the rotation of the earth on its axis makes all the stars appear to rotate counterclockwise around the celestial north pole. Today, the position of Polaris is so close to the pole that its rotation around it is too small (30′ of arc) to be discerned by the naked eye. If one were to use Polaris to determine latitude, a reasonably accurate position fix could be made even without applying any correction factor. In the early centuries of Atlantic exploration, however, Polaris was not as close to the north celestial pole as it is today. At that time it described a polar circle of 3°30′, a distance too great to be ignored. To correct for this, navigators used the two outer stars Kochab and Pherhad, the guard stars of Ursa Minor (Little Dipper), to define the position of Polaris in its nightly circle. They compared their observations with tabulations on "Polaris Wheels" or "Wheels of Altitude." The wheels gave the correction factors they needed to calculate their latitude. With increased mathematical ability, mariners could convert altitude observation of Polaris directly into latitude.

The Greeks developed a very simple instrument to determine the altitude of a celestial body. It consisted of a hemispherical bowl (scaphe) which had a vertical rod (gnomon) at its centre. The shadow cast by the rod on the side of the bowl could be read directly in degrees from a scale on the interior of the bowl. Eratosthenes, Hipparchus

Fig. 3-1.
Astrolabe. Line P-G is the angle of the axis of the earth at the time the celestial observation is made, obtained from astronomical tables; Z equals zenith; and D is the observed altitude of the sun. To obtain a noon position fix of the sun at its meridian passage, the observed altitude of the sun is subtracted from 90°, and the declination of the sun is added (algebraically) to this result.

and Ptolemy all used this device to determine the latitude of various geographical points.

In the Middle Ages, the instrument used for measuring the angular height of a celestial body above the horizon was the planispheric astrolabe. This instrument developed into one more suitable for "taking the height" while at sea, the nautical astrolabe. It was a perforated disc made of bronze or brass (which gave it weight), and it could be suspended from a ring at the top. A sighting bar, called the alidade, was affixed to the centre of the disc and could be moved in a complete circle. The navigator aimed the alidade at the heavenly body, aligning it by sighting through holes or notches in plates at each end. He read the altitude in degrees directly off a scale inscribed around the circumference of the disc.

The cross-staff appeared later than the astrolabe, sometime around the first quarter of the sixteenth century. It was the ultimate in simplicity, being but a long stick with a movable cross-bar. The navigator aimed the lower point of the cross-bar at the horizon and moved the cross-bar until the upper tip touched the celestial body; then he read the altitude on the scale inscribed along the length of the staff. To prevent painful damage to the eyes by having to look directly at the sun, a small shield blocked the sun, and the navigator subtracted a correction value to find the true reading. A modification of the cross-staff was the back-staff. Essentially it was the same instrument, but instead of aiming it directly at the sun, the observer turned his back toward the sun and took readings through an appropriately positioned mirror.

Fig. 3-2.
Cross-staff.

In spite of the knowledge of how to determine latitude by means of celestial observations and the existence of nautical instruments to take these measurements, there was a vast difference between theory and practice. The instruments themselves caused a certain amount of error. They were finely crafted yet lacked the advantage of present-day optics. It was no small feat for the navigator to keep the cross-staff aimed at the horizon, while at the same time moving the crossbar so as to have its upper tip touch the celestial body, all the while trying to brace himself on the pitching and rolling deck of a ship. Under these conditions, maintaining a star or the sun in the sighting holes of the alidade of the astrolabe was no easier.

Polaris, the celestial body used most often at night, is easy to identify from the pointer stars of Ursa Major (the Big Dipper), but it is not always easy to see. Polaris is not a first-magnitude star, and its dim appearance makes keeping it in the sights of any nautical instrument difficult. This problem gets worse the farther south one sails, for Polaris becomes lower on the horizon and must be viewed through a much thicker layer of the earth's atmosphere, and so it appears even dimmer. At the equator, it disappears altogether beneath the horizon, leaving the navigator to search for other stars in other constellations from which to make his observations. Whereas in the Mediterranean sailors could become "disoriented" when losing their east-west position, in the Atlantic they could become "disnorthed" by sailing too far south and losing the North Star. The Portuguese had a specific word for this — *disnorteados*.

Altitude sights of the sun at its meridian passage also become much more difficult as one moves into southern latitudes. When the declination of the sun is close to the latitude in which one is sailing, its appearance directly overhead makes it very difficult to determine the altitude at meridian passage. Then too, if the sailing route is south of the sun when the sun is in the northern hemisphere, a different set of mathematics has to be applied to determine latitude, which was beyond the ability of most navigators.

While it is true that, because of the greater reliability of celestial observations, position fixes in northern latitudes were more accurate than those closer to the equator, navigators in the north Atlantic were confronted with other problems. Fog, a frequent occurrence in northern waters, especially where warm and cold currents meet, was as much a culprit as continuous cloud-cover in masking the sun and stars from the navigator's eyes.

Temperature inversions, a meteorological phenomenon common to the offshore archipelagos of Africa, produce an extremely thick haze akin to fog.

Normally, the highest peaks of these volcanic islands are visible up to fifty miles away. Yet so effective is this haze in hiding the islands that it is possible to be within five miles of them and be totally unaware of their presence. Nineteenth-century *Coast Pilot* books warn mariners to keep a careful watch, for often "the sound of breakers upon the shore will be the first indication that land is near." Satellite photographs confirm that this is even more true today, due to the addition of atmospheric polution drifting over from the mainland of Europe.

In navigating long distances, the compass was as important an instrument as the sand-glass was for marking time. The compass developed in China around AD 1100 and independently in northern Europe shortly thereafter. By the end of the twelfth century the compass was used for navigation by mariners in western Europe, and at the beginning of the thirteenth century it was used by the Arabs when navigating in the Indian Ocean.

Viking mariners used lodestone, a naturally occurring magnetic iron ore, which they floated on a board in a water-filled wooden bowl. This arrangement was subsequently improved by magnetizing a needle with the lodestone; the needle then could float on a splinter of wood or reed. Later, the floating needle gave way to one that pivoted on a pin rising from the bottom of the bowl. The principal points of direction were marked on the bottom of the bowl, with the north point under the north-seeking end of the needle. Finally, in the evolution of the compass, a card was mounted on the needle, and navigators could read the direction off the the top of the card.

As long as voyages in the Atlantic were confined to routes along the west coasts of Africa and Europe, the compass served mariners well in guiding their course. But when they began to venture west *across* the Atlantic, it no longer seemed to read correctly. Until then, everyone had assumed that magnetic north coincided with true north at the geographical pole. They soon found out this was not so. Not only did the two norths not coincide, but the difference between them increased the farther west and north they sailed; but in northern waters east of Ireland, the change was in the opposite direction. The closer one approaches the magnetic north pole, the greater is the amount of difference between the two norths. This discrepancy between magnetic north and geographic north is called magnetic variation.[3] Furthermore, magnetic variation is not a consistent pattern; it varies in different parts of the world according to regional influences.

Up until the mid-sixteenth century, mariners were unaware of magnetic variation; consequently, as they sailed west they found their position did not correspond with where they ought to be according to the charts. The farther

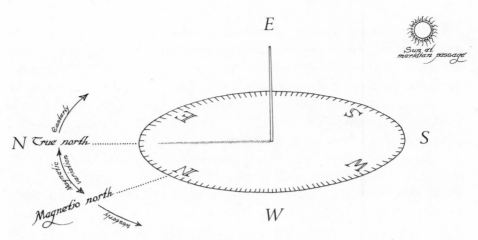

Fig. 3-3.
Meridianal compass.

west one sails, the greater the magnetic variation becomes. If a navigator departed England and followed his compass due west, his course would take him on a gradual curve south; instead of arriving in Newfoundland as he intended, his landfall would be somewhere along the mid-Atlantic coast of the United States. The confusion caused by magnetic variation, plus the inability to determine longitude, prevented mariners from using the compass to determine their position.

In 1580, Robert Norman published *The New Attraction*, containing observations on the variation and dip of the magnetic compass. Twenty years later, a general concept of the world distribution of magnetism was postulated in *De Magnete*, by William Gilbert. He attempted to explain planetary motions on the principle that the earth is a magnet, and he described the importance of this magnetism in practical problems of navigation.

Mariners attempted to correlate the amount of easterly or westerly variation of the compass with longitude. But they were unsuccessful, and the method was finally discredited in 1634. Still, there was some value to it, for knowledge of the amount of variation at a particular geographic locale could be useful as a general guide to the mariner's proximity to that site. Knowing that he was in the correct latitude of a certain island but not in the proper region of variation would enable him to determine the appropriate east-west corrections.

More importantly, measuring the amount of variation of the compass enabled the navigator to continually correct his magnetic course heading relative to true north. Since maps and charts are drawn with meridian lines of *true* north and south and parallels of true east and west, the mariner needed to know the amount of magnetic variation at his position to correctly plot the ship's course.

In order to keep track of the ship's position and progress, navigators carried more than one type of compass. The meridianal compass, used for the daily reading of magnetic variation, had a special attachment which cast a shadow to true north when the sun reached its meridian at noon. With this arrangement, the amount of variation could be read directly off the compass card, and the ship's heading could be properly corrected. Knowing that true or geographic north was not the same as magnetic north, instrument makers in some of the northern countries produced compasses in which the compass card (the flye) was mounted on the magnetic needle in alignment with the amount of magnetic variation. Thus the needle pointed to magnetic north while the fleur-de-lis on the compass card indicated true north. By this arrangement the compass had a built-in correction value for the amount of magnetic variation. This was fine, as long as voyages were limited to regions where the amount of variation did not change appreciably. On other compasses, the position of the card on the needle as it pointed to magnetic north could be changed according to the amount of local variation. These were called "true compasses," whereas on the "varied compass" the fleur-de-lis always pointed to magnetic north.

Another type of compass measured the magnetic field of the earth, a phenomenon quite different from the magnetic north and south pole. Measurements of this field were taken with the magnetic dip compass. Whereas the needle on a regular magnetic compass was mounted to swing in a circle in the *horizontal* plane, with its positive end seeking the north magnetic pole, the magnetic dip compass needle was mounted to swing in the *vertical* plane. The vertical swing of the needle pointed to the direction of the earth's magnetic field and was measured on a card calibrated in degrees. At the magnetic equator, which approximates the earth's geographic equator, the needle would rest in its horizontal position. But as one travelled farther north, the north-seeking end of the needle would dip below the horizon in increasing amounts. In southerly regions

Fig. 3-4.
Wind rose found on portolanos. The eight letters on the rose come from the ancient Greek system of eight named Mediterranean winds. These winds were transposed onto the compass rose to indicate the eight principal points of direction: *Tramontana* (north), *Ostro* (south), *Levante* (east), *Ponente* (west), *Greco* (northeast), *Africo* (southwest), *Maestro* (northwest), *Sirocco* (southeast). The fleur-de-lis, as an embellished symbol for north, developed from the combination of a broad spearhead (resembling the flattened iron leaf used as a needle in early compasses) with the letter "T" for *Tramontana*, the north wind. East was also given special emphasis with a cross.

the opposite end of the needle dipped downward. It was thought that these measurements could serve as a new means to determine position at sea, but they were found to be of little use and discarded.

By the fourteenth century, the eight primary points of the compass were subdivided into sixteen and then thirty-two points. This arrangement remained until the first half of the twentieth century, when it was replaced with the degrees of a circle. When the 360 degrees of a circle are divided into thirty-two points, each point is equally spaced at 11°15′. By the end of the sixteenth century, compass cards carried a dual system of points and degrees. Any good sailor could "box the compass," giving the name of each point in its turn: north, north by east, north northeast, northeast by north, etc., until all thirty-two points were covered.

The Enigma of Currents

As if all the perils, fears and hardships were not sufficient reasons to prevent mariners from venturing out across the Atlantic, there was yet another problem to contend with, one that could not be seen or measured but had a definite effect on their progress — ocean currents.

Latitude sailing was not the only means of keeping track of the ship's position. Continuous records were made of the vessel's speed, the direction travelled and the time elapsed, which the navigator used to plot the vessel's course on the chart. This system is known as dead reckoning. When conditions were right for taking celestial sightings, the dead reckoning course was updated and corrected. Optimally, sights were taken once a day at noon, but frequently many days would go by without the navigator's being able to correct the ship's position. When he could make an accurate latitude fix, the navigator would sometimes find it did not match the dead reckoning position.

Navigators recognized the problem and assumed that currents had altered the ship's course. Journal entries typically read: "Taking the sun's height, we found we were before ourselves by 8 leagues [24 miles]." The journal from Henry Hudson's 1609 voyage notes, "We perceived that the current had hindered us in fortie-eight houres to the number of 16 leagues [48 miles] to our best judgement."

Well into the seventeenth century, there simply were neither enough voyages made nor a sufficient number of observations taken of these currents to construct a general pattern of the ocean's circulation. Their general set (direction) and velocity were virtually unknown, and the navigator's estimate of position could be thrown off by as much as thirty miles in one day. Though they seemed random, currents had to be taken into careful account to enable proper course headings and hence accurate landfalls.

In simple terms, the general surface current of the North Atlantic Ocean is one large clockwise gyre which has several segments. The southern portion of this gyre, sweeping across from east to west, is the North Equatorial Current, a very consistent current both in set and velocity. Within its central axis the speed is about 0.5 knot. Upon reaching the Caribbean and Bahama Islands the current curves northward and is joined by the Florida Current, which originates in the Caribbean, and shoots through the narrow strait between Florida and the western edge of the Bahama Islands. At this point the Florida Current achieves its maximum velocity, reaching 3.0 knots. As it heads northward, paralleling the United States coastline, it is properly called the Gulf Stream; its velocity ranges from 2.0 knots at its southern end to about 0.6 knot where it is deflected by the southern edge of Cape Cod to begin its journey eastward. But at this point the boundaries of the Gulf Stream and the patterns within it change considerably; they start to fan out and become more complex. In the movement of the Gulf Stream from west to east there are large north-south meanders, loops and whorls. Some of these loops break off and become their own, self-contained eddies — some clockwise, others counterclockwise, but all generally moving from west to east.

At about 45°00′W longitude, the Gulf Stream divides into two major parts: a more northerly one, called the North Atlantic Drift Current, which heads toward the British Isles, and a southerly one, moving toward the Iberian Peninsula, where it begins a southward journey along the northwest coast of Africa to become the Canary Current. The Canary Current, attaining a velocity of 0.5 knot, changes its course westward in the vicinity of the Cape Verde Islands (about 15°00′N latitude), where it becomes the North Equatorial Current. Thus, the circle is completed.

In 1593, Sir Richard Hawkins left England on a voyage "to the kingdoms of China and the East Indies by way of the Strait of Magellan and the South Seas." In his observations on the voyage, published in 1622, he had this to say about the Gulf Stream:

> The currant that setteth betwixt, *New-found-land* and *Spaine* [the Gulf Stream], runneth also East and West, and long time deceived many, and made some to count the way longer, and other shorter, according as

the passage was speedie or slowe; not knowing that the furtherance or hinderance of the currant, was cause of the speeding or slowing of the way.[4]

When Martin Frobisher was about to seek the Northwest Passage to the Indies (1578) and Arthur Pet to search for the Northeast Passage (1580), Gerardus Mercator had written a letter to Richard Hakluyt requesting that "whatsoever observations of both these voyages shall come to your hands, you will impart to me." Mercator was particularly interested in whether the currents constantly flowed in one direction to the east or west, or whether they flowed according to the tides, that is, six hours in one direction and then six hours in the other direction, "for thereupon depend other speculations of importance."

Hawkins summed up the difficulties created by the Atlantic currents:

When the current runneth north or south, it is easily discovered, by augmenting or diminishing the height [finding latitude by celestial observation], but how to know the setting of current from east to west in the mayne sea is difficult. I have not knowne any man, or read any author, that hath prescribed any certaine meane or way to discover it; and that therefore the best and safest rule to prevent the danger is carefull and continuall watch by day and night, and upon the east and west course ever to bee before the shipp.[5]

In other words — always be on watch, anticipating an early arrival at land on account of the currents, lest you run aground thinking you still have sea-room.

Development of Mapmaking

Without maps or charts, the mariner could not plot a proper course to his destination, nor, upon his return, could he report to cartographers the location of his discoveries, so that they might be incorporated into a new view of an expanding world. It was recognized from the very start that geographical positions could be recorded only if there was a grid system in which to place them, but mapmakers had to struggle with how to represent, with a minimal amount of distortion, the spherical form of the earth on a flat plane, a piece of paper. Ptolemy, the greatest of all cartographers of classical antiquity, found one way of solving the problem.

For the master map in his atlas, showing all that was known of the inhabited world, Ptolemy devised a conical projection of the earth's surface; that is, he projected on the globe a cone, with its axis from the peak to the centre of the base aligned with the axis of the earth. When the cone is un-rolled and becomes a flat plane, the parallels of latitude are represented as curved lines maintained equidistant from north to south, while the meridian lines of longitude are widely spaced at the base and converge to a point at the pole.

Curiously enough, Ptolemy did not use this system for the remaining twenty-six maps, reverting instead to the grid system of earlier map-makers, where lines of latitude and longitude are all at right angles to each other and all equidistant. Obviously, this system created deforma- tion in the size and shape of land and sea, and Ptolemy himself criticized it for this reason. Shortly after 1472, the projection plan of these twenty-six maps was modified by Nicolaus Germanus (Donis), making them consistent with the main map, and subsequent editions of Ptolemaic maps used the Donis projection. The maps in Ptolemy's atlas continued to be re-produced in many editions throughout the sixteenth and early seventeenth centuries, forming the basis for all future advances in cartography. As new information became available, additions and corrections were made to them. Even today, Ptolemy's dominance is still felt and many of his practices are fol-lowed. Differentiating land from sea by shading is unchanged, as well as orienting north at the top of the map. His method of representing a spherical surface on a flat plane by a conical projection is still in use.

Fig. 3-5.
Conical projection plan.

While European maps based on the Ptolemy atlas and its modifications continued to flourish during the fifteenth and sixteenth centuries, there also existed a parallel cartographic development: the portolano. Unlike the Ptole-my maps, which originated from classical concepts of cosmography and were enhanced by tales and legends brought back by travellers, the portolano re-sulted from the experiences and observations of countless mariners and merchants and depicted the sea routes of their commercial voyages. Essentially, it was a chart derived by empirical means and intended for the very practical purpose of getting from one port to another — hence the name *portolano*.

These charts came into being in Italy around the beginning of the twelfth century. *Portolano* originally signified a book of courses or a sailing directory, but because these charts contain elaborately drawn "compass roses" they are sometimes called compass charts. No matter what designation is used, they all have a distinctive appearance. They were generally drawn on parchment, with the shoreline and towns in the immediate vicinity of the sea painted in brilliant colours and richly ornamented. Every headland, cape, inlet or any other geographical feature that had a name was identified on the chart. Overlaid on this was a complicated pattern of lines radiating from one or more "compass roses."

These "compass roses" were *not* divisions of the horizon into degrees of arc, as on today's compass. Instead, they represented the ancient eight-wind system of the Mediterranean, with north being Tramontana, east, the Levant, and so forth. The mariner used the lines from the "compass rose" to help project his course, according to the destination and the direction from which the wind was blowing. Most often, the portolanos contained no grid system for longitude and latitude, for none was required. The navigator needed only a ruler, a pair of dividers, and a compass to keep his course steady and arrive at the goal.

For the most part, these charts covered the Mediterranean and the Black Sea, though there were some of Antwerp and the North African coast. Portolanos were sufficiently accurate for navigation of this limited region and continued to be used for three centuries. They did not have to deal with the problem of transformation, since they were already plane maps and the area represented was small enough to be free of distortion. But when cartographers attempted to make them cover a larger area their usefulness diminished, since, without a grid, the topography was markedly distorted.

Solutions to representing a spherical surface on a flat plane based on geometry or trigonometry of the sphere took many forms. Conical projections, cordiform (heart-shaped) projections, and the use of gores (cutting the spherical surface into a number of segments which are then splayed out flat) were all tried. The problem had no perfect answer; all in some way caused distortion and skewed relationships and distances. Finally, in 1569, Gerardus Mercator came up with a brilliant solution.

Born in 1512 in the small Flemish town of Rupelmonde, Mercator attained his academic degree in the study of philosophy at the University of Louvain. Later, his interests expanded to include copper-plate engraving, mapmaking and the construction of nautical instruments. At this time, the dominion of Charles V, Emperor of Spain, extended all the way to Flanders

Fig. 3-6.
Mercator projection plan
as first presented in his
1569 atlas.

and the Netherlands. Mercator could not have had better circumstances for his education; not only could he exchange ideas with the most important scholars of geography from the Low Countries, but he also had access to all the documentary resources of Spain, which balanced in practical experience the theories of the academicians.

Mercator's most influential achievement is the map of the world he created and published in 1569; on it he first presented his new projection of the earth's surface. He kept all the meridional lines (lines of longitude) parallel and equidistant from each other, instead of converging at the pole. To compensate for the greater space between the lines of longitude near the pole, he increased the distances between the lines of latitude proportionately from the equator toward the pole. Thus he created a *rectangular* grid of intersecting right-angle lines. In a long inscription on the 1569 map, he explained the mathematical principles of its construction and how it would be used in navigation. Technically called an isogonic cylindrical projection, it is now simply referred to as Mercator's projection, and it has not been improved upon to this day.

Although the relative sizes and shapes of landmasses are markedly enlarged and distorted as they become closer to the polar region, the Mercator projection has one distinct advantage over all other projections: it allows the navigator to plot a ship's course (rhumb line) that remains a straight line and a constant angle, no matter how it cuts across the meridians.

But the map which was to change the future of cartography and navigation so profoundly received scant attention when it was published; Mercator's theories were too advanced for popular acceptance. Another map in the same atlas attracted far more attention. It showed the polar regions and emphasized the feasibility of a Northwest Passage and a Northeast Passage to the Orient — a concept that had its roots in Aristotelian geography.

Chapter IV

Rediscovery of the Atlantic Archipelagos

AT THE BEGINNING OF THE FIFTEENTH CENTURY, the greatest intellectuals of Europe, the Byzantine world and Arabia were grappling with the cosmography of the earth. By the end of the century, however, Portuguese and Spanish mariners were venturing out into the Sea of Darkness. The first voyagers brought back with them new information and observations from unknown lands. New maps portrayed the geography of this expanded world and were illustrated with the scenes and people encountered. Extensive embellishment with beasts, combining real and imaginary features, heightened the storytelling character; legends and myths collided with new perceptions.

By the mid-sixteenth century, the major powers of the world — Spain, Portugal, France and England — were all sending forth their ships. Islands of tradition in the Atlantic archipelagos were rediscovered, and new lands were found.

Spanish explorations revealed the existence of an entire New World. The voyages of Christopher Columbus gained for the Spanish monarchy a vast Caribbean empire, and in 1519 the Spanish conquistador Hernando Cortés captured Tenochtitlán (Mexico City), the capital of the Aztec empire. Other Spanish explorers extended this dominion from Florida in the north to the Yucatan in the south, and to Peru on the west coast of South America. After rounding Cape Horn, Spanish ships reached the Philippines and the Spice Islands, there to establish ports of trade.

Meanwhile, Portugal made considerable progress to the southeast, exploring the African coast and its offshore islands. Eventually, Portuguese ships doubled the Cape of Good Hope to reach India, thus giving Portugal a sea route to the East Indies. By the middle of the sixteenth century, Portugal had more than fifty forts and factories, ranging all the way to Macao on the mainland of China and Nagasaki, Japan. France and England also explored the New World, but mostly in northerly latitudes.

The primary cause and the greatest driving force behind this outburst of oceanic activity was the search for a sea route to the Far East, to the territories of Cathay[1] and Cipangu (Japan), to gain better access to the treasures sought by all of Europe — silks, spices, precious stones and perfumes. For centuries these goods travelled overland by caravan to Alexandria and Mecca, there to be bartered for western goods and transported farther northward. In the Mediterranean, Venetian ships monopolized the spice trade, while Genoese ships handled the silk trade through their merchant colonies in Constantinople and Kaffa. The Genoese carried their trade not only from east to west, but from west to east as well. They transported goods from northwest Africa through the Strait of Gibraltar and sold them at the eastern end of the Mediterranean and in the Black Sea. But when the Turks conquered Constantinople in 1453 and Alexandria shortly thereafter, this major trade route from the Levant, if not altogether cut off, was at least severely limited. The nations of Europe had to search for other routes to the riches of the Orient; patterns of trade established since the thirteenth century now changed to new ones based on Atlantic routes. Genoa lost its access to the eastern markets, but rather than see that trade fall into the hands of Venice, Genoa financially backed the Portuguese in their search for an alternative sea route.

The Iberian Peninsula, Europe's westernmost land, thrusts far out into the Atlantic. With overland travel eastward to Asia blocked by the Pyrenees mountains, and with the Muslim centres of trade in the Mediterranean virtually monopolized by Venice and Genoa, Spain and Portugal had to turn toward the west, to the uncharted Atlantic, in order to seek riches and expand their empires. Tumultuous events followed their discoveries, and through colonial conquest they created a new world order of unbounded empires.

Prince Henry the Navigator

Prince Henry the Navigator, the Infante Dom Henrique, was the son of John I, surnamed "The Avenger," and Philippa of Lancaster, sister of Henry IV of England. His determination, drive and support for Portuguese mariners were unflagging, in order that Portugal might be foremost among nations in the exploration of the sea. He established a great centre for the study of navigation and other maritime sciences at Sagres, on Cabo St. Vincent, the most extreme southwest promontory of Portugal; it commanded an unobstructed horizon of the western sea. Whether the large complex of buildings actually served as a school of navigation and an astronomical observatory or whether it was a more informal gathering place for scholars in these disciplines is uncertain. Definitely, mathematicians, astronomers and geographers gathered at Sagres to discuss their theories and work out new techniques in celestial navigation. There, mariners found the latest charts and information from the most recent voyages. A contemporary chronicler, Gomes Eanes de Azurara, described his Prince as:

> . . . a noble spirit ever urging himself both to begin and to carry out great deeds. . . . He had also a wish to know the land that lay beyond the Isles of Canary and that Cape called Bojador, for that up to his time, neither by writings, nor by the memory of man, was known with any certainty the nature of the land that lay beyond that Cape. . . . It seemed to him that if he or some other lord did not endeavor to gain that knowledge, no mariners or merchants would ever dare to attempt it, for it is clear that none of them ever trouble themselves to sail to a place where there is not a sure and certain hope of profit.[2]

Portuguese mariners sailed the Atlantic coast of Africa, where they established colonies and trading stations. Each voyage advanced a little farther before turning homeward, and by 1434 Gil Eanes (a navigator from the Algarve) had made an unprecedented journey as far south as Cape Bojador on the western bulge of Africa. Before this, seamen feared travelling so far south, for they knew the prevailing northeast trade winds and the south-setting Canary Current would be against them and make the return voyage very difficult. Moreover, they were still apprehensive about entering the torrid climate zone.

When sailors found they could survive such hazards, they pushed the limits of voyages still farther, until they passed Dakar, Guinea, and reached as far south as Sierra Leone, only 10°00' above the equator. Prince Henry died in 1475, not living to achieve his goal, the doubling of the Cape of Good Hope. It took twelve more years before two Portuguese mariners, Bartholomeu Dias and Pèro da Covilhã, were able to double the cape and enter the Indian Ocean. In 1498, Vasco da Gama not only rounded the Cape of Good

Hope but sailed all the way to Calicut, India. The explorations and discoveries directed by Prince Henry raised Portugal to a world power, extracting wealth from gold mines, the sale of ivory and the trade in black slaves in its colonies along the African coast.

Portuguese sailors also gained experience with the wind and current systems in the waters off the African coast. These systems were favourable for the outbound (south) passage, but on the return passage the caravels could not beat against the prevailing winds and currents. By making a wide sweep, however, tacking far out to sea, they were able to make enough northing to obtain the latitudes of the prevailing westerly winds. When they reached the latitude of Lisbon or Lagos, the sailors "ran their easting down."

In attempting to circumnavigate Africa, these long voyages led to the rediscovery of the Atlantic archipelagos, enabling Spain and Portugal to claim Madeira, the Canary Islands, the Cape Verdes and the Azores. These archipelagos became well established, both in identity and in location, and the islands of legend slowly gave way to islands of reality. No longer was their existence dependent on vaguely remembered myths and legends of the distant past or on tales brought back by some errant mariner whose ship was blown off course by an ocean storm.

Since the two nearest of the Canary Islands lie only sixty miles off the African coast, they were the first islands to be rediscovered. In 1278, Lancelot Malocello, a Genoese nobleman, built a fort on one of the islands. Thereafter, the charts not only label the island with his name, Lanzarote (retained to this day), but display the Cross of Genoa upon it. Lanzarote remained in relative obscurity until 1420, when Spanish vessels came upon it and Fuerteventura and claimed them for Castile. Later, in voyages initiated by Prince Henry, the outer islands of Gran Canaria, Palma, Tenerife, Gomera, and Hierro were also explored and claimed for Portugal. They remained Portuguese colonies until 1479, when the Treaty of Alcáçovas established Spanish sovereignty over all the Canary Islands.

With the voyages of João Conçalves Zarco and Tristão Vaz Teixeira in 1425, the Madeira archipelago was also rediscovered, and the islands became Portuguese colonies.

Like the Canary Islands, the Azores had been visited centuries before by Carthaginians and Arabs; their positions were charted on a map in 1381. But it remained to the courageous Portuguese mariners, in their great crescent sweep of the Atlantic, to rediscover and colonize the Azores. The earliest dated document referring to the rediscovery of the Azores is the map of Gabriel de Vallseca (1439), which contains the legend: "These islands were found by Diogo de Silves, pilot of the King of Portugal in the year 1427." Santa Maria, the most southeasterly island in the archipelago, was the first to be found, followed by São Miguel (St. Michael) in 1444. By 1452, the remaining seven islands, which lie more to the west, were explored and finally colonized.

At the time of Portugal's annexation to Spain, Alfonso V of Portugal presented the Azores to his aunt Isabella, the Duchess of Burgundy, which brought them under the authority of Spain for a brief time (1580-1640). The Low Countries were also under Spanish control; so many Flemish traders and settlers colonized the islands that maps of the period call the Azores the Flemish Islands. Indeed, windmills on the islands of Corvo and Faial still stand today, and traditional dances, seen during festival times on São Miguel, are living scenes from the paintings of Pieter Bruegel the Elder. Eventually, the Azores reverted to Portuguese control and became the crossroads of ocean traffic, where Portuguese and Spanish galleons stopped off on their return voyages from India, Africa, Brazil and the Caribbean.

Islands of Legend, Islands of Reality

With these momentous changes in the geography of the Atlantic, Europeans were now forced to revise their concept of the world, both physically and philosophically. All that remained for geographers and cartographers was the process of refinement of the maps and charts, and the filling in of empty spaces. No longer could the almost-unknown Atlantic archipelagos serve variously as legendary islands such as Brazil, Saint Brendan or Antillia. Still, these islands continued to appear on maps, sometimes complete with well-defined geographical features and even cities. How could this be?

History and geography are so entwined that the study of one is scarcely possible without the other. Captain John Smith of the famed Virginia Colony said, "As geography without history seems like a carcass without motion, so history without geography wanders as a vagrant without habitation." Fortunately, there is no need to separate the two, for cartography expresses history and geography simultaneously. Although the passage of time, so essential to history, is absent from any single map, it is readily observed in a group of maps; patterns emerge that show the appearance, change and eventual disappearance of these phantom islands.

Undoubtedly, many illusory islands appearing on early maps of the Atlantic were the result of the same island's being repeatedly discovered over a long period of time. As mariners began to navigate the Atlantic with greater predictability, they rediscovered legendary islands from a dimly remembered past and superimposed the new islands over the legendary ones. With the islands now fixed in reality, the imaginary ones, rather than being replaced, were thought of as being even further west, at the outermost margin of the known world. Increased knowledge about the Atlantic archipelagos necessitated a continual westward migration of mythical islands. Gradually, however, a geography of legend gave way to a geography of reality.

Some phantom islands may be accounted for by the numerous offshore banks and seamounts which extend from the Färoe Islands to Spain. Possibly, at one time portions of these subaqueous grounds surfaced as islands; temporary uprisings and subsidences of the ocean floor provide support for this speculation.

Other phantom islands are not so easy to explain, or explain away. In spite of new discoveries and advances in cartography, belief in islands now known to have been phantoms persisted for centuries or even millennia. The search for fragments of historical truth reveals a strong underpinning of verity beneath the legends; myth and reality are not as disparate as one might think.

Chapter V

Isle of Demons

*"A legend may not be a record of facts, but the existence of a legend
is itself a fact, and requires an explanation."* (G. Ashe)

OF THE MANY ISLANDS ONCE SCATTERED ACROSS the Atlantic Ocean and now
lost to memory, one of the most intriguing is Isola des Demonias — Isle of
Demons. Located at the bleak and savage northern extremity of Newfoundland, Isle of Demons was reputedly inhabited by a curious mixture of wild
animals: bear and walrus, plus mythological creatures such as the gryphon.
Evil spirits or demons, being of a nature intermediate between gods and
men, abounded. These beasts and malignant spirits had one activity in common — "vying with each other to torment civilized man."

Tales of the island were recounted from the time of the first voyages to
the cod-fishing grounds off Newfoundland, but André Thevet, a French
scholar and writer, Franciscan friar and chaplain to Catherine de' Medici,
gives the most complete and vivid description. "True it is, and I myself have
heard it, not from one, but from a great number of sailors and pilots with
whom I have made many voyages, that when they passed this way, they heard
in the air, on the tops or about the masts, a great clamor of mens' voices,
confused and inarticulate, such as you may hear from the crowd at a fair or
market place; whereupon they well knew that the Isle of Demons was not far
off."[1] He allows that he himself had been on this very island and seen how
malicious these demons were, but he warded them off by repeating the Gospel of Saint John.

Thevet encountered the Isle of Demons on a voyage he made in 1555,
when he signed on as almoner to Nicholas Durant (called the Chevalier de
Villegagnon). They sailed the entire east coast of North and South America
as far north as Newfoundland, or Baccalaos (Codfish-land), as it was then
called. Upon his return, he published an account of his travels, *Les Singulari-*

téz de la France Antarctique, Autrement Nommé Amérique (The Peculiarities of Antarctic France, Otherwise Called America).

Much of what André Thevet wrote about the lands he visited was regarded later by historians as showing "excessive credulity" and including "drolleries, everywhere full of humor." Marc Lescarbot, a seventeenth-century French historian, condemned the credibility of Thevet as "suffering from his mendacity."

From Legend to Reality

Thevet's Isle of Demons may be the product of his imagination, but he was not the first to claim to have visited such a place. On October 17, 1540, Jacques Cartier received royal commission from Francis I, King of France, for his third voyage to Canada to colonize the new lands. The King resolved to send him far inland to live among the inhabitants and extend the knowledge of God. Appointed Captain-General and Master-Pilot of all the ships necessary for this enterprise, Cartier was also given fifty prisoners he considered "suitable and proper and capable to serve in the said expedition." Unless there was a profit to be made from the cod fishery, sufficient people to voyage to New France could be recruited only by beating, bribing or dragging those who had no choice; it was a land of "inhospitable climate, savage people and soil barren of gold."

Shortly afterward, Jean-François de La Rocque, Sieur de Roberval received a similar commission. He was to sail with Cartier "for conquest of these lands and to make settlements in the said country." Given the titles of Lieutenant-General, Chief, Commander and Captain of the enterprise, his authority exceeded that of Cartier. Roberval also received complete command over the new lands and the power to grant lands in feudal tenure. In effect, Roberval's commission annulled Cartier's, allowing him only so much authority as Roberval chose to tolerate. Fortunately, Cartier did not have to suffer this indignity, for when he had made all his preparations and the ships were ready to sail, Roberval was unable to accompany him. So the expedition of five ships filled with mariners, convicted criminals of both sexes, horses, cattle, swine, sheep, goats, poultry and twenty-five "persons of quality" departed in 1541 without Roberval.

The following year, Roberval, well armed and provisioned, sailed from La Rochelle, France, with his own fleet of three ships and two hundred colonists. By chance, the two parts of the expedition met in the harbour at St. John's, Newfoundland. Cartier had already abandoned his attempts at colonization and was returning to France. He tried to persuade Roberval of the uselessness of such a venture, but Roberval, determined to continue as originally planned, set sail toward the St. Lawrence.

Roberval's niece, Marguerite de La Roque, accompanied him on this journey, during which she injudiciously entered into a passionate love affair with one of the young officers on board. This perfidy so inflamed Roberval's religious principles that upon reaching the Isle of Demons he immediately put her ashore, along with four guns and an old nurse as a companion. It was not pity that moved Roberval to give the nurse to Marguerite, but vengeance: she had pandered to her mistress's illicit love. The young officer, who was about to be put in irons, seized the moment and jumped overboard to join Marguerite. Fate did not intend theirs to be a romantic idyll, for the demons at once beset them day and night. The young couple and their retainer drove the demons back only through readings from the New Testament and intercession by the Virgin Mary. Their religious fervour may have kept the demons at bay, but it did nothing against the other creatures, "beasts or other shapes abominably and unutterably hideous, the brood of hell, howling in baffled fury," which tore at the dwelling to get at the lovers.

Though Marguerite and her lover repented their sin, they did not abandon it, and Marguerite became pregnant. The infuriated tormentors redoubled their efforts. Eventually they won, for Marguerite's lover sickened and died, soon to be followed by the child, and finally by the old nurse. Now Marguerite faced her agony and despair alone. The demons were unscathed by her bullets, but the other creatures were "vulnerable to mortal weapons," and she killed three bears, all "as white as an egg." In this manner, she struggled to maintain her existence, until, two years and five months later, a passing fishing boat rescued her and brought her back to France. Not only did Marguerite survive her ordeal, but later she met Thevet in Périgord and told her tale to him.

André Thevet's tale is considered the product of invention, whereas Marguerite's is well substantiated. Yet the island upon which Marguerite de La Roque was banished and Thevet's Isle of Demons both contained the same evil spirits or demons, wild animals and mythological creatures. Can this varied group of beasts, common to both stories, be given credence? Surprisingly, the answer is Yes. The key element, and the one probably responsible for the island's name, is the "confused and inarticulate voices" that emanated from the island.

Portuguese and French mariners carefully timed their departure from European ports so as to arrive at Newfoundland when an ice-free passage through the Strait of Belle Isle into the Gulf of St. Lawrence could be assured. Coincidentally, this timing brought them to these shores during the nesting and breeding season of gannets and other pelagic birds. Consider the impact a large gannet colony must have made upon the passing mariner who had spent a long and lonely passage at sea, hearing only wind and wave, seeing nothing but the monotonous infinity of sky and water. Suddenly he would be engulfed in a cacophony of sound. The fog or mist he would encounter as he approached land would undoubtedly add a sense of apprehension and an aura of mystery to the clamorous event.

Normally, gannets are silent, but on their breeding grounds "males give a whistling call, and the females a resonant trumpeting." Auks, too, are seldom heard at sea, but when nesting they "utter low moans, guttural growls, quacks and croaks, a few species giving piping cries."[2] Imagine the din created by thousands of great white gannets nesting on the top of an island, while on the cliff-side, murres, auks, kittiwakes, black guillemots and Atlantic puffins add their raucous cries. This indeed would frighten anyone. Is it any wonder that this chaos of sound of an almost human nature would cause Friar Thevet, in his piety, to think he was hearing demons?

In 1534, when Captain Jacques Cartier made his first voyage to "explore the New-found-land of the cod fisheries, and the great river of Canada, called by him *Hochelaga* [St. Lawrence]," he made landfall at Cabo de Bona Vista (Cape Bonavista). From there, Cartier set a northerly course, making a second landfall at l'Isle des Ouaisseaulx (Isle of Birds, now called Greenly Island). He set the location of this island at 49°40′ N latitude and 14 leagues (42 miles) off the east shore of Newfoundland. L'Isle des Ouaisseaulx is so full of birds, he said, that "all the ships of France could easily load themselves there, without any difference being seen. The island was covered with snow-white, nesting birds, while a feathered umbrella of thousands more were flying and screeching." Among these birds were *margaulx* (gannets) and other members of the Alcid family which comfortably cohabit in gannet breeding sites: *apponatz* (great auk) and *godez* (either murre or razorbill auk). Cartier recorded the location of another island, on the south shore of Labrador, that was thickly covered with nesting birds — Bouyas (Isle au

Bois), as well as three small islets, Isles des Margaulx, which he named after the birds as "thick ashore as a meadow with grass."

These islands were shown on many of the sixteenth-century maps. On Ortelius's *Americae Sive Novi Orbis Nova Descriptio* (America, with a New Description of the New World), Isle of Birds is placed near Newfoundland, where it is labelled Des Oyseaux. An earlier map of 1555, by Guillaume de Testu more prosaically calls it I. Puanto (Stinking Island), because of the large quantities of guano there. Today, this offshore bit of land is called Funk Island.

Cartier describes the walrus as "a beast big as an ox, with two teeth in its mouth like an elephant, who lives in the sea." This fantastic and improbable creature certainly sounds like a mythological beast. As for other wild animals, fox and bear commonly raid these islands, easily swimming the great distances offshore to gorge themselves on the bounteous feast of fowl provided there. Nor were Marguerite's tormentors ordinary bears; they were "big as a cow, and white as a swan" — polar bears.

A Place on the Map

Confusion about the location of Isle of Demons is not surprising, for in the sixteenth century the northeast coast of North America was imperfectly understood. Inlets which cleft deeply into Newfoundland were originally thought to be straits leading into the Gulf of St. Lawrence. It was not until the beginning of the seventeenth century that the multiple "islands" of Newfoundland, as shown on the maps, coalesced into a single entity. The task would have been easier if early explorers had given cartographers reliable and consistent coordinates of latitude and longitude. But longitude calculations were beyond their ability, and latitude determination was often in error.

The first depiction of Isle of Demons may be on the world map drawn by Andrea Bianco in 1436, labelled Y.ª de la Satanaxio, or on the 1435 map by Beccario, where it is called Satanagio. The names are the Genoese and Venetian versions of the Portuguese word *satanazes*, which means satans or devils. Neither of these may actually represent the Isle of Demons, for there are no nearby landmasses to fix the island's position. From its placement at the very edge of the map and north and west of the Sargasso Sea, it may have been in-

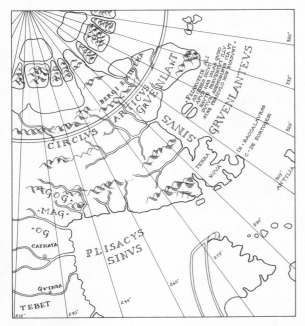

Fig. 5-1.
Detail of map by Johannes Ruysch, *Universalior Cogniti Orbis Tabula.* Published in 1508 in *Geographia*, it incorporated the North American discoveries made by Columbus and Cabot into the old geography of Ptolemy. Greenland is shown continuous with the northern portion of the New World, which merges in its western part with Cathay. See *Fig. 8-4* for a view of the entire map.

tended to border on the New World. But its demonic character may be more a coincidence of names than a true geographical relationship.

There is no ambiguity, however, on the 1508 map of Johannes Ruysch. In the large bay between Gruenlant and Terra Nova is a pair of islands accompanied by the legend: "*Apud has insulas quando naute perveniunt illuduntur a demonibus ita ut sine periculo non evadunt*" (Demons assaulted ships near these islands, which were avoided, but not without peril). These islands are north of the Strait of Belle Isle, near the entrance to Hamilton Inlet and Groswater Bay, roughly at 54°00′ N latitude and 56°30′ W longitude.

An undated (c. 1540) Portuguese map by Sebastian Lopes is more primitive in its display of geographic information, yet key landmarks and place-names are evident: Bacalhaos, Cabo Raso (Cape Race), I. de Aves (Island of Birds), and, at the mouth of Hamilton Inlet, I. de Tormenta (Isle of Demons). Perhaps its companion island, I. de Fortuna (Isle of Fortune), is placed there to point a Christian moral.

Later maps (such as the Pseudo-Agnese map of 1556) shifted the position of the island, or pair of islands, closer to the eastern shore of Labrador. Elsewhere, the Isle of Demons, or Island of the Tormented, as it was sometimes called, is variously shown at the entrance to the Strait of Belle Isle at the northern tip of Newfoundland, as on the Mercator world map of 1569, or slightly farther north near the entrance to Hamilton Inlet. Gannet Island on contemporary maps closely corresponds to this position. Isle of Demons is prominently shown on the Abraham Ortelius map of the New World, where it is placed in a position similar to that on the Lopes map. Though these maps never precisely locate the Isle of Demons, nonetheless they present evidence of a persistent and pronounced belief, lasting well over a century, in an island of diabolical evil on the shores of North America.

In 1544, Roberval's pilot, Jean Alphonse, published an account of the voyage in *La Cosmographie*. It contains detailed descriptions of the coast, its navigational hazards, and relevant information about distances and directions. With all the material provided in *La Cosmographie*, it should be easy to retrace the exact route of Roberval's vessels and determine the true position

I. de tormenta
I. de fortuna

C. Raso

Fig. 5-2.
Portuguese map by
Sebastian Lopes, c. 1540.

of Marguerite's island. Alphonse pays elaborate attention, with precise nauti-cal details, to two small islands he called Isles de la Demoiselle. He makes no explicit statement about putting Marguerite de La Roque ashore here, but the name suggests the interpretation. Alphonse places these isles at 50°45′N latitude. From this position and the stated relative distances to other land-marks, the American historian Samuel Eliot Morison concluded that Isles de la Demoiselle is among the Harrington Islands on the south shore of Labra-dor, the same as Ysles Saincte Martre (Isles of Saint Martha), named many years earlier by Cartier.

Therefore, it seems that the Island of Demons shown off the east coast of Labrador could not be the same island where Marguerite de La Roque was deposited. But deducing the course of Roberval's voyage from *La Cosmo-graphie* is as perilous for the historiographer as shoals and ledges are for the mariner. With no means to calculate longitude, Alphonse could only approxi-mate the distances Roberval travelled using the combination of latitude fixes

Fig. 5-3.
Pseudo-Agnese map of
1556-1560. The size of Ysala
de Demon on this map
reflects its importance in the
mind

and dead reckoning. He could not even rely on the most simple instrument, the compass, due to the proximity of this region to the magnetic pole.

Nor is Alphonse's account in *La Cosmographie* quite as first-hand as one would suppose. He gives distances between landmasses which he could not have measured directly; his information could have come only from someone else who had been there before. And indeed records show that some of the men from Cartier's first voyage were aboard Roberval's ships. In other instances, Alphonse gives directions that he could have taken only from another map. W.F. Ganong studied this problem carefully and diligently. In *Crucial Maps*, he concludes that Alphonse's description of the southern portion of the Gulf of St. Lawrence and Cabot Strait "is so brief, generalized, and erroneous, as to show he never passed that way."[3] Most likely, then, Roberval returned home the same way he entered the St. Lawrence — through the Strait of Belle Isle.

After Marguerite's return to France and her meeting with Thevet, the tale was published in *Le Grand Insulaire et Pilotage d'André Thevet, Cosmographe du Roy* (1586). Here, Thevet variously calls the Isle of Demons Isle de Fiche, Isle de Roberval and Isle des Démons, saying, "It is a small island situated near the north extremity of Newfoundland." This does not tell us whether it is the same as Cartier's Island of Saint Martha, as S.E. Morison concludes; in fact, it suggests another site altogether. Saint Martha (in the Harrington Islands) is directly off the *Labrador* shore. From St. Martha to the nearest Newfoundland coast is fully a hundred miles; moreover, it is roughly opposite the middle of the western shore, a long way from the "north extremity of Newfoundland."

Francis Parkman, in his *Pioneers of France in the New World* (1865), says only that Roberval set sail from St. John's, Newfoundland, "steering northward to the Straits of Belle Isle and the dreaded Isle of Demons. After depositing these unfortunates to the devils and wild beasts, the ship weighed anchor, receded and vanished . . . Roberval held his course up the St. Lawrence." There are two ways Parkman's statement could be interpreted: either Roberval *entered* the Strait of Belle Isle, deposited his niece, and continued

Fig. 5-4.
Detail of map titled *Americae Sive Novi Orbis Nova Descriptio,* from the atlas *Theatrum Orbis Terrarum* by Abraham Ortelius (1570). As well as the Isle of Demons (Des Demonias), it shows many of the other phantom islands of the Atlantic: Saint Brendan (S. Brandani), Frisland, Antillia or Island of Seven Cities (Sept Cites), and Santana (a variant of Satanazes), an island usually shown on charts as a companion island north of Antillia.

Fig. 5-5.
Present-day map of Canada's Atlantic provinces. Fichot Island, the presumed Isle
of Demons, is near the northern tip of Newfoundland.

up the St. Lawrence; or, after depositing his niece at the Isle of Demons, he *then* entered the Strait of Belle Isle and continued his course up the St. Lawrence.

Obviously, Des Demonias near Hamilton Inlet could not be the same Isle of Demons of Marguerite's exile. If Roberval was so incensed by the behaviour of his niece that he "immediately put her ashore," it is hardly likely he sailed along 210 miles of uninhabited coastline, dropped her off, and then backtracked the same distance, travelling a total of 420 miles out of his way, before resuming his course through the Strait of Belle Isle into the St. Lawrence.

In a brief but significant footnote, Parkman says the island is the same as Isle Fichet — Fichot Island on some modern maps. This comes from Thevet's 1586 account, which came directly from Marguerite de La Roque. Even though André Thevet exaggerated or enhanced elements of her experience for storytelling purposes, the underlying basis of truth cannot be ignored.

Certainly any of the numerous gannet breeding colonies off the east coast of Newfoundland or Labrador could be the Isle of Demons, but two are most probable: Fichot Island, close to the entrance of the Strait of Belle Isle, and a more southerly island, Isle of Birds (Funk Island); Fichot Island, which lies near the northern extremity of Newfoundland, best fits the evidence. Fichot Island is but a tiny speck of land, flung far out to sea, in a most inhospitable climate. Pity, then, poor Marguerite de La Roque, who endured her hellish torment throughout her sojourn there. For her, truly it was the Isle of Demons.

The Tale Transformed

As well as having a cartographic existence, the Isle of Demons became firmly established in literature. André Thevet was not alone in spreading the story of Marguerite's woe. Marguerite de Navarre, Queen of Navarre and sister of Francis I, used it in her book, *Histoires des Amans Fortunez*. First printed in 1558, this collection of stories contributed by a number of people was structured like Boccaccio's *Decameron* or Chaucer's *Canterbury Tales*, in which fictional characters "find themselves in dangerous or unusual situations." The *Heptameron*, as the book is commonly called, contains seventy-two stories; number sixty-seven is about Marguerite de La Roque. In essence, the story does not wander greatly from historical facts, especially where it recounts Captain Roberval's voyage to Canada to create a new colony. Where it markedly differs is in the role of Marguerite de La Roque; Marguerite de Navarre says she was left on the island through no perfidy on her part but because she wept and pleaded with the captain not to separate her from her husband, though he was a "wicked traitor."

Alone on the desolate island, Marguerite and her husband fought off the wild beasts as best they could — not the gryphon, walrus or polar bear, but creatures more familiar to the story's audience: lions, in spite of the wildly improbable habitat. Eventually, her husband died and Marguerite had to endure her hardships alone, "her bodily existence no higher than that of the beasts, but her soul in the sphere of the angels; for she spent her time in reading the Scriptures, contemplation, prayer and other devotions." Marguerite de Navarre heaps on her the highest praise and makes her a shining example in her fidelity to her husband and in her steadfast belief in God.

Chapter VI

Frisland

ONE OF THE MOST UNUSUAL AND CONTROVERSIAL MAPS in the chronicles of cartography resulted from a voyage made in 1380 by a Venetian nobleman, Nicolò Zeno. A violent storm in the North Atlantic cast Nicolò upon the island of Frisland. There he met Zichmni, a great lord and owner of Frisland. Zichmni desired to conquer and possess more territory; with Nicolò as counsel, and the Venetian mariners as pilots, he won many lands with little effort. As a reward he made Nicolò a knight and gave him gifts. Nicolò wrote to invite his brother, Antonio, in Venice, to join him, and both brothers lived in Frisland for four years. Nicolò died there, but Antonio, remained for another ten years in the service of Zichmni. During his stay, Antonio met another sailor whose boat had been driven by a gale to lands much farther west than Frisland. This sailor told him about encounters with a civilized people in Estotiland who could speak Latin but not Norse. There were other lands, too, much farther south, which had great towns and temples.

Antonio returned to Venice, where he died. Most of the story about the voyage and the events that occurred during those fourteen years is contained in letters written by Antonio to a third brother, Carlo. These letters and a map of the region remained in the Zeno family, neglected and unpublished, for several generations. Then Nicolò Zeno the younger, a descendant of the voyager Nicolò, collected all the documents that were available. As a youth, he had read the letters, but when he was finished he had torn them up. In compiling the narrative, Nicolò the younger used the few remaining scraps of letters he could find and augmented them with what he could remember. The story of the Zeno brothers' voyage, accompanied by a map redrawn as well as possible from the aged and partially obliterated original, was finally published in Venice in 1558 by Francesco Marcolino. Marcolino's work was translated into English and appeared in 1660 in Richard Hakluyt's *Voyages, Navigations, Traffiques, and Discoueries of the English Nation*.[1]

The Discouerie of the Isles of Frisland

The discouerie of the Isles of Frisland, Iseland, Engroneland,
Estotiland, Drogeo and Icaria: made by two brethren,
namely M. Nicholas Zeno and M. Antonio his brother:
Gathered out of their letters by M. Francisco Marcolino.

. . . M. *Carlo Il grande* [was] the famous Procurator and Captain general against the *Genoese* in those cruel wars, when almost all the chief Princes of *Europe* did attack and seek to overthrow our Empire and liberty, wherein by his great valiance and prowess, as *Furious Camillus* delivered *Rome*, so he delivered his country from the present peril it was in, being ready to become a prey and captive of the enemy: wherefore he was afterward surnamed the *Lyon* in his arms. M. *Carlo* had two brothers, M. *Nicolò* the knight, and M. *Antonio* the father of M. *Dragon*, of whom issued M. *Caterino*, the father of M. *Pietto da i Crocecchieri*. This M. *Pietro* had sons M. *Caterino*, that died the last year, being brother unto M. *Francisco*, M. *Carlo*, M. *Battista*, and M. *Vincenzo*: Which M. *Caterieno* was father to M. *Nicolò* (the younger) that is still living.

Now M. Nicolò the knight, being a man of great courage, after this previously mentioned *Genoan* war of *Chioggia* that so troubled our predecessors, had a great desire and fancy to see the fashions of the world and to travel and acquaint himself with the manners of sundry nations and learn their languages, whereby afterwards upon occassions he might be the better able to be of service to his country, and create for himself credit and honour. Wherefore he caused a ship to be made, and, having furnished her at his proper charges (as he was very wealthy), he departed out of our seas, and, passing the Straits of *Gibraltar*, he sailed for certain days upon the Ocean, keeping his course still to the Northwards, intending to see *England* and *Flanders*. Where being assaulted in those Seas by a terrible tempest, he was so tossed for the space of many days with the sea and wind, that he knew not where he was, till at length he discovered land, and, not being able any longer to sustain the violence of the tempest, the ship was thrown upon the Isle of *Frisland*. The men and most part of the goods that were in the ship were saved. This was in the year 1380.

The inhabitants of the Island came running in great multitude with weapons to set upon M. *Nicolò* and his men, who, being badly weather-beaten and over-worked at sea, and not knowing in what part of the world they were, were not able to make any resistance at all, much less to defend themselves courageously, as it behooved them in such a dangerous case. And they should have been doubtless very discourteously treated and cruelly handled, if by chance there had not been close by the place a prince with armed people. Who, understanding that there was presently a great ship cast away upon the Island, came running at the noise and outcries that they made against our poor Mariners, and driving away the inhabitants, spoke in Latin and asked them what they were and where they came from, and perceiving that they came from *Italy* and that they were men of the said Country, he was surprised with marvellous great joy. Wherefore promising them all that they should receive no discourtesy, and that they had come to a place where they would be well used and very welcome, he took them into his protection upon his faith. This was a great Lord, and possessed certain Islands called *Porland*, lying on the South side of *Frisland*, being the richest and most populous of all those parts. His name was *Zichmni*: and besides the said little Islands, he was Duke of *Sorani*, lying over against *Scotland*.

Of these North parts I thought it good to draw the copy of a Sea card, which among other antiquities I have in my house, which although it is rotten through many years, it still appears quite well: and to those that are delighted in these things, it may give some light to the understanding of that, which without it cannot so easily be conceived. *Zichmni* being Lord of those Signories (as is said) was a very warlike and valiant man and above all things famous in Sea causes. And having the year before overthrown the king of *Norway*, who was Lord of the Island, desired to win fame by feats of arms, and landed with his men on *Frisland*, which is an Island much bigger than *Ireland*, in an attempt to win it. Wherefore seeing that M. *Nicolò* was a man of judgement and discretion, and very expert both in sea matters and martial affairs, he gave him commission to go aboard his Navy with all his men, charging the captain to honour him and in all things to use his counsel.

This Navy of *Zichmni* had thirteen vessels, whereof only two were rowed with oars, the rest were small barks, and one ship with which they sailed to the Westwards and with little effort won *Ledouo* and *Ilose* and various other small Islands: and turning into a bay called *Sudero*, in the haven of the town named *Sanestol*, they took certain small barks laden with fish. And here they found *Zichmni*, who came by land with his army, conquering all the country as he went: they stayed here for a while, then continued their course to the Westwards till they came to the other Cape of the gulf or bay, then turning again, they found certain Islands and broken lands which they reduced all unto the Signorie and possession of *Zichmni*. These seas, for as much as they sailed, were in manner nothing but shoals and rocks, and if M. *Nicolò* and the Venetian mariners had not been their Pilots, the whole fleet in judgement of all that were in it, would have been lost, so small was the skill of *Zichmni's* men, in respect of ours, who had been trained in the art and practice of Navigation all the days of their life.

Now the fleet having done such things as declared, the Captain, by the counsel of M. *Nicolò*, determined to land at a town called *Bondendon*, to understand what success *Zichmni* had in his wars: they heard, to their great content, that he had fought a great battle and put to flight the army of his enemy: by reason of which victory, they sent Ambassadors from all parts of the Island to yield the country up into his hands, taking down their ensigns in every town and castle: they thought it best to remain there for his arrival, it being reported for certain that he would be there very shortly. At his coming there was great congratulations and many signs of gladness showed, both for the victory by land, as well as that by sea: for which the Venetians were honoured and extolled of all men, in so much that there was talk only of them, and of the great valour of M. *Nicolò*. Wherefore the prince, who greatly favoured valiant men and especially those that could behave themselves well at sea, caused M. *Nicolò* to be brought before him, and after having commended him with many honourable speeches, and praised his great industry and dexterity of wit, by which two things he acknowledged himself to have received an inestimable benefit, as the saving of his fleet and the winning of many places without any great trouble, he made him knight, and rewarded his men with many rich and bountiful gifts. Then departing from thence they went in triumphal manner toward *Frisland*, and the chief city of that Island, situated on the Southeast side of the Isle, within a gulf, as there are many in that Island. In this gulf or bay there is such great abundance of fish taken, that many ships are laden therewith to serve *Flanders*, *Britain*, *England*, *Scotland*, *Norway* and *Denmark*, and by this trade they gather great wealth.

And this much is taken out of a letter that M. *Nicolò* sent to M. *Antonio* his brother, requesting that he would seek some means to come to him. Wherefore *Antonio*, who had as great a desire to travel as his brother, bought a ship and directed his course that way: and after he had sailed a great while and escaped many dangers, he arrived at length in safety with M. *Nicolò*, who received him very joyfully, for he was his brother not only in flesh and blood, but also in valour and good qualities.

M. *Antonio* remained in *Frisland* and dwelled there for the space of fourteen years, four years with M. *Nicolò*, and ten years alone. Where they came in such grace and favour with the Prince, that he made M. *Nicolò* Captain of his Navy, and with great preparation of war they were sent forth for the enterprise of *Estland*, which lyeth upon the coast between *Frisland* and *Norway*, where they caused much damage: but hearing that the king of *Norway* was coming towards them with a great fleet, they departed with such a terrible wind that they were driven upon certain shoals: where a great part of their ships were lost, the rest were saved upon *Grisland*, a great Island but uninhabited. The king of *Norway*'s fleet, encountering the same storm, did utterly perish in those seas: Whereof *Zichmni* having notice, by a ship of his enemies that was cast by chance upon *Grisland*, having repaired his fleet, and perceiving himself Northerly close to the Islands, determined to set upon *Island*, which together with the rest, was subject to the king of *Norway*: but he found the country so well fortified and defended, and his fleet so small and very ill appointed with weapons and men, he was glad to retire. And so he left that enterprise without performing anything at all.

And in the same channels he assaulted the other Isles called *Islande*, which are seven, *Talas, Broas, Iscant, Trans, Mimant, Dambere* and *Bres*: and having ravaged them all, he built a fort in *Bres*, where he left M. *Nicolò*, with certain small barks and men and ammunition. And now thinking he had done well for this voyage, with those few steps which were left he returned safely to *Frisland*. M. *Nicolò*, remaining now in *Bres*, determined in the spring to go forth and discover land: wherefore arming out three small barks in the month of July, he sailed Northwards, and arrived in *Engroneland* [Greenland]. Where he found a Monastery of Friars, of the order of the *Predicators*, and a Church dedicated to *S. Thomas* close to a hill that cast forth fire like *Vesuvius* and *Etna*.

There is a fountain of hot burning water, with which they heat the Church of the Monastery and the Friar's chambers, it also comes into the kitchen so boiling hot that they use no other fire to prepare their meat: and putting their bread into brass pots without any water, it bakes as though it were in a hot oven. They have also small gardens covered over in the wintertime, which being watered with this water, are defended from the force of the snow and cold, which, in these parts, being situated far under the Pole, is very extreme, and by this means they produce flowers and fruits and herbs of sundry sorts, even as in other temperate countries in their seasons, in such sort that the rude and savage people of those parts, seeing these supernatural effects, do take these Friars for Gods, and bring them many presents, as chickens, meat, and various other things, and hold them all in great reverence as Lords. When the frost and snow is great, they heat their houses in the manner before said, and, by letting in the water or opening the window, at an instant temper the heat and cold at their pleasure.

In the buildings of the Monastery they use no other matter but that which is ministered unto them by the fire: for they take the burning stones that are cast out as it were sparkles or cinders at the fiery mouth of the hill, and, when they are most enflamed, cast water upon them, whereby they are dissolved and become excellent white lime, so tough that, being used in building, it lasts forever. And the very sparkles, after the fire is out of them, do serve instead of stones to make walls and vaults: for being once cold they will never dissolve or break, except when cut with some iron tool, and the vaults that are made of them are so tight that they need no substance or support to hold them up, and they will endure continually very fair and whole. By reason of these great commodities, the Friars have made there so many buildings and walls that it is a wonder to see. The covers or roofs of their houses for the most part are made in the following manner: first they raise up the wall up to its full height, then they make it incline or bow in by little and little in some form of a vault. But they are not greatly troubled with rain in those parts, because the climate (as I have said) is extremely cold: their winter endures so long that when the first snow falls it does not thaw for nine months.

They feed off the flesh of wild fowl and of fish: where the warm water falls into the sea, there is a large and wide harbour, which by reason of the heat of the water never freezes all winter, by means whereof there is such concourse and flocks of sea fowl and such abundance of fish, that they take thereof infinite multitudes, whereby they maintain a great number of people round about, which they keep continually working, both in building and taking of fowls and fish, and in a thousand necessary affairs and business about the Monastery.

Their houses are built about the hill on every side, in form round, and 25 feet broad, and in mounting upwards they go narrower and narrower, leaving at the top a little hole, where the air comes in to give light to the house, and the floor of the house is so hot that, being within, they feel no cold at all. In the Summertime many barks come from the Islands thereabout, and from the cape above *Norway* [North Cape], and from *Trondon*, and bring to the Friars all manner of things that may be desired, taking fish in exchange, which they dry in the sun or in the cold, and skins of various kinds of beasts. For which they have wood to burn, and timber very artfully carved, and coin, and cloth to make them apparel. For in exchange for the two aforesaid commodities all the nations bordering around about them covet to trade with them, so the Friars, without any travel or expenses, have that which they desire.

Friars of *Norway*, of *Suetia* and of other countries, but the most part from *Island*, retire to this monastery. There are continually in that part many barks, which are kept in there by reason of the sea being frozen, waiting for the spring of the year to dissolve the ice. The fishermen's boats are made like a weaver's shuttle: taking the skins of fishes [seals], they fashion them with the bones of the same fishes, and sewing them together in many doubles they make them so sure and substantial that it is marvellous to see, how in tempests they will shut themselves closed within and let the sea and wind carry them they care not where, without any fear either of the boat breaking or their drowning. And if by chance they are driven upon any rocks, they remain sound without the least bruise in the world: they have as it were a sleeve in the bottom, which is tied fast in the middle, and when any water comes into the boat, they put it into the one half of the sleeve, then fastening the end with two pieces of wood and loosening the band beneath, they convey the water forth from the boat: and this they do as often as they have occasion, without any peril or impediment at all.

Moreover, the water of the Monastery, being sulphurous or brimstoney in nature, is conveyed into the lodgings of the principal Friars by certain vessels of brass, tin or stone, so hot that it heats the place as it were a stove, not carrying with it any stink or other annoying smell.

Besides this, they have another conveyance to bring hot water through an underground tunnel, so that it should not freeze, into the middle of the court, where it falls into a great vessel of brass that stands in the middle of a boiling fountain, and this is to heat the water they drink and to water their gardens, and thus they have from the hill the greatest commodities that may be wished: and so these Friars labour and study for the most part in tending their gardens and in making fair and beautiful buildings, especially handsome and commodious: neither are they destitute of ingenious and diligent craftsmen for the purpose; for they give very large payment to those that bring fruits and seeds that are very bountiful, and give they care not what. So that there is great resort of workmen and masters in various faculties, by reason of the good gains and large allowance that is there.

Most of them speak the Latin tongue, and especially the superiors and principals of the Monastery. And this is as much as is known of *Engroneland*, which is all related by M. *Nicolò*, who makes also particular description of a river that he discovered, as is to be seen in the card that I drew. And in the end M. *Nicolò*, not being used to and acquainted with this cruel cold climate, fell sick, and a little while after returned to *Frisland*, where he died. He left behind him in *Venice* two sons, M. *Giovanni* and M. *Toma*, who had two sons, M. *Nicolò* the father of the famous Cardinal *Zeno*, and M. *Pietro* of whom descended the other *Zenos* that are living at this day.

Now M. *Nicolò* being dead, M. *Antonio* succeeded him both in his goods and in his dignities and honour: and although he attempted various ways and made great supplication, he could never obtain permission to return to his country. For *Zichmni*, being a man of great courage and valour, had determined to make himself Lord of the sea. Wherefore using always the counsel and service of M. *Antonio*, he determined to send him with certain barks to the Westwards, for towards those parts some of his fishermen had discovered certain Islands very rich and populous: this discovery M. *Antonio*, in a letter to his brother M. *Carlo*, recounts from point to point in this manner, except for some old words which we have changed, leaving the matter entirely as it was.

Twenty-six years ago there departed four fishing boats, which, when a mighty tempest arose, were tossed for the space of many days very desperately upon the Sea. When at length the storm ceased and the weather became fair, they discovered an Island called *Estotiland*, lying to the Westwards more than a 1000 miles from *Frisland*, upon which one of the boats was thrown, and six men that were in it were taken by the inhabitants and brought to a fair and populous city, where the king of the place sent for many interpreters, but there was none who could be found that understood the language of the fishermen, except one that spoke Latin, who was also cast by chance upon the same Island, who on behalf of the king asked them what countrymen they were: and so understanding their case, repeated it to the king, who willed that they should remain in the country: wherefore they obeyed his commandment, for they could not do otherwise; they lived five years on the Island, and learned the language, and one of them was in various parts of the Island, and reports that it is a very rich country, abounding with all the commodities of the world, and that it is little less [in size] than *Island* but far more fruitful, having in the middle of the land a very high mountain, from which there spring four rivers that pass through the whole country.

The inhabitants are very wise people, and have all the arts and aptitudes that we have: and it is credible that in past times they have had traffic with our men, for he said that he saw Latin books in the king's Library, which at the present time they do not understand: they have a peculiar language, and letters or characters [known] to themselves. They have mines of all manner of metals, but especially they abound with gold. They have their trade in *Engroneland*, from where they bring furs, brimstone and pitch: and he says that to the Southwards, there is a great populous country very rich in gold. They sow corn, and make beer and ale, which is a kind of drink that North people use as we do wine. They have mighty great woods, they make their buildings with walls, and there are many cities and castles. They build small barks and have sailing, but they do not have the lodestone, nor know the use of the compass. Wherefore these fishermen were held in great estimation, in so much that the king sent them with twelve barks Southwards to a country which they call *Drogio*: in their voyage they had such contrary weather, that they thought they would perish in the sea: but escaping that cruel death, they fell into another more cruel: for they were taken [captive] in the country and most of them were eaten by the Savage people, which feed upon man's flesh as the sweetest meat in their judgement that there is. . . .

Now this fisherman, having dwelt so many years in those countries, decided, if it were possible, to return home to his country, but his companions, despairing of ever seeing it again, let him go in God's name, and they kept themselves where they were. Wherefore he bid them farwell, fled through the woods towards *Drogio*, and was very well received by the Lord that dwelled next to that place; who knew him and was a great enemy of the other Lord: and so, running from one Lord to another, being those by whom he had passed before, after a long time and many travails he came at length to *Drogio*, where he dwelt three years. When by good fortune he heard from the inhabitants that there were certain boats arrived upon the coast; wherefore, entering into good hope to accomplish his intent, he went to the seaside and asked them of what country they were; they answered, of *Estotiland*, whereat he was exceedingly glad, and requested that they would take him with them, which they did very willingly, and since he had the language of the country and there was none there that could speak it, they used him for their interpreter.

And afterward he frequented that trade with them in such sort that he became very rich, and so, furnishing out a bark of his own, he returned to *Frisland*, where he reported to the Lord about that wealthy country. . . .

Wherefore retaining only the barks with *Dares* and such as were willing to stay with him, [Zichmni] sent all the rest with the ships back again, and willed that I [Antonio], (though unwilling) should be their captain. Therefore departing, because I could not choose otherwise, sailed for the space of twenty days to the Eastwards without sight of any land; then turning my course towards the Southeast, in five days I discovered land, and found myself upon the Isle of *Neome*, and, knowing the country, I perceived I was past *Island*: wherefore taking in some fresh victuals from the inhabitants being subject to *Zichmni*, I sailed with a fair wind in three days to *Frisland*, where the people, who thought they had lost their prince because of his long absence in this our voyage, received us very joyfully.

What followed after this letter I know only by conjecture, which I gathered from a piece of another letter, which I will set down here as follows: That Zichmni built a town in the port of the Island that he discovered, and that he searched the country very diligently and discovered it all, and also the rivers on both sides of *Engroneland*, for that I see it particularly described in the sea cards. But the discourse or narration is lost. The beginning of the letter is thus:

Concerning those things that you desire to know of me, as of the men and their manners and customs, of the beasts, and of the countries adjoining, I have made thereof a particular book, which by God's help I will bring with me: wherein I have described the country, the monstrous fishes, the customs and laws of *Frisland*, *Island*, the kingdom of *Norway*, *Estotiland*, and in the end the life of M. *Nicolò*, the knight our brother, with the discovery which he made and the state of *Groneland*. I have also written the life and acts of *Zichmni*, a prince as worthy of immortal memory as any that ever lived for his great valiance and singular humanity, wherein I have described the discovery of *Engroneland* on both sides, and the city that he built. Therefore I will speak no further hereof in this letter, hoping to be with you very shortly, and to satisfy you in sundry other things by word of mouth.

A Local Habitation and a Name

The tales recounted in this document and the map which accompanied it created an immediate interest in Italy and the rest of Europe. Previously, lands in the far North Atlantic had not been shown so completely, nor had their geography been described in such detail. The most eminent cartographers of the sixteenth century accepted this new information without question and incorporated the newly displayed lands, especially Frisland, into their maps. Frisland is included on Gerardus Mercator's influential map of 1569, which showed for the first time his new projection plan (see *Fig. 3-6*), as well as on his later maps, published in 1587 and 1595. It was this 1569 map, considered the finest at the time, that Martin Frobisher carried with him on his voyages in 1576-1578 in search of the Northwest Passage. Frisland was shown on the Molyneux globe of 1592, on the Petrus Plancius map *Orbis Terrarum Typus* in 1594, and on Hessel Gerritsz's map of 1612 used to illustrate Henry Hudson's last voyage. The famous Flemish cartographer, Abraham Ortelius, displayed Frisland on the map of America in his *Theatrum Orbis Terrarum* atlas of 1570 (see *Fig. 5-4*).

Estotiland, which by implication on the Zeno map is an island, is identified with Labrador by Ortelius. This is proof, he says, that America was not first discovered by Christopher Columbus, "as all the writers of our time ascribe." Ortelius goes on to say that Columbus is certainly worthy of this distinction, but as "for the North part, called *Estotiland* which most of all extendeth toward our Europe, and the islands of the same, namely, *Groneland, Island* and *Frisland*," they were first found by the fishermen of Frisland, and then they were rediscovered by Antonio Zeno while he was in Zichmni's service. Even before the time of Columbus, Ortelius says, "our European pilots sailed those seas by the help of the lodestone . . . concerning the use thereof, I suppose there is not to be found a better proof than this ancient testimony [of Zeno]."

Unlike the other phantom islands, which continually shifted their position on maps of the Atlantic, Frisland remains fixed; shown south of Iceland, its southern coast was roughly at 60°00′ to 61°00′ N latitude. The constancy of the island's location is not surprising, since it was derived from a single common source.

Drogeo, like Estotiland, had not been heard of before the Zeno document. The position of these two lands relative to each other suggests that Drogeo is the land later called Terra Nova — that is, Newfoundland. If this

Fig. 6-1.
Carta da Navegar of M. Nicolò the Chevalier and M. Antonio Zeno as it first appeared in 1558 (adapted). Forty place-names cover the island of Frisland, including seven towns. Many of the geographic features depicted on Engroneland (Greenland), particularly promontories, are also identified with names, the farthest north being Neum Promontor, fully 540 nautical miles north of the Arctic Circle.

identification is correct, it is hard to reconcile it with the description of its inhabitants, cannibals "who feed upon man's flesh, as the sweetest meat in their judgement that there is."

The Zeno map shows Greenland attached at its northern end to the continent of Europe. In the sixteenth century, cartographers were perplexed about where to place Greenland. Part of the problem arose from the extreme magnetic variation in this region; close to Greenland the difference between magnetic north and true north is as much as 30°00′ to the west, and in the Labrador Sea it increases up to 40°00′. Consequently, as mariners sailed west in the high latitudes of the Atlantic they found that their position did not correspond with where they ought to be according to the chart. This confusion, plus the inability to determine longitude, prevented any accurate determination of Greenland's position.

Apart from the pragmatic problem of compass variation, there was a philosophical problem about Greenland's inhabitants. Fourteenth-century Scandinavian stories relate the invasion of Norse settlements in Greenland by a large group of Eskimos. A battle was fought in which the Eskimos were the victors. If, as it was believed, all mankind originated from one source, then the Eskimos could have reached Greenland only by way of some kind of land-bridge from Eurasia. The various postulations about this land-bridge account for the unusual locations for Greenland on maps of this period; sometimes it was attached to Europe, other times it was attached to the northeast part of Asia (as on the Johannes Ruysch map of 1507), and on occasion it was an appendage to a polar continent.[2] When the Zeno map was introduced into the Ptolemy Atlas of Girolamo Ruscelli in 1561, an important change was made: Greenland was severed from Norway, resulting in a strait of open water between the two. This new depiction of Greenland was repeated thereafter in many other editions of the Ptolemy atlas.

Fact or Fiction?

Some historians, however, did not entirely believe the Zeno story. The Reverend Samuel Purchas, a compiler of English maritime history, added other relevant documents to the Hakluyt records in *Hakluytus Posthumus, or*

Purchas his Pilgrimes (1625). Into the 1626 edition of his book, Purchas inserted a large section of the Zeno narrative. He cautiously concludes:

> This History I have thus inserted at large, which, perhaps, not without cause in some things, may seem fabulous; not in the *Zeni,* which thus writ, but in the Relations they received from others. Howsoever; the best Geographers are beholden to these Bretheren, for that little knowledge they have of these parts; of which none before had written: nor since have there been any great in-land Discoveries.[3]

As fifteenth-century maps containing many of the same features as the Zeno map were rediscovered by cartographers, doubts arose about the authenticity of Nicolò Zeno's narrative and map. The attachment of the northern end of Engroneland (Greenland) to the northern coast of Eurasia, which at first seemed unique to the *Carta da Navegar* of Nicolò, was found on four other earlier maps. A 1467 map in the Zamoisky Majorat Library at Warsaw was like the Zeno map not only in the location of Greenland, but in the various names and legends for rivers and islets, which seemingly were of Scandinavian origin. Missing, though, from the Zamoisky map were the islands of Podanda, Neome, Icaria and Frisland, as well as the monastery of Saint Thomas in Greenland which Nicolò Zeno describes in such detail. Adolf E. Nordenskiöld, the famous Arctic explorer and historian, contends that both of these maps were derived from some earlier prototype which derived its information from Norse voyages.

As additional maps were found, over four hundred books and articles were written analysing the Zeno story and map. Debate over authenticity versus forgery continued to the very end of the nineteenth century, when it then polarized around the writings of two historians — Richard Henry Major and Frederick W. Lucas — who exhaustively researched the problem. Each writes convincingly in support of his belief. Lucas accuses Nicolò Zeno the younger "of the perpetration of a contemptible literary fraud — one of the most successful and obnoxious on record." He bases this conclusion on the number of earlier sources (written accounts and maps) which contain almost all the geography and place-names found on the Zeno map, purported there to be "new discoveries." Lucas's work is so thorough and complete that it is difficult to keep from being swept away by the tidal wave of documentation.

The general configuration of the island of Frisland duplicates in all respects that of Fixlanda, displayed on two earlier maps: a fifteenth-century

Catalan map in Milan, and the Matheus Prunes map of 1553 in Sienna. On these maps the general outline of Fixlanda, as well as the disposition of the smaller isles surrounding it, are the same as represented for Frisland. The cluster of islands south of Frisland correspond to the Westmann Islands off the south coast of Iceland; the solitary island north of Frisland can be correlated with Grimsey; while the several peninsulas, bays and numerous isles on the west coast closely match the contour of Iceland. Lucas leaves no doubt that in physical resemblance, Frisland, Fixlanda and Iceland are all the same island. However, when it comes to the place-names shown on Frisland the evidence is less compelling. Seven of the forty names on Frisland are found on early maps of the Färoe Islands: Farre Insula, Monachus, Sudero, Nordero, Dumo or Duino, Faren or Farre, and Streme. None of these names appear on Fixlanda. Of the remaining thirty-three names on Frisland, some have been traced to Icelandic names, others indicate physical features such as promontories, and the rest have not been deciphered. Thus, according to Lucas, the island of Frisland is a concoction of portions of earlier maps of various dates and nationalities; it never had an existence of its own, and the entire story of the Zeno voyage "is a pure fiction."

If Nicolò the younger intended to convince the rest of the world that a Venetian mariner was the first to discover America, he did not succeed. England was quick to assert prior ownership of all the islands between Scotland and Iceland, including Frisland, and territory extending from Russia in the east to Labrador in the west. On November 28, 1577, Dr. John Dee wrote in his diary, "I spake with the Quene hora quinta. I spake with her secretary Walsingham. I declared to the Quene her title to Greenland, Estetiland, and Friseland." And on June 30, 1578, he says, "I told Mr. Daniel Roger and Mr. Hack-

Fig. 6-2.
Comparison of the island of Fixlanda as shown on the Matheus Prunes map of 1553 (B) with Frisland as presented by Nicolò Zeno the younger (A), and a present-day map of Iceland (C). The many islets surrounding Fixlanda and Frisland correspond with isles around Iceland.

luyt . . . that King Arthur and King Maty, both of them did conquer Gelinda, lately called Friseland." On a map prepared by Dr. Dee in 1580, his contention about British ownership of these lands is more explicit. The map shows Iceland, Icaria, Groeland, Engroneland, Estotiland, Friseland, Neome and Podalida/Podanda. In a legend on the map, he explains:

> Circa Anno 530 King Arthur not only Conquered *Iseland*, *Groenland*, and all the Northern Iles compassing unto Russia, but even unto the North Pole (in manner) did extend his jurisdiction: and sent Colonies thither, and unto all the isles between *Scotland* and *Iseland*, whereby yit is probable that the last-named Friseland Island is of the Brytish ancient discovery and possession: and allso seeing *Groeland* beyond *Groenland* did receive their inhabitants by Arthur, it is credible that the famous Iland Estotiland [Labrador] was by his folke possessed. Circa A° 1350. . . . The Latin books in the Kyng's Library in Estotiland, by no history (yet heard of) can most probably be ascribed to any other Mens bringing Thither than by the Foresayd Colonies sent by Kyng Arthur.[4]

Discounting the claim that Frisland was really discovered by King Arthur in 530, and mindful of the careful studies made by Frederick Lucas which destroy the credibility of Nicolò the younger, what support can be produced for the authenticity of the Zeno story?

R.H. Major supports the veracity of the Zeno narrative in equally expressive terms, and with evidence as strong as that of his antagonist. He contends that Frisland in the Zeno narrative does not refer to some previously undiscovered island south of Iceland, but to the Färoe Islands, and that Nicolò's voyage was within the straits and gulfs and between the islands of this archipelago. Major believes that Nicolò called the major island of this group, as well as its capital city, Frisland; today the town is called Thorshan, and the island is Stromoe, the largest of the Färoes. Antonio joined Nicolò, and together they sailed with Zichmni's navy to wage war on Estland, an island lying between Frisland and Norway. They "caused much damage" there, and Zichmni "determined to set upon *Island*" to conquer more lands. But he found the country there too well fortified and was unable to accomplish anything. He "assaulted the other Isles called *Island*, which are seven." According to Major, *Island* does not refer to Iceland, but to the Shetland Islands.

There is much to support Major's correlation of Frisland with the Färoes

Fig. 6-3.
Map of the island of Frisland, drawn by an anonymous Italian cartographer, c. 1560. The tilled fields and towns indicate that the island has been populated for some time. The capital, also named Frisland, is shown on the western shore.

(Reproduced courtesy of the Newberry Library, Novacco Collection.)

and *Island* with the Shetland Islands. The southern boundary of the Färoes at 61°28′ N latitude corresponds well with the southern edge of Frisland at 61°20′ N, although Frisland's northern boundary extends 125 nautical miles beyond the northernmost of the Färoe Islands. However, in longitude there is a great discrepancy, for the centre of Frisland lies at 20°00′ W longitude — 780 nautical miles west of the Färoes. This can be explained by Nicolò's being "tossed for many days by the sea and wind . . . not knowing in what part of the world" he was in, until he was cast ashore upon Frisland. At that time, calculation of longitude was not possible, and the fury of the storm undoubtedly prevented any sensible keeping of a dead-reckoning position.

Identifying Frisland with the Färoe Islands also explains how it was possible for Nicolò to be able to dispatch a letter to his brother Antonio in Venice to join him, and how Antonio could accomplish it. Obviously, the island's location was well known, and boats frequently sailed there. This is confirmed by Nicolò's disclosure that the capital of Frisland is situated on a gulf or bay where "many ships are laden thereof [with fish] to serve Flanders, Britain, England, Scotland, Norway and Denmark."

It also explains the forty place-names shown on the map of Frisland, which indicate that this land was already well known, settled with towns, and lay within established sea-routes.

There is corroboration for Major's belief that the *Island* which Zichmni decided to conquer was really the Shetland Islands, and not Iceland as the name suggests. The Shetland archipelago is at the entrance to the North Sea, close to the stated position of Zichmni's navy; it does not stretch the imagination to accept his decision to go there after leaving Estland to wrest the land from the King of Norway. That Zichmni's ships sailed "in the same channels" shows clearly that *Island* is an island group, not a solitary island, and, indeed, seven other islands are named: Tales, Broas, Iscant, Trans, Mimant, Dambere and Bres.[5] Late fourteenth-century maps, such as the Catalan *Mappemonde* in Florence and the Catalan world map in the Biblioteca Estense, Modena, show a group of seven or eight islands a great distance northwest of Scotland. The legend on the Florence map says that these islands are called *Islandes*. On the Modena map all eight islands are named; two of the names are the same as those in the Zeno account and the rest are similar. The southeasternmost island on the Modena map is called *Islanda*; the rest are: Daubert (Dambere?), Tranes (Trans), Cales (Talas?), Brons (Broas?), Bres (Bres), Minanj (Mimant) and Bicam. Reference to the Shetlands as *Islanda* goes back as far as 1154. The map Idrîsî made for King Roger of Sicily was accompanied by a text in which Idrîsî stated: "From the end of *Squôzia* [Scotland] to the island of *Islânda* [is] two-thirds of a day's sail in a northern direction. From the end of *Islânda* to the great Island of *Irlânda* [is] one day." Early cartographers had a hazy notion about the various island groups north of the British Isles, and Idrîsî may have been referring here partly to the Orkney Islands. Nonetheless, the Shetlands are a mere ninety nautical miles north of Scotland, convincing evidence that Idrîsî's *Islânda* was not Iceland.

When Zichmni left *Island* having "spoyled them all," he built a fort in Bres where Nicolò remained. In the spring, Nicolò sailed northward in three barks to discover land, "and arrived in Engroneland." Although the text states that Engroneland (Greenland) was his destination, this is obviously an error on the part of Nicolò the younger when he compiled the letters. Geographically, it makes sense that the next major land on his voyage would be Iceland. Nicolò says that, in the summertime, "many barks from the Ilands thereabout and from the Cape above Norway and from Trondon come here to exchange their goods for the fish and skins of various kinds of beasts." By the middle of the thirteenth century, Norwegian vessels had well-established routes between Norway and the Shetlands, Färoes and Iceland. At first, Trondheim was the centre in Norway for the Icelandic trade, the principal sea-route being from Trondheim to Eyjafjörd on the north coast of Iceland. Later, Trondheim was superseded in importance by Bergen as the principal port of trade.

Iceland, instead of Greenland, is confirmed as the destination of Nicolò in other parts of the story: the volcanic mountains that throw forth fire "like *Vesuvius* and *Etna*"; the description of the monastery of friars and of how they heat their houses with the hot water from thermal springs; and the use of Latin as a common tongue — all are in keeping with Iceland.

Veritas Filia Temporis

Now that sufficient time has elapsed for a dispassionate view to be taken of the Zeno story, the truth can emerge. This much seems certain: Nicolò Zeno made a voyage in the North Atlantic in the year 1380. Nicolò reached England and possibly Flanders, as he intended. Nicolò and Antonio's sojourn on Frisland was actually on one of the Färoe Islands; the other islands to which

Nicolò travelled while in the service of Zichmni were the Shetland Islands or possibly the Orkney Islands, north of Scotland. The distance between the Shetlands and the Färoes is only 165 nautical miles; from the Färoes to Iceland is an additional 240 nautical miles. By 1380, passages among all these island groups, Iceland, Norway and Greenland were frequently made by English and Norwegian ships. There is nothing improbable about Nicolò's visit to Iceland; the distance from Frisland (the Färoes) was short, and the routes, harbours and general weather patterns at that time were all well known. The description of the land, its inhabitants and all manner of daily life is too detailed and specific to have been made up, or pieced together from narratives of voyages prior to 1380.

Nicolò's visit to Greenland changes from the realm of probability to that of possibility, and the discovery (or news) of other lands beyond Greenland — that is, Estotiland and Drogeo — is subject only to conjecture. That Irish monks reached Iceland in 770, sixty-five years before the Norse arrival, is well documented in the Icelandic sagas. When Eirík Raudi (Erik the Red) arrived from Iceland in 982 to explore Greenland, he found on the shores "stone implements and fragments of boats, scattered along the shores of the fiords." Whether this was evidence of Christian missionaries who preceded him or remnants of Eskimo habitation is uncertain. But by the beginning of the twelfth century Greenland not only had priests, but a bishop as well. In 1112 Bishop Eirík Upsi arrived in Greenland, but he left in 1121 "in search of Vinland." Christianity took hold in Greenland, and by the end of the twelfth century there were twelve parish churches in the East Settlement and four in the West Settlement. In 1200 a large cathedral was built at Gardar. Since these events all precede the date of Nicolò Zeno's voyage, it is possible that he really did visit Greenland, where he could have found monasteries and people who spoke Latin. However, two important elements in the story reinforce the probability that Iceland was Nicolò's destination: the volcanic and geothermal activity for which Iceland is so well known, and the lack of documentation of any monastery on Greenland by the name of Saint Thomas. Furthermore, the Greenland settlements were at the southern end of that land, and no habitation, let alone a monastery, is known to have existed halfway between the seventy-fourth and seventy-fifth parallels of latitude, where the monastery of Saint Thomas appears on the *Carta da Navegar* of Nicolò and Antonio Zeno.

Estotiland, lying a thousand miles west of Frisland, appears to be Labrador. Here too, the Irish monks in their travels may have preceded other

European mariners; although the inhabitants of Estotiland had a language of their own with "peculiar letters or characters [known] only to themselves," they also spoke Latin, and the king's library contained books written in Latin. It is also reasonable to assume that they had trade with Greenland, as the narrative asserts, for "furs, brimstone and pitch."

South of Estotiland is a "great populous country, very rich in gold," with "many cities and castles." Is this the mythical kingdom of Saguenay, peopled with winged men and rich with jewels and spices, that Jacques Cartier sought in 1535? Or is it the fabled land of Norumbega, with its rich and noble city, that Giovanni da Verrazzano first charted after his voyage to North America in 1524? After Verrazzano's voyage, Michael Lok, "citizen of London," created a map depicting the geography of northern regions. On the map he shows Norumbega as a large island bordering the southern shore of Grand Bay (Gulf of St. Lawrence), with the land of Corte Real on the north shore of Grand Bay. Geographically, these two lands correspond with Drogeo and Estotiland on the Zeno map. It could well be that Nicolò the younger had heard tales about these mythical lands and incorporated them into his narrative. Lands still farther south, where savage natives "feed upon man's flesh, as the sweetest meat in their judgement there is," hints of Mayan and Aztec sacrificial practices, which Nicolò the younger may have learned about from the Spanish explorers and thought fit to add to his own version of the narrative.

Few cartographers had the luxury of being able to personally visit all the lands they depicted on their maps. They had to rely on the new information brought to them by explorers, and integrate it as best they could with the existing geography. The original map made by Nicolò and Antonio Zeno was rotten with age; in order to depict Frisland on the *Carta da Navegar*, Nicolò the younger had to resort to filling in the partially obliterated sections with lands shown on other maps. In adopting parts of other maps to fill in the empty spaces, and harmonizing his map with what he had read in the letters of his forbears, Nicolò the younger only followed common procedure among cartographers — hardly a reason to vilify him.

Why was there such a long delay between the time the fabulous tales of the Zeno brothers' adventures were brought back and their publication 164 years later? And what was the motive for Nicolò the younger to engage in duplicity (if such it was)? He came from one of the most socially prominent Venetian families; as a member of the Council of Ten he held the highest political office in Venice; and, through his great-grandmother, he was "connected with the reigning families of Persia and Cyprus." The answers to these questions can only be surmised. Justin Winsor, in his *Narrative and Critical History of America*, suggests that the driving force behind the story may have been a belated patriotism. Spanish discoveries in the New World had gained international recognition and praise; the glory, though, was the result of expeditions by Italian explorers (Columbus and Vespucci) sailing under the Spanish flag. The insult to the prowess of Venetian mariners was heightened by the fact that Columbus was a Genoan, and the city-state of Genoa was a fierce rival of the state of Venice. Publishing the Nicolò and Antonio Zeno story would assuage family pride and personal vanity; most important, honour for the discovery of America would be restored to Italy.

As a phantom island, Frisland was a case of mistaken identity on two counts; it was a curious hybrid, with the geography of the Färoe Islands and the contour of Iceland. But cartographers and historians were reluctant to give up on the existence of Frisland. Some believed that the "Sunken Land of Buss" was the last remnant of Frisland. Others thought that Frisland and its satellite islands of Porlanda, Grislanda, Neome and Ilose were once a single, united land, and that parts of it became submerged. Iceland, portions of the Färoes, North and West Ireland, and islands off the east coast of the Orkneys all had their advocates for identification with Frisland. But, like the other phantom islands, Frisland too was eventually removed from the face of the map.

Chapter VII

Buss Island

SO THOROUGHLY IS BUSS ISLAND EMBEDDED in a matrix of verifiable facts and events that it is difficult to believe it never existed. It appeared fairly late on maps compared to other phantom islands, but it remained there the longest, so firmly accepted that, even when cartographers finally removed it from maps for lack of substantiation, they still showed its location as the "Sunken Land of Buss." Cartographers and mariners alike preferred to credit its disappearance to some geological cataclysm, rather than admit it was never present.

Buss Island was first reported by one of the passengers on Martin Frobisher's third voyage into the Arctic in 1578. In the closing decades of the sixteenth century, interest in the Northwest Passage, which had lain dormant since the expeditions of John and Sebastian Cabot at the start of the century, revived in England. Voyages of exploration were prompted by Sir Humphrey Gilbert in his *Discourse of a Discoverie for a New Passage to Cataia* (1576), by William Bourne (1580), and by other leading theorists on world geography. Gilbert believed that simply by "entering a wide passage between Baccalaos [Newfoundland] and Canada, one would sail into an immense sea leading into the Strait of Anian."[1] From there it would be but a "short sail to Japan, China and the Moluccas," where there would be a lucrative trade in goods. These writings, reinforced by maps made by the most influential cartographers of the time, prompted a group of merchant adventurers of London to organize and finance Martin Frobisher's voyage to find the North-west Passage.

Fig. 7-1.
Sir Martin Frobisher.

That all previous endeavours to find the passage had failed did not diminish the strength of the concept or deter further expeditions. As difficult as encounters with the polar sea could be, with its crushing ice, bitter cold and blinding snow, the immense rewards for finding a northern route to Cathay far outweighed the attendant problems. Nor was it just financial benefits that spurred the English to seek the passage. As well as intellectual curiosity about the geography and navigational problems of the far north, Martin Frobisher pronounced, "It is *still* the only thing left undone, whereby a notable mind might be made famous and remarkable."

Frobisher sailed westward in June of 1576, and on July 11 he sighted the southern tip of the coast of Greenland. He assumed it was Frisland, since it was in the latitude of 60° as shown on his chart. Greenland, he believed, was 360 miles farther north at 66°. Though the map he carried with him, prepared by Gerardus Mercator in 1569, was the finest of its kind, in this region the geography was faulty.

At the end of July, Frobisher arrived at the southern end of Baffin Island, then known as Meta Incognita. He explored its coast and sailed a considerable distance into a deep inlet. Frobisher was unable to investigate the full length of this bay, but he assumed that the open sea to the west lay between the two headlands he saw at its far end. Believing he had found the Northwest Passage, where he could pass to Cathay and the East Indies, Frobisher named this body of water Frobisher Strait, likening it to its southern counterpart, Magellan Strait, leading to the Pacific Ocean. Before returning home with news of the discovery, his crew threw a few pieces of black stone into the ship as a souvenir of their having landed on these far shores.

In England the stone was analysed by three different experts, all of whom said it was of no value. Later, however, an Italian goldsmith, perhaps inspired more by self-delusion than by an urge to deceive, claimed the stone was rich in gold ore. Once the news spread, Frobisher had no trouble obtaining backing for another voyage. Merchants formed the Company of Cathay and provided capital for a second expedition. With the promise of immediate profit from the mining of gold ore, they apparently forgot about continuing the search for the Northwest Passage.

This time, Frobisher brought back 160 tons of the black rock to England. Processing it was delayed, so that its true value — absolutely nothing — was not known when Frobisher set out on his third expedition in 1578. He had organized the largest fleet ever assembled for a single Arctic expedition. It comprised fifteen ships, of which eleven were newly commissioned and the remaining four hired from private owners. One of these four was the *Emma-*

nuel, a type of boat known as a "busse," a vessel used by the Dutch and English in the herring fishery. Busses were two- or three-masted, of 50-70 tons burden and strongly built. Since the *Emmanuel* came from Bridgewater in Somersetshire, England, she was frequently called the *Busse of Bridgewater*.

When the fleet arrived at Baffin Island, they encountered the worst weather of any of the three voyages. Frobisher wrote, "In this storme, being the sixe and twentith of July, there fell so much snow, with such bitter cold air, that we could scarce see one another for the same, nor open our eyes to handle our ropes and sayles . . . everyman persuading himself, that the wynter there must need be extreme, where they found so unseasonable a summer."

Throughout the month of August, Frobisher's men mined various sites on Baffin Island, and loaded 1136 tons of ore into the ships. The *Emmanuel* was filled "up to the full Sea Marke" with 110 tons of rock. Earlier in the summer she had suffered damage to her prow and leaked badly, so she could not accompany the rest of the vessels when they left Baffin Island in a howling gale. The next day, separated from the rest of the fleet, she too headed back to England.

Discovery of Buss Island

On September 12, James Newton, captain and owner of the *Emmanuel*, came upon an island where none had previously been known. He named it Buss Island, after the ship. News of his discovery was published that very same year (1578) in George Best's *A True Discourse of the Late Voyages of Discouerie for Finding of a Passage to Cathaya by the North-Weast, under the Conduct of Martin Frobisher, Generall*. The entire report of Buss Island reads:

> The *Busse*, of *Bridgewater*, as she came homeward, to ye South Eastwarde of *Freseland*, discoured a great Ilande in the latitude of ___ Degree, which was neuer yet founde before, and sayled three dayes alongst the coast, the land seeming to be fruiteful, full of woods, and a champion countrie.[2]

The brief and fanciful characterization of the island may be attributed to the account's being second-hand; presumably, omission of the latitude numbers would prevent anyone from discerning the location of the gold mines on Baffin Island.

Buss Island went unnoticed by the public until eleven years later, when Thomas Wiars told his story in Richard Hakluyt's *Principall Navigations, Voiages, and Discoveries of the English Nation, made by Sea or on Land*:

The Report of Thomas Wiars, passenger in the Emmanuel
(otherwise called the Busse of Bridgewater, wherein Iames Leeche was Master, one of the Shippes in the last voyage of Master Martin Frobisher, 1578), concerning the discouerie of a great Island in their way homeward, the 12 of September

The Busse of Bridgewater was left in Bear's sounde, at *Meta Incognita*, the second day of September, behinde the Fleete, in some distresse through much winde, ryding neere the Lee shoare, and forced there to ride it out upon the hazard of her cables and ankers, which were all aground but two. The thirde of September, being fayre weather, and the wind North-north-west, she set sayle and departed thence, and fell with *Frisland* on the 8 day of September, at 6 of the clocke at night; and then they set off from the Southwest poynt of *Frisland*, the winde being at East and East-south-east; but, that night the winde veared Southerly, and shifted oftentimes that night; but, on the tenth day, in the morning, the wind at west-north-west, fayre weather, they steered south-east by south, and continued that course until the 12 day of September; when about 11 a clocke before noon they descryed a lande, which was from them about fiue leagues [15 miles]; and the Southernmost part of it was South-east by East from them, and the Northernmost next North-north-east or North-east. The Master accompted that *Frisland* (the South-east poynt of it) was from him, at that instant when hee first descryed this newe Island, North-west by north 50 leagues [150 miles]. They account this Island to be 25 leagues long, and the longest way of it South-east and North-west. The Southerne part of it is in the latitude of 57 degrees and 1 second part, or thereabout. They continued in sight of it from the 12 day, at 11 of the clocke, til the 13 day [at] three of the clocke in the after noone, when they left it; and the last part they saw of it bare from them North-west by north. There appeared two harboroughs upon that coast, the greatest of them seven leagues to the Northwardes of the Southermost poynt, the other but foure leagues. There was verie much yce neere the same lande, and also twentie or thirtie leagues from it; for they were not cleare of yce till the 15 day of September, after noone. They plied their voyage homewards, and fell with the west part of Ireland, about *Galway*, and had first sight of it on the 25 day of September.[3]

Unlike George Best's few sentences, Thomas Wiars's account is full of explicit detail (including the latitude). He describes Buss Island as surrounded by a vast field of ice, implying that the land is cold and barren rather than "fruitful" and "full of woods." Both men sailed along the southern edge of its extensive coastline, but apparently neither attempted to make a landing. The ice field noted by Thomas Wiars presumably prevented his anchoring in either of the two harbours.

Luke Foxe reviewed the brief history of Buss Island in his book *North-West Fox*, published in 1635. He said, "If this Iland were found againe, there is a great store of Fish about it." To help him in his own search for the Northwest Passage, Foxe had gathered the latest charts and talked to as many persons as he could who had had Arctic experience. One of the passengers aboard the busse *Emmanuel*, or perhaps Captain Newton himself, had told Luke Foxe about the quantity of fish.

Later Sightings

James Hall, Chief Pilot in the service of King Christian IV of Denmark, next reported having seen Buss Island while on an expedition to Greenland. In 1605, Hall looked for the island in its presumed position but could not find it. Hall remarked, "I doe verily suppose the same to be placed in a wrong latitude in the marine charts." The following year, on a second expedition, his search was more rewarding:

On the 1st of July wee saw Land, being eight leagues off, with a great banke of Ice lying off South-west; wee, setting our tacks aboord laid off East and by South and East South-east, to double the same. About two a clocke having doubled the same, wee went away West and by South all this evening and the night following. This Land I did suppose to be *Busse* Iland; It lying more to the Westwards than it is placed in the Marine Charts.[4]

On his voyage to America in 1609, Henry Hudson also kept a lookout for Buss Island. The journal states:

[June 2, 1609] . . . mystie weather, the wind at North-east. At noone we steered away West Southwest, to find *Busse* Iland, discouered in the yeere 1578, by one of the ships of Sir *Martin Frobisher* to see if it lay in her true latitude in the Chart or no: we continued our course as before all night, with a faire gale of wind: this night we had sight of the first stars, and our water was changed colour to a white greene. The Compasse had no variation. The third [of June], faire Sun-shining weather; the wind at North-east. We steered on our course Southwest and by West, with a stiffe gale of wind. At noone we observed and found our height to bee 58. degrees 48. minutes. And I was before the ship 16. leagues, by reason of the Current that held us so strong out of the South-west. For it is eight leagues in foure and twentie houres. We accounted ourselves neere *Busse* Iland: by mid-night we looked out for it, but could not see it.[5]

The North Atlantic Current, a branch of the Gulf Stream that pushes all the way into the Barents Sea, had set Hudson's ship off course. Hudson started a lookout for Buss Island when his ship, the *Half Moon*, was only two days' sail southwest of the Färoe Islands. Though he was in the proper latitude for his search, he was too far east. Between the reported location of Buss Island southeast of Greenland and the place where Henry Hudson looked for it is a gap of fully 960 miles. Hudson reported a change in the water colour that would indicate shallowness, but, judging from the position of the *Half Moon*, what he observed was Rockall Bank, one of the many banks and ridges rising from the ocean floor northwest of Ireland. Although Henry Hudson never saw Buss Island, at least he attempted to prove its existence and to reconcile the disparate positions given for it.

The next recorded sighting of Buss Island came sixty years later, in part because of lessened interest in the search for the Northwest Passage and in part because of the paucity of records made by those who may have passed its way. Then, in 1671, with the publication of John Seller's *The English Pilot* (Book IV), Buss Island sprang fully to life again with reports of sightings on *two* different expeditions. According to Seller, while Captain Thomas Shepherd was on the way to Hudson Bay, he not only saw the island but partially explored it.

A Description of the Island of Buss

This Island lieth in the Latitude of 58 deg. 39 min. It bears W. by N., half a point Northerly, from the *Mizen-head,* in *Ireland,* distant about 296 leagues. This Island was first discovered in Sir *Martin Frobisher's* third and last Voyage to the North-West, in the Year 1578, by one of his Vessels that strai'd from his Fleet in their Home-ward-bound Passage, who accidentlly discovered it, and called it after the name of the vessel, which was the *Buss of Bridgewater,* and therefore they called it *Buss* Island. They judged it to be about 25 leagues long, lying the longest way, S.E., and N.W. They found two Harbours in it; and, according to the account they give of it, that the greatest of them is about seven Leagues to the northward of the Southermost Point of the Island, [and that it is] called *Rupert's Harbour;* and the other, four Leagues to the N.W. of that, called *Shaftsbury's Harbour.* There are two small Islands that lie off the East Point of the Island. This Island was further Discovered by Captain *Thomas Shepherd,* in the *Golden Lion,* of *Dunkirk,* in the year 1671, at the charge of Mounsier[s] *Kiel, Spawlding,* and *Kicquerts,* Lords of that Town. The said Captain *Shepherd* brought home the Map of the Island that is here annexed; and reports that the Island affords store of Whales, easie to be struck, Sea-horse, Seal, and Codd in abundance; and supposes that two Voyages may be made in a year. The sea is clear from Ice, unless in *September.* The Land low and level to the Southward, and some hills and mountains on the N.W end. The Variation was here, in the Year 1671, 9 degrees west. There lieth a Bank about 12 Leagues to the southward of the Island that hath good store of Fish upon it, and is about 15 Leagues in length, lying chiefly N.N.W. and S.S.E., having 40 fathom and 36 fathom Water upon it. This Island hath several times been seen by Captain *Gillam* in his Passages to and from the North-West.[6]

Two maps of the island accompanied the description, one a general chart of the North Atlantic, drawn on a small scale, and the other a larger, more detailed map. Both thoroughly identified the island's main features with place-names, though there was some variation between the two maps in the number and in the persons after whom they were named.

The very brief reference at the end of the narrative to Captain Zachariah Gillam was expanded in later editions of *The English Pilot*:

> On the first day of August following, [Gillam] saw Land bearing west from two miles off, and judged it to be an island, being dark and foggy weather, having sailed due west 524 leagues and a half, seeing many great Flocks of small Birds; and, in sounding found 120 fathom Water, the Land or Island (which he rather supposed it to be) bearing west 2 miles from them, being in Lat. 59 deg. 35 min.

> The second of *August*, having still steered away west 528 leagues and a half, he saw a small Island, being then in the Latitude of 59 deg. 43.min.

> The third day, he saw the Land bearing from the W.N.W., to the S.W. by W., with one Island lying about four Leagues from the Main, being then in the Latitude of 59 deg. 34 min.

> . . . After six of the Clock, he ran N.W. by W. 3 leagues, and then W. by S. 11 Leagues, and then found his whole Westing 539 Leagues and a half.[7]

Captain Gillam made these sightings in 1668, in command of the *Nonsuch*, when he sailed to Hudson Bay on a trading voyage. Gillam's was the first voyage made to Hudson Bay specifically for the purpose of trade (rather than exploration), and it resulted in the establishment of the Hudson's Bay Company. Buss Island is not specifically mentioned by name here, but elsewhere Seller says of Captain Gillam's voyage, "The ketch *Nonsuch,* in her way, made the Land of *Buss,* lying betwixt Iseland and Groenland." Whether Captain Shepherd indeed saw a plenitude of whales, walrus, seal and cod, or whether they were an extravagance of his imagination, he was sufficiently persuasive to arouse the Hudson's Bay Company to seek a Charter of Buss Island. He had easy access to the Company's confidence, for, before his voyage in the *Golden Lion*, Thomas Shepherd had worked for them.

On December 22, 1673, three years after the Hudson's Bay Company's incorporation, its members resolved "That his Royall Highnesse [James, Duke of York], his Highnesse Prince Rupert, the Earle of Arlington and Mr. Vice Chamberlain bee desired to Moove his Maj^tie [Charles II] for a pattente for Busse Island." On May 13, 1675, King Charles II granted a charter of Busse Island to the Hudson's Bay Company; having spent £65 for charges, they received:

> . . . All that Island called the Busse Island lying betweene fifty seaven and fifty nyne Degrees of Northerne Latitude or thereaboutes, and the sole trade and commerce of all the Seas Bayes Islettes Rivers Creekes and Sounds whatsoever lying within neare or about the said Island with the fishing of all sortes, of Fish as well Whales Sturgeons and all Royall Fishe as all other sortes of fish. . . . And all mynes Royall as well discovered as not discovered of Gold Silver Gemmes and Precious Stones to bee found or discovered within the Island aforsaid.[8]

The king granted the island in perpetuity to the governor and the company and their successors in terms almost identical to those of the original charter of the Hudson's Bay Company. On the same day that the company requested the patent for Buss Island, they also ordered:

> Mr Shepherd forthwith [to] give an estimate to the Committee, or one of them, of what ship & of what burthen & what number of men of the charges and Wages which may grow due to the same, & what other thinges may be necessary for a Voyage & for discovery & fisheing at Buss Islande, at the cheapest rate it can be computed.[9]

The company prepared to explore its new property. Captain James Golding, in command of the *Prince Rupert*, would sail to Buss Island, and, upon his arrival, Captain Shepherd, with the *Shaftesbury*, would join him. But both vessels arrived so late at Hudson Bay from England that they had to over-winter in the Bay. There are no records of whether they actually set out for Buss Island in the spring, and any further interest by the company in Buss Island remained dormant until 1720.

Fig. 7-2.
Map drawn by Henry Hudson on his voyage to Hudson Bay in 1610-11. Published by
Hessel Gerritsz in 1612, it shows only the southern coast of Buss Island, in accordance

with the description of its discovery by Thomas Wiars. The southern tip of Greenland is now in its proper geographical position on the map, but it contains some features transported from the discoveries near Baffin Island made by Martin Frobisher.

A Place on the Map

Remarkably, Buss Island was not shown on maps or marine charts until a considerable time after its reported discovery. George Best, the first to describe it, did not show it on either of the two maps included in his *True Discourse. Nor did it appear in the original published account (1589) of Tho*mas Wiars or in the subsequent edition (1599-1600) of Hakluyt's *Principall Navigations.*

It wasn't until fourteen years after the island was first reported that it was shown on a map. In 1592, William Sanderson financed the construction of a globe by Emery Molyneux, a distinguished mathematician and draftsman. This was the first globe ever constructed in England, and, coincidentally, it included the first cartographic depiction of Buss Island. It was shown as a fairly large island, lying 58°30′N to 59°00′N latitude and 27°00′W to 30°00′W longitude. Its general shape closely corresponded to the description given by Thomas Wiars — from which Molyneux most likely derived it. Though the *Emmanuel* sailed only along the island's southern shore, the Molyneux globe showed it with a complete coastline, as if it had been circumnavigated.

Petrus Plancius, the noted Dutch geographer and friend of Henry Hudson, included Buss Island on his general map of the world, printed in 1594.

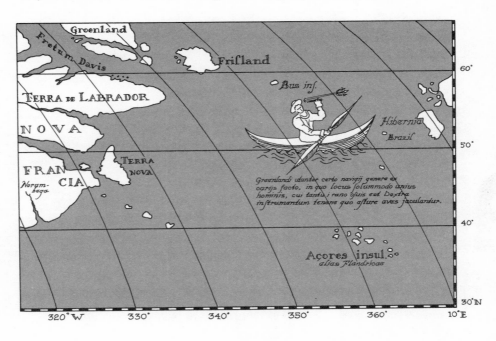

Fig. 7-3.
Detail of a map titled *America* by Jodocus Hondius, published in 1607. Buss Island is shown in its customary position southeast of Frisland. The inscription beneath the illustration of the Eskimo in a kayak reads: "The Greenlanders use a special kind of boat made of skins, in which there is a place for one man alone, who needs only one oar. In the right hand they hold a weapon with which they cleverly spear birds."

118

Shown at roughly the same latitude — 57°30′ N to 58°30′ N — it, too, had a complete coastline. But Plancius placed it much farther east, at 23°00′ W longitude, a difference amounting to 120 nautical miles.

When Hessel Gerritsz published a map in 1612, depicting the geography explored and discovered by Henry Hudson on his voyage to Hudson Bay, he kept the latitude and longitude of Buss Island much the same as that laid down by previous cartographers. He made one important change, however. He delineated only the southern coast of Buss Island, the shore of which trended southeast and northwest, with entrances to two inlets or harbours; he left the northern coast undefined. This representation was in keeping with the description given by Thomas Wiars, published twenty-three years earlier. Gerritsz's widely acclaimed chart served as the prototype, with minor variations, for all subsequent representations of Buss Island throughout the seventeenth century.

The general location of Buss Island remained unchanged on the charts, based on Wiars's account that his ship was about fifty leagues southeast of Frisland when Buss Island was sighted. Buss was an island of considerable size, extending over sixty miles in a north-south direction, and roughly the same distance east to west. It had two, or sometimes three, harbours along its southern shores; at the eastern end were one or two very small islets. The centre of Buss Island was commonly shown at about 58°00′ N latitude, and somewhere between 27°00′ and 31°00′ W longitude.

None of the maps exceeded in detail of topography and identification by place-names the one accompanying Captain Shepherd's 1671 description of Buss Island. The large-scale map showed twelve place-names on the island, plus one on the sandbank to the south of it. The small-scale map showed an even greater number of names, of which twelve of the nineteen were derived from the names of the directors in the original charter of the Hudson's Bay Company. Apparently these were not the names used by Shepherd but were bestowed by the company, evidence of their firm belief in the existence of the island they owned.

The line far exceeds the word in its authority, and once Buss Island was firmly established on the map, it continued to be unquestioningly accepted well into the eighteenth century. But at the beginning of the eighteenth century the

Fig. 7-4.
The Island of Buss, by John Seller, "Hydrographer to the King." This map accompanied Captain Thomas Shepherd's description of his 1671 voyage.

representation of Buss Island began to undergo a change. Lacking any further confirmation of its existence from the numerous voyages made through these waters in search of the Northwest Passage, and no longer certain about the island's geography, some cartographers eliminated the island altogether, while others reverted to showing a fully circumscribed island instead of an indeterminate coast. Some kept Buss Island at 58°00′ N latitude but elongated its southern coast to extend over 006° of longitude — a distance of 190 miles. This is how De l'Isle showed it on his 1720 map, *Hemisphere Occidental*. Even more interesting is the way he identified it: "*Isle de Bus, ci devant Frislande*" (Isle of Buss, formerly Frisland). By the middle of the century, further changes were made; the legend now read, "The submerged Land of Buss is now-a-days nothing but surf, a quarter of a mile long, with a rough sea. Most likely it was originally the great island of Frisland." Thereafter, its place became simply the "Sunken Land of Buss."

Mariners and cartographers alike accepted the notion that Buss Island had sunk beneath the sea as the result of volcanic action. They preferred this theory to discarding outright what had been so firmly believed for so many years.

Could the disappearance of Buss Island possibly be explained by the submergence of land? Prior to the melting of the ice cap some 11,000 years ago, land now submerged beneath the ocean floor once stood far above the water. The Atlantic bed has risen and fallen constantly, even since the last ice age. Icelandic records dating back to the very beginning of the thirteenth century confirm the tremendously eruptive nature of the region. Undersea volcanic eruption has suddenly created entirely new islands. In 1830, volcanic activity accounted for the vanishing of Geirfugla Skjer, a group of rocks off the southwest coast of Iceland, and in 1968 a new island — Surtsey — rose from the depths of the sea off the coast of Iceland.[10] Viking sagas tell of rocky islets, Gunnbjörn's Skerries, between the coasts of Iceland and Greenland, that have long since disappeared. When Henry Hudson explored the Arctic to the farthest limits the ice-pack would allow, he had with him notes from "a Greenlander named Iver Boty" describing islands midway between Iceland and Greenland which at one time were large enough to support farming communities, but which by then were totally gone. The notes warned that this place was so shallow that the water would freeze quicker than in the surrounding area, and that this ice would prevent using the same old passage as before.

Enticing as it may be to believe that Buss Island once stood above water but then sunk beneath the sea, the notion has its drawbacks. Summits of even the highest ocean mountain peaks in the reported vicinity of Buss Island are no higher than 700 fathoms from the water's surface. It is difficult to embrace the idea that land which was once above the sea could have subsided to such great depths in so short a time, geologically speaking.

Evidence Pursued

Buss Island may have disappeared beneath the surface of the waves; it did disappear off the face of maps; but it did not disappear from the minds of seafarers. On the contrary, their desire to find it was only renewed and strengthened. If Buss Island was under water, sightings were out of the question, but there was still the possibility that soundings would reveal a shallow bank or shoal, some subaqueous remains to corroborate that the island had once existed.

Johan Anderson recounted in 1746 how an unnamed skipper of an unnamed vessel "took much trouble to find the vestiges of the Sunken Land of Buss, which are clearly indicated on the charts." He did not get soundings, the water being deep everywhere except in one place where he observed "an inexplicable surf extending over a short distance, notwithstanding a depth of 100 fathoms."

Lieutenant Richard Pickersgill believed in the continued existence of both Buss Island and Frisland, and in 1776, in support of his contention, he said, "A master of a Greenland-man (called the British King) once told me that, being by his reckoning near that place [Buss Island], he was alarmed by breakers, and, sounding, found at 59 *fathoms depth*, a rocky bottom. He also says that many vessels had seen breakers thereabout." That very same year, while on a voyage to Davis Strait to protect the interests of British whalers, Pickersgill took soundings when he thought his vessel was over the submerged island. He wrote, "June 29th, 3 P.M. — Calm. Tried soundings, and got ground at 230 fathoms; drifted to the N.E. about 2 miles and sounded again in 290 fathoms; fine, white sand. At the same time, saw a shag, gulls, and other signs of land not far hence." Pickersgill thought that if he had had more time, he might even have found land. "If it be again discovered . . . our ships bound to the northward might winter there and it would prove a nursery for hardy seamen."[11]

Pickersgill named the shoal he found Lion's Bank, after his vessel, H.M. Brig *Lion*. What he reported neither confirmed nor contradicted the finding of a sunken land, for he did not give exact coordinates. Records vary as to Pickersgill's position, but evidently he was farther east than he supposed. From the depths he recorded, it appears that he took soundings of the westernmost portion of Rockall Bank, the same shallow bank Henry Hudson passed over two hundred miles northwest of Ireland.

Soundings continued to be made in the supposed vicinity of Buss Island well into the nineteenth century. More systematic searches with better equipment did not change the results. On a voyage to Baffin Bay in 1818, Captain Sir John Ross altered course when he was near the charted position of Buss Island to determine if it existed. At 57°27′N and 29°45′W he kept a good lookout, and, "being near the spot, shortened sail and hove to in order to sound, but found no bottom in 180 fathoms."[12] Sir William Parry on his voyage in search of the Northwest Passage the following year had no better luck; though 1120 fathoms of line were let out, bottom was not found.

The last time Buss Island appeared on a map was on the 1856 *Physical Atlas* by Keith Johnston. There, 264 years after its first appearance on the Molyneux globe, it was shown as a tiny, nameless speck at about 57°00′N latitude and 25°00′W longitude.

Even after representation of Buss Island, sunken or otherwise, ceased, the belief lingered. In 1903 Captain DeCarteret, in command of the S.S. *Minia*, was engaged in laying a trans-Atlantic cable. Midway between Ireland and Newfoundland he found "the existence of a mountainous district in a locality where ocean depths were assumed to be those of a fairly level plateau with its shallowest waters 1550 fathoms."[13] Taking numerous soundings on a line north from the Azores, DeCarteret discovered rapid changes in depths, with precipitous mountain peaks rising above the deep ocean floor by as much as 1200 feet.

Only a few years earlier, a similar discovery was made in a spot directly north of the Azores. There, where the charts marked the "Doubtful Chaucer Shoal," a mountain range was found whose tops exceeded 8000 feet above the general bottom of the ocean and lay only 714 to 730 fathoms deep. No longer a doubtful shoal, it was renamed the Faraday Hills. To Captain DeCarteret, his soundings of 630 fathoms in the region marked "A Doubtful Shoal — The Sunken Land of Buss" proved the existence of that submerged land.

As well as the soundings, the investigations by the S.S. *Minia* included an analysis of rock specimens and mud brought up from the ocean floor. The results were published in 1904 in *Transactions of the Nova Scotia Institute of Science*. The article included a chart, "The Sunken Land of Bus," with detailed depth contour lines and all of the mountain peaks with their heights.

Perhaps if the author who wrote up the research had known more about the history of Buss Island and of the long search for it, he would have loudly proclaimed the discovery. Instead, he simply concluded, "In that locality [Buss Island], recent investigations have proved the presence of shallower waters than those about it, if not of a shoal, in the usual acceptance of the term."[14]

The author noted that the shoaler waters between the fortieth and sixtieth parallels of latitude lay in a due north and south course of the mean longitude of 32°00′W. The obsidian in the samples told him that the mountains were volcanic in origin. Actually, the S.S. *Minia* had found the Reykjanes Ridge. This underwater mountain chain extends from the Azores to Iceland and is a section of the Mid-Atlantic Ridge. These mountains are the adjoining edges of two huge tectonic plates of the earth's crust, where the ground has been thrust upward by volcanic forces from deep inside the earth. Faraday Hills, at the northern end of the Mid-Atlantic Ridge, remains today on nautical charts as the Faraday Seamount. But the name of Buss, even as a doubtful shoal, has quietly slipped away — it is no longer on any map. Soundings by the S.S. *Minia* failed to convince the rest of the world of the island's existence.

Perceptions and Deceptions

Though it is easy enough to explain what the S.S.*Minia* found, what about the earliest reports? What, if anything, did these mariners see that created the legendary Buss Island?

At first glance, Captain Shepherd's narrative of "further discovery" best answers this question, for it contains the most information. It enlarges upon Wiars's description of the island's physical characteristics and natural resources, and it is accompanied by two maps. However, Captain Shepherd's veracity is suspect, not because of what he says, but because of what he leaves unsaid. It is surprising that in his report of a totally "new land" (though it was already on some maps) all concrete information is missing: he gives no date when he first saw it, does not tell how long he stayed there, and records no position, either by latitude and longitude or by reference in distance and heading from a known landmark. His only new and specific information is the magnetic variation (9°W) at Buss Island, which is of little use by itself. Captain Shepherd does not even divulge the purpose of his expedition.

A great many named bays, headlands and harbours appear on Shepherd's map, but he does not mention anchoring in any of the harbours or exploring the interior of the island. Nor does he tell if he circumnavigated the island. How did Shepherd arrive at the contours of the island's coastline and obtain knowledge of its diverse inland topography?

Within two years of his "discovery" of Buss Island, Captain Shepherd was back in the employ of the Hudson's Bay Company. Having convinced the company to obtain a charter for Buss Island, he was now in charge of further exploration. In arguing for the advantages of owning the island, Shepherd had emphasized the increased potential for profit to be gained — "two voyages may be made in a year," because "the sea there is clear of ice, unless in September." This has the faint echo of the words of Thomas Wiars, who proclaimed that "there was verie much yce neere the same land [Buss I.] . . . for they were not cleare of yce till the 15 day of September." The ice encountered by the *Emmanuel* was reported by Wiars to surround the island, and it wasn't until two days' sail toward Ireland, after leaving the island, that the sea was clear of ice. Nor is Shepherd's mention of the vast numbers of whale, walrus, seal and cod entirely fresh to the eye: in *North-West Fox*, printed thirty-six years earlier, Luke Foxe says, "If this Ilande were founde again, there is a great store of Fish about it."

In all, Captain Shepherd's account contains little other than what was previously known; he appears to have fabricated his re-discovery of Buss Island in order to further his own financial interests and gain re-employment with the Hudson's Bay Company.

The brief narratives of Zachariah Gillam and James Hall are an entirely different matter. On his voyage to find the Northwest Passage, Captain Gillam reported seeing land somewhere between Greenland and Iceland and "judged it to be an island." It was about two miles away, and had a great many small birds around it. In taking soundings he found 120 fathoms of water. The weather was "dark and foggy"; nonetheless, he reported a position of 59°31′N. Obviously, with such limited visibility, he must have estimated his position based on dead reckoning. Even though his latitude was 120 miles north of the charted position of Buss Island, it was sufficiently close that he believed that is what he saw.

On the first of James Hall's two Greenland expeditions, he kept a lookout for Buss Island when near its marked position, but, not seeing it, he concluded that his chart was wrong. During his second voyage, however, he saw

Fig. 7-5.

Reconstruction of the route of the "busse" *Emmanuel* from the time she left Bear's Sounde on Baffin Island until the sighting of Buss Island. Solid lines are coastlines as shown on present-day maps and nautical charts, while dashed lines show the position on the Gerardus Mercator map that Martin Frobisher carried with him. Frisland is indicated here in two positions; the dashed line represents the placement as Frobisher knew it, and the dotted line represents its most commonly shown position. This map also includes the Faraday Hills on the Mid-Atlantic Ridge and soundings taken at the lower end of the Reykjanes Ridge near the "Doubtful Shoal of Chaucer," where Captain DeCarteret believed he had found Buss Island.

land, but from a distance of 24 miles; it was farther west than shown on his chart, and there was a great bank of ice to the southwest of it.

Given the region of their sightings, what Captains Gillam and Hall likely saw was a fog-bank or ice-field that gave the appearance of land. This had happened to James Hall before, when he was in the southern part of Davis Strait. Land was sighted, but when he and the captain went in the ship's longboat to explore it, they found they had been deceived by a fog-bank, which came upon them so fast they could "scarce see one another."

Faulty perception — mistaking icebergs, fog-banks or ice-fields for land — is a possible explanation for the sighting of Buss Island by those aboard the *Emmanuel*. However, it seems unlikely that they would confuse a fog-bank with land for three continuous days of sailing along a supposed coast. Shifting outlines or alteration of the form would have shown them what they were really seeing.

By the end of the nineteenth century, most writers on the subject of Buss Island believed it to be an error of perception on the part of those aboard the *Emmanuel*; they had mistaken congeries of icebergs or a fog-bank for land. Some historians, however, came to a different conclusion. Sir John Richardson, in *The Polar Regions* (1861), proposed that "this land [Buss Island] was, no doubt, the southern extremity of Greenland."

After the *Emmanuel* crossed Davis Strait and approached land thought to be Frisland, contrary winds drove the ship northward. When the weather improved, the ship resumed its course toward England and once again came upon land. The mariners thought they were clear of Frisland by fifty leagues, and since their charts showed nothing but open ocean south of Frisland, it was only natural to believe they had discovered a new land. Actually, they had regained the southernmost part of Greenland.

To understand how this happened, it is necessary to reconstruct from the ship's log the route of the *Emmanuel*. When the *Emmanuel* left Bear's Sounde on the north shore of Frobisher Bay, she had fair weather and a north-northwest wind. In order to avoid the southern tip of Greenland her heading would have to be greater than 107°true; but as the Greenland side of Davis Strait was approached, the West Greenland Current deflected her onto a more northerly course. Although the captain intended to entirely miss Greenland, unknown to him, the current had placed his vessel at, or near, Cape Desolation at the southwest extremity of Greenland. Most likely, this is where land was first sighted. Believing that Greenland had already been passed, the mariners thought they had reached the shores of Frisland. Cape

Fig. 7-6.
Detail of the reconstructed
route of the *Emmanuel.*

Desolation juts far out to sea, and with poor visibility — a frequent occurrence in this region — it would appear to be an island. At the latitude of Cape Desolation, 61°00′ N, they were at the same latitude as Frisland on their chart. In those five and a half days, the *Emmanuel* had covered roughly 500 miles, or 90 miles per day, at an average speed of 3.7 knots, with the West Greenland Current deflecting her east southeast course by 25 miles to the north.

Then, at six o'clock on the evening of September 8, the wind shifted and came out of the east and east southeast — an unfavourable direction for their course. So for the next six hours the *Emmanuel* headed west, keeping as much southing as possible. Sometime in the night, the wind veered to the south — an even worse direction. Now the *Emmanuel* was forced to head north northwest for the next thirty-six hours, until fair weather and west northwest winds allowed a resumption of the proper course. For the duration of the ship's contrary heading, the captain probably ordered sail to be reduced as much as possible to slow the speed. At an estimated 2.3 knots, the ship would have gained 83 miles under sail, plus 21 miles augmented by the current.

When the wind shifted to the west northwest the mariners headed southeast by south. If they also resumed the average speed they made with a favourable wind as they crossed Davis Strait, they sailed 196 miles less the 32 miles lost to the contrary current, or 163 miles. When they sighted land, the position of the *Emmanuel* would have been about 59°50′N latitude and 47°30′W longitude. Considering the variables of wind, heading, speed and current, this estimate places the vessel close to the southwest part of Greenland, just north of Cape Farwell, rather than to a newly discovered island.

The direction of Buss Island's shore, trending northwest and southeast, corresponds with the geography of Greenland in that region, while the two harbours could be any of the deep indentations along this part of the Greenland coast. Furthermore, the immense quantity of ice about the Greenland coast is compatible with the description of ice extending twenty or thirty leagues from the shore of Buss Island.

But Wiars says that the latitude of Buss Island is 57°30′N. The difference of 02°10′ between this and the southern tip of Greenland, at 59°40′N, amounts to 130 nautical miles — a considerable error in navigation. Wiars and his men may have taken the celestial observation readings from a false horizon created by the tricks and deceptive appearances of the Arctic atmosphere. Or they may only have estimated their latitude based on their supposed distance of fifty leagues from the southeast point of Frisland.

The type of error — duplication in geography — that created Buss Island is not unique in the history of cartography. Matsyn Island, for example, was but a double image of the northern tip of Nova Zembla that was transposed to the west of Nova Zembla as an island. In 1553, Sir Hugh Willoughby, attempting to find the Northeast Passage, "discovered" a group of islands in an empty area of the Barents Sea and called them Sir Willoughbys Land. In reality, they were a section of the Costin Char shore, misapprehended in the same way as the coast of Greenland was misjudged in Wiars's account.

Samuel Purchas was the first to recognize this problem of duplication in regard to Buss Island. As early as 1613, he wrote, "Frisland is in length 25 leagues. The southern part of it is in the latitude of 57 degrees and one second part."[15] These are the same words used by Thomas Wiars to describe Buss Island and are evidence that Purchas regarded the two as indistinguishable. The notion that Buss Island was identical with Frisland was also accepted by some cartographers. Guillaume De l'Isle, in his atlas published in

1720, shows Frisland on a map of the northern hemisphere and calls it "Fris-lande," while on a map of the western hemisphere he gives an island identical in appearance and location the label "*Isle de Bus, ci devant Frislande*" (Isle of Bus, formerly Frislande). A 1745 map by the Dutch cartographer Van Keulen shows Buss Island with the inscription, "The submerged Land of Buss is now-a-days nothing but surf, a quarter of a mile long, with a rough sea."[16]

It may seem senseless to validate the existence of one phantom island with another equally imaginary island. But inadvertently Purchas and the carto-graphers who equated Buss Island with Frisland came close to the truth. Buss Island was indeed a duplication of another land — not Frisland, as they sup-posed, but the southern tip of Greenland.

Fruitless Efforts

On her return passage to England, the *Emmanuel* was continuously beset by tempestuous weather and contrary winds, until finally, without masts, sails, boats or anchors, she was driven upon the sands at Smerwick Harbour on the southwest coast of Ireland. In an attempt to lighten the ship and facilitate re-pairs, the crew transferred a hundred tons of the ore to shore to be "preserved for the Queen." Later, the ore was given to Richard Newton, the captain and owner of the *Emmanuel*, as compensation for his expenses in the voyage to the northwest.

The crew eventually made their way back to England, but the ship did not fare as well. Barely two years later, she was a hollow wreck, exposed to the re-lentless pounding of the Atlantic surf and prey to local inhabitants salvaging timbers. By this time Newton recognized that the black ore was worthless; it remains today where it was taken ashore, buried beneath the fort of Dun-an-Oir, the Fort of Gold. Captain Newton remained in Bridgewater in charge of barge traffic, his fortunes substantially reduced by the loss of his vessel and the lack of compensation (other than useless rocks) for his part in the voyage.

The Hudson's Bay Company abandoned its interest in exploration and trade with Buss Island after attempts in 1676 to reach it failed. The company expelled Captain Shepherd 1681, "on account of bad behaviour."[17] In 1720, in order to "extend and enlarge their trade" in Hudson Bay and Buss Island, the Company wrote a letter to Whitehall requesting an increase in the Company's capital from £31,500 to £378,000, citing great operating expenses and losses to the French as reasons for the insufficient funds. But upon reconsideration they withdrew their request. Thereafter the Hudson's Bay Company said nothing more about Buss Island, directing its efforts toward profitable trade within its more tangible domains. But in 1770 an anonymous author accused the company of keeping the location of Buss Island secret in order to maintain financial control and profits.

The question of Buss Island lay dormant for another twenty-one years, until 1791, when the Office of Trade, Whitehall, wrote the Governor of the Hudson's Bay Company to learn "by what description Busse Island is known at present on the maps." Captain Charles Duncan, then temporarily employed by the Hudson's Bay Company to search for the Northwest Passage, replied: "I strove as much as the Winds would permit me to keep in the supposed Lattd. of the *supposed* Buss Island. But it is my firm Opinion that no such Island is now above Water if ever it was."[18] As far as the Hudson's Bay Company was concerned, the existence of Buss Island was in the "gravest doubt."

The last words in the company's archives on the subject of Buss Island are in a memorandum to the secretary from Mr. Leveson Gower, dated June 21, 1934. After a brief history of the "Grant of Busse Island to Hudson's Bay Company," Gower concludes "that it was a mythical island in the North Atlantic, and that it was alleged to have been first seen by one of Frobisher's vessels in 1578."[19] After more than three centuries of fruitless efforts to validate its existence, Buss Island had, finally and officially, become a phantom.

Chapter VIII

Antillia: The Isle of Seven Cities

THE LEGEND OF THE ISLE OF SEVEN CITIES starts with the history of early medieval Spain. The Visigoths, a barbaric group of Germanic tribes whose rule had dominated Spain since their expansion into that country in 507, were weakening, their disintegration the result not so much of attacks from outside forces as of their own corruption and immorality. At the very beginning of the eighth century, contemporary chroniclers describe Witiza, the Gothic King, as "a reprobate . . . disgraceful in his habits. He dissolved the councils. He sealed the canons. He took many wives and concubines. Witiza ordered all the bishops and priests of his realm to follow his example and marry."[1]

Witiza's conduct set the pattern for Roderick, his son and successor, "a warlike man" under whose rule "Spain grew even worse in its iniquity." When the Moors from North Africa invaded Spain they easily demolished the Gothic army. In this they were aided by the treachery of Roderick's brothers, who, in their rivalry for the kingship, sided with the enemy. The chroniclers, however, attribute their defeat to their being "weighed down by the quality of their sins . . . because they forsook the Lord, and did not serve him in justice and truth." Roderick either fled or was killed in 711, thus ending the Gothic monarchy in Spain. Not that the Moors delivered divine retribution in ridding the Spanish of the sins of Witiza and Roderick, for their own behaviour was far from exemplary. They "ruined beautiful cities, burning them with fire; condemned lords and powerful men to the cross; and butchered youths and infants with the sword."[2]

The story goes that after the fall of the Goths, an archbishop, along with six other bishops and a multitude of followers, fled from Spain to a Portuguese port, where they set sail. Guided by heaven, they settled on Antillia, an island far out in the Atlantic, where they founded seven cities — one for each bishop. Several versions of the tale vary the point of departure and the date (714 or 734), but the basic story remains the same. How the bishops and their flocks prospered and their fate on their island are unknown. After seven centuries of silence, the subject re-emerges in cartographic and written documents.

Even the very name "Antillia" is the subject of speculation. Armando Cortesão, an authority on the history of early navigation and cartography of Portugal, has postulated that Antillia is the contraction of two Portuguese words: *ante* or *anti*, meaning opposite, and *ilha*, meaning island. Therefore Antillia could be taken to mean an island lying opposite the European continent and in front of another continent — presumably Asia. If Cortesão is correct, then some navigator, probably Portuguese, must already have crossed the Atlantic and discovered unknown lands in its far western reaches fully sixty-eight years (at the very least) before the voyage of Columbus.

Alternatively, it is possible that *Ante ilhe* was intended as the opposite of the island of paradise, which geographically and symbolically lay to the east. Antillia would be its western counterpart, associated with Satan because of its proximity to another island called Satanaxio. The Greek concept of symmetry and balance in geography fit well with the Christian sciences of the Middle Ages and may support this derivation of the name of Antillia.

The first representation of Antillia appears on the nautical chart of 1424 in the Bibliotheca Phillipica, England. It is labelled *ista ixola dixemo Antilia*, and although no accompanying inscription proclaims it to be the Island of Seven Cities, obviously that is the intention, for it carries seven place-names within its border. Unfortunately, these names yield no clues as to their identification or meaning. They appear with minor variations in spelling on subsequent maps well into the seventeenth century.

Later maps, such as the Martin Behaim globe of 1492, eliminate any doubt about linking the island of Antillia with the legend of the seven bishops and their seven cities. A label next to Antillia reads:

> In the year 734 of Christ, when the whole of Spain had been won by the heathen of Africa, the above island Antilia, called seven cities, was inhabited by an archbishop from Porto in Portugal, with six other bishops, and other Christians, men and women, who had fled thither from Spain by ship, together with their cattle, belongings and goods. In 1414 a ship from Spain approached very close to this island.[3]

Clearly, by the end of the fifteenth century it was known that Antillia existed and that it could be reached by sailing west from Iberia.

Ferdinand Columbus, in his book on the history and life of his father,

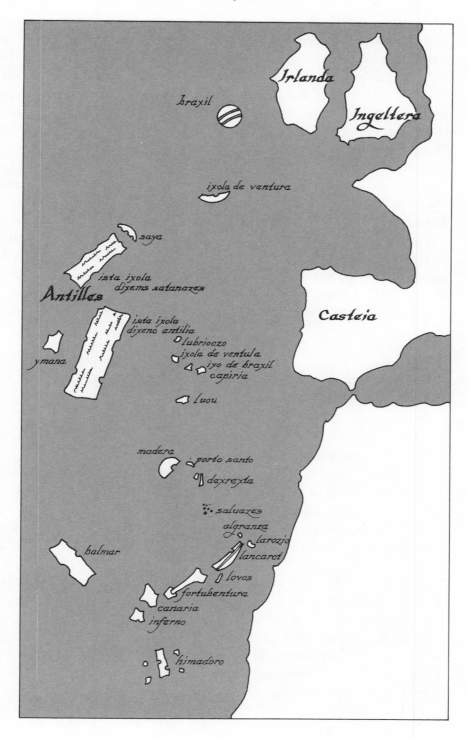

Fig. 8-1.
Nautical chart of 1424,
the first chart to show
the island of Antillia.

adds a few more details to the somewhat cursory legend. He says that the island of Antillia was located 200 leagues (686 nautical miles) due west from the Canaries and the Azores. Once the bishops had built their cities, they burned their ships and all aids to navigation to prevent them from ever thinking of returning to Spain again. In addition, Ferdinand Columbus reports, in the time of Prince Henry the Navigator (about 1430), a Portuguese ship was blown off course by a violent storm but as a result found Antillia. The crew attended church on the island and quickly departed. They sailed home and informed the Prince of their discovery, but when he requested them to return and bring back proof, they made themselves scarce. Not much credence was given to their story. However, the legend did not die, probably because of one more element in the tale: sand brought back for use in the cooking hearth of the ship turned out to be one-third gold. There is nothing like the promise of wealth to perpetuate a legend, and, in this case, to assure a continuing search for the Island of Seven Cities.

Antonio Galvão presents an even more detailed version of the same story:

> In this yeere also, 1447, it happened that there came a Portugall ship through the streight of Gibralter; and being taken with a great tempest, was forced to runne westwards more than willingly the men would, and at last they fell upon an Island which had seven cities, and the people spake the Portugall toong, and they demanded if the Moores did yet trouble Spaine, whence they had fled for the losse which they received by the death of the King of Spaine, Don Roderigo. The boateswaine of the ship brought home a little of the sand, and sold it unto a goldsmith of Lisbon, out of the which he had a good quantity of gold. Don Pedro understanding this, being then a gouernour of the realme, caused all the things thus brought home, and made knowne, to be recorded in the national archives.[4]

Prompted by these reports, Diogo de Teive, a Portuguese nobleman, decided to search for Antillia. He received letters of patent from the king of Portugal granting him lord of any new land discovered, and he set out in 1452 for the Island of Seven Cities, no doubt also enticed by the possibility of finding gold. The details of this voyage are somewhat confused, even at times contradictory. According to the nineteenth-century historian Henry Harrisse, Diogo de Teive sailed "after 1452, one hundred and fifty leagues southwest of Fayal, to find the Antilia island, said to have been sighted by a Lusitanian [Portuguese] vessel."[5] Bartolomé de Las Casas, in his *Historia de las Indias*, says that Teive departed from Fayal, and "proceeded 150 leagues with the wind *lebechio*."[6]

Since the *lebechio* is a northwest wind, and a caravel needs to have the wind abaft its beam in order to sail, Las Casas's report might be construed as saying that Teive sailed southwest, as stated by Harrisse. If so, it must have been a difficult voyage on several counts: this direction would have led Teive into the Sargasso Sea, where he would be frustrated by the heat and calms as much as by the failure to find Antillia. Or possibly Teive had to tack his vessel against the wind in order to sail *toward* the northwest. This is what Jaime Cortesão believes, and concludes that in 1452 Diogo de Teive reached the Grand Banks of Newfoundland, a distance of 1450 miles.[7] If this is true, it would make him one of the earliest European discoverers of America. Whichever direction Teive took, the voyage was not a total failure, for on the return passage he discovered Flores and Corvo, the two most westerly islands of the Azores group.

Between 1462 and 1487 there were at least eight Portuguese voyages whose primary objective was the discovery of new Atlantic islands. Sometimes Antillia was specifically referred to by name, but even when it wasn't, it was undoubtedly implied, for this island was significant in Portugal's history and firmly implanted on the map. Spain, too, was strongly interested in possessing the Isle of Seven Cities, claiming it in the Treaty of Evora, with Portugal, among "the islands which had not been found."[8]

Antillia was a geographic concept much like the Northwest Passage, always assumed to be there, just beyond the horizon, waiting only to be corroborated rather than discovered. There was no question about the authenticity of Antillia in 1475, when King Afonso V of Portugal granted to Ferdinando Teles "the Seven Cities or some other islands" that he might find in the Atlantic.[9] In 1486, Ferdinand d'Ulmo wrote to King João II of Portugal informing him of *his* intent to find "a great island or islands or coast of a continent which presumably is the Isle of the Seven Cities"; the king gave him permission "to go and discover the island of the Seven Cities."[10] However, no further records exist on this projected voyage.

A Stepping-stone in the Atlantic

Antillia featured prominently in the travels of Christopher Columbus, if not as a goal in itself, at least as a means to that goal. Columbus's extensive library of books on cosmography and geography attest to the many years he spent in gathering information and assimilating current geographical concepts before he came to his own decision to reach the East Indies by sailing west. Though for the most part his theories were correct, unfortunately they were based on serious misconceptions. By accepting the circumference of the world based on the Posidonius-Ptolemy calculations, he underestimated the size of the world by 28%. The *Book of Marco Polo (Il milione)* also significantly influenced his theory about the size of the world. When Marco Polo travelled beyond what Ptolemy considered the farthest limit of land, he concluded that, because the landmass was greater in size than Ptolemy had thought, the intervening ocean between Europe and Asia must be correspondingly smaller.

Columbus's second serious misconception was that in the western Atlantic he would find many islands. Marco Polo's report of 1378 islands off the coast of Asia encouraged Columbus to believe that even before reaching the far shore he could easily make some sort of landfall. But to Columbus, Marco Polo's most convincing and enticing statement was: "Cipangu [Japan], an island toward the east in the high sea, [is] 1,500 miles distant from the continent": convincing, because it was one more "proof" of the shortness of a voyage required; enticing, because Marco Polo added that the "Lord of the island lived in a great palace, wherein its roof, pavement and floors were entirely of gold, a good two fingers thick."[11]

The Florentine cosmographer Paolo del Pozzo Toscanelli also contributed to Columbus's misconception about the width of the Atlantic. Sometime before 1492, Toscanelli had sent a letter to Ferdinand Martins, Canon at Lisbon.[12] In a recapitulation of this letter addressed to Columbus, Toscanelli estimated the distance between Lisbon and the great city of Quinsay (the capital of China) to be 6500 miles, one-third of the circumference of the earth. This he showed on an accompanying map, where each meridian space represented 250 miles. The distance on this map from the westernmost of the Canary Islands to Antillia was a little over 1000 miles. Marco Polo had estimated the distance from Japan to the shores of the Asian continent to be 1500 miles But, Toscanelli continues in his letter, "from the island of Antillia, known to you, to the most noble island of *Cipangue* there are ten spaces." With Antillia used as a stepping-stone, the greatest distance to be sailed would be the segment between Antillia and Japan — 2500 miles. Thus, concludes Toscanelli, "the spaces of the sea to be crossed in the unknown parts are not great."

Even though the geographic position of Antillia was unknown (other than that it lay somewhere in the western part of the Atlantic) and the only tales about its existence were vague and unsubstantiated, Columbus did not consider it a difficult task to find Antillia and stop off there en route to Asia. In 1491, Columbus visited the friary of La Rábida. There he consulted with those who were to help him with his forthcoming venture, most notably the shipowner, Garcia Fernández, and Pedro de Velasco, pilot to Diogo de Teive on his voyage thirty-nine years earlier. Undoubtedly, Velasco related many tales about their discovery of Flores and Corvo and their exploits in search of Antillia. Columbus added another goal to his ambitious plans: to discover Antillia among the islands in the Atlantic.

Although Columbus probably didn't see the globe constructed in 1492 by Martin Behaim before he set off on his first voyage, there is no doubt that he had communication with Behaim (who lived for a while in Portugal) and discussed with him his views on geography and cartographic projects. Behaim's globe displayed the full extent of geographical knowledge of the time, including the multitude of Atlantic islands. Like other great cartographers, Martin Behaim brought to his work remarkable craftsmanship; he was regarded as an important mathematician; and he had actually sailed the western coast of Africa in 1484 and 1485, which enabled him to bring such accuracy to his work. The geography and legends on Behaim's globe synthesize information from three major sources: Ptolemy's atlas, accounts of medieval travellers to Asia (chiefly Marco Polo) and discoveries by Portuguese voyagers. The extensive topographical detail of rivers and mountains and the use of many place-names is evidence of the contribution of merchant caravans to Asia. On Behaim's globe, the vast archipelago of the East Indies is strewn in the western ocean separating Europe and Asia, and the largest of the islands, Cipangu Insula, is shown a considerable distance from shore. Near the tropic of Cancer, these islands reach out and all but touch those extending west from Europe — the Azores and the Madeira and Canary islands. Antillia is shown south of the Azores, with the legend of the seven bishops. Near the equator are the Cape Verde Islands, as well as a much more detailed outline of the west coast of Africa than had ever before appeared on a map.

By spreading the islands across the open spaces of the Atlantic, Martin Behaim effectively diminished the immensity of the ocean; his globe visually matched the verbal assertions of Columbus. Thus, Christopher Columbus cannot be entirely faulted in his belief in a "small world" and "narrow Atlan-

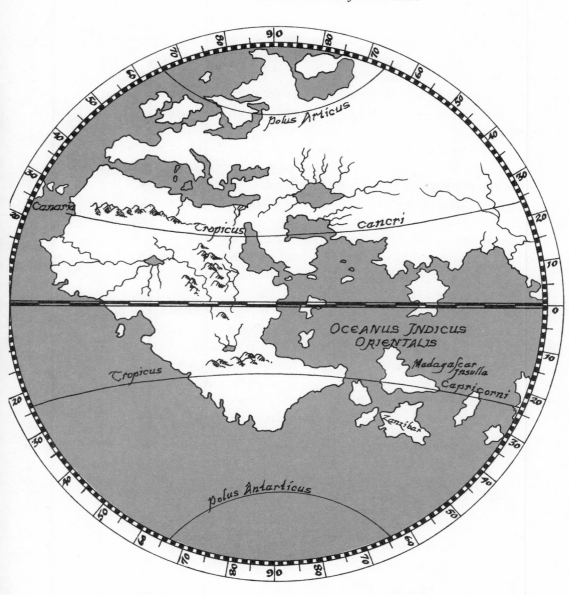

Fig. 8-2.
Martin Behaim globe,
1492. This illustration
is based on an engraving
made of the Behaim globe
by John Gabriel
Doppelmayer in 1730.

tic," for the preponderance of texts and maps available to him was in accord
with his flawed mathematical geography.

In the second half of the fifteenth century, England, too, was expanding
the horizons of the known world, but in more northerly latitudes. Mariners
of Bristol, the second largest port in England, sailed south to Spain, Portugal, and possibly Madeira and the Canaries in their merchant ventures. In the
1480s and 1490s, Bristol handled more cloth, wine and dutiable goods than

any other English port. However, it was in the other direction — northwest to Iceland, Greenland and the Banks of Newfoundland — that England contributed the most in exploration. At first, the rich cod fishery in this region was the impetus for these expeditions. Profits were sufficiently great to offset the difficulties of sailing in such a harsh climate, with its navigational problems, tempestuous seas and dangerous icebergs.

Though the northern fishing grounds and the routes there and back were well known and heavily trafficked, it was thought possible that somewhere along the way the legendary islands of Brazil and Seven Cities could still be found. Then they could serve as way-stations to and from the fishing grounds, shortening the distance and easing the difficulties of the voyage. In a letter dated July 25,1498, Pedro de Ayala, Spanish envoy in London, informed Ferdinand and Isabella that "for the last seven years the Bristol people have equipped, every year, two, three or four caravels to go in search of the islands of Brazil and Seven Cities."

After Columbus's triumphal return in 1493, bringing with him news of "having reached the Indies" and of starting a colony on an island "off the coast of Japan," John Cabot thought he could do as well, if not better, sailing a shorter route to China by crossing the Atlantic in very high latitudes. It had even been rumoured that Columbus, upon his return from Hispaniola in 1496, had found Antillia. Now England's objective shifted from trade and fishing to a bolder one, involving greater risk but also the potential for even greater profits — a search for the Northwest Passage leading to the riches of Cathay.

Whether Giovanni Cabato was of Venetian or Genoese birth is uncertain, but he was a citizen of Venice, where he resided until 1490. There, he traded in the spices, silks and dyes brought by Arab traders from Asia to Mecca and the port of Alexandria. When Cabot moved to Valencia, Spain, he retained his interest in the Far East. He knew of Cathay from the travels of Marco Polo, and he had become knowledgeable in cartography and navigation. When his approaches to Spain and Portugal for support of his plan to reach the Orient were rejected, he turned to Henry VII of England for patronage.

In his proposal to King Henry, Cabot outlined several advantages to a northern passage: the route to Asia in higher latitudes would be shorter and hence cheaper and more profitable, and reaching China would help counteract some of the initial advantages Spain had as the result of Columbus's discoveries. Henry VII, mindful of the fact that he had previously turned down the entreaties of Columbus's brother, decided not to let a second chance slip by. He granted a patent to John Cabot including ships, men and the authority to "saile to all parts, countrys and seas of the East, of the West and of the North," under the banners and ensigns of England, and "to seeke out, discover, and find whatsoever isles, countrys, regions or provinces . . . in what part of the world soever they be, which before this time have bene unknowen to all Christians."[13]

Cabot sailed from Bristol in May of 1497 in a single small ship, the *Mathew*, to find his short ocean route to the Indies. He made landfall on June 24 and took formal possession of this "Newe-founde-ilande" for Henry VII. From the northern tip of Newfoundland, his general course was a southerly coasting of the island until he passed Cape Race at its southern end, whereupon he returned to England. John Cabot did not achieve his goal of reaching China, but he did accomplish something perhaps more important: as the result of this voyage, England claimed possession of the entire North American continent.

News of Cabot's successful voyage quickly spread. Raimondo de Soncino, a Milanese envoy to London, a chronicler and a confidant of Cabot, quickly dispatched a letter to the Duke of Milan. Dated August 24, 1497, it reads:

> . . . Also some months ago his majesty the king [Henry VII] sent out a Venetian who is a very good mariner and has considerable skill in discovering new islands, and he has returned safe, and has found two new very large and fertile islands, and also discovered the Seven Cities, 400 leagues [1200 miles] from the island of England on the western passage. This next spring his majesty the king means to send him out with fifteen or twenty ships.[14]

Soncino was not frugal in his hyperbole. Not only did he claim that the island of Seven Cities was found by Cabot, but he overstated the king's interest in a second voyage. King Henry was interested in backing a second voyage and in being a winner in the race to the Indies, but not to the extent of financing fifteen or twenty ships. Instead, Cabot left England with five ships. For this second voyage, Henry VII advanced Cabot considerable sums of money, as did the Bristol merchants, in hopes of a large profit when he returned with his ships filled with spices and gems of the Orient.

The plan of this new voyage, Soncino said, was: "to keep along the coast from the place at which he touched, [sailing] more and more toward the East, until he reaches an island which he calls Cipango, situated in the equinoctial region where he thinks all the spices of the world have their origin, as well as the jewels." There he will "form a colony" and London will "become a more important mart for spices than Alexandria."

Almost immediately, one of Cabot's ships was forced by a storm off Ireland to return to England. The rest of the fleet proceeded until they reached the east coast of Greenland. They followed the coast north in the hopes of finding a passage to the west, but as the cold grew more intense and the icebergs more numerous, the crew refused to proceed any farther toward the North Pole. Thereupon Cabot turned south until he reached Cape Farewell at the southern tip of Greenland; then he explored the western shore of that land until once again ice forced a change in course. He crossed Davis Strait and followed the coast of Baffin Island, Newfoundland, Nova Scotia and New England until eventually he reached the 38th parallel of latitude, near Chesapeake Bay. Low provisions and the disappointment of finding no evidence of eastern civilization finally forced him to return to England. The disappointment of the Bristol merchants certainly matched that of John Cabot and his men, for instead of great profit they received only a few furs and heard tales of a barren land. This disappointment put a stop to similar expeditions for the next few years.

While Cabot was engaged in exploration, Spanish ambassadors in England relayed letters about his activities to their Catholic sovereigns. Ruy Gonzalez de Puebla, in a letter of July 25, 1498, said:

> The King of England sent five armed ships with another Genoese like Columbus [John Cabot] to search for the island of Brazil and others near it, and they were provisioned for a year. It is said that they will return in September. Seeing the route they take to reach it, it is what your Highnesses possess. The King has spoken to me at various times about it, he hopes to derive great advantage from it. I believe that it is not more than 400 leagues distant from here.[15]

Pedro de Ayala, like Gonzalez de Puebla, believed that Cabot had found the islands of Brazil and Seven Cities. In his dispatch to Ferdinand and Isabella dated the same day, Ayala said: "the land they have found or seek" already belonged to Spain, "for it is at the end of that which belongs to your Highnesses by the convention with Portugal."[16]

Both men based their conviction that, although the islands were discovered by an Englishman, they actually belonged to Spain, on the 1494

Treaty of Tordesillas between Spain and Portugal. In this treaty, Portugal and Spain had divided the world between them with a line "running from pole to pole [at 47°27'W long.] on the Ocean Sea, from the Arctic to the Antarctic pole"; everything east of the line belonged to Portugal, while lands to the west of it were the property of Spain. Ayala told King Henry several times that the islands and mainland that John Cabot testified he found did not belong to England; according to the treaty, they already belonged to Spain. But the king would not hear anything about it.

Both of the Spanish ambassadors and Soncino, the Milanese envoy, were all of the opinion that whatever Cabot had claimed lay 400 leagues (1200 miles) west of Bristol.[17] Since Soncino, Cabot's friend, expressed this first, it is reasonable to suppose that Cabot gave him this information. Unfortunately, it is useless for resolving the location of Brazil and Antillia. Brazil was traditionally placed about one hundred miles southwest of Ireland, while the coast of Newfoundland is some six hundred miles distant; these are generous margins of error, even when taking into account the problem of determining longitude. After the beginning of the sixteenth century, no one claimed again that John Cabot, or any other mariner, had discovered the Island of Seven Cities. But belief in the existence of this island had not ended. At mid-century, historians declared the island "to be present, though . . . no longer visible," and cartographers continued to show the island of Antillia on their maps until 1587.

Antillia and the Antilles

Throughout the fifteenth and early sixteenth centuries, Antillia's position on maps is consistent, and its unique physical characteristics vary so little that a single map, that of Grazioso Benincasa (1470), can be taken as representative. Antillia is so huge that it dwarfs all other islands of the Atlantic archipelagos. Using the geography of Iberia as a guide for calculation, Antillia would be about 50 nautical miles wide and 210 nautical miles long — roughly three-quarters the size of Portugal. Its greatest length is aligned in a north-south axis. North of Antillia, separated by a wide strait, is a second island, Saluaga, variously labelled on other maps Satanaxio or Satanazes. It is not quite as large as its companion, but like Antillia it is rectangular and

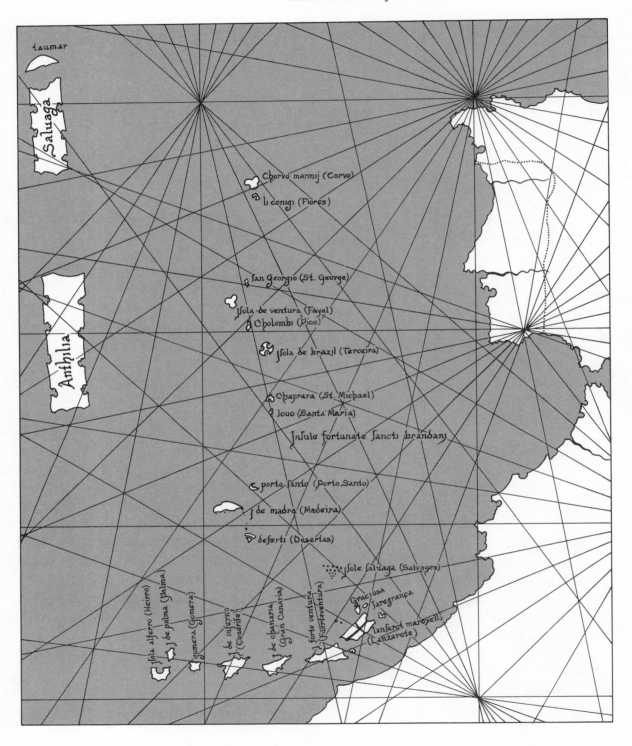

taumar

Saluaga

Antßlia

Chorvo marinij (Corvo)

li conigi (Flores)

san georgio (St. George)

Isola de ventura (Fayal)

Cholombi (Pico)

Isola de brazil (Terceira)

Chaprara (St. Michael)

Iouo (Santa Maria)

Insule fortunate fancti brandan)

porto fanto (Porto Santo)

J de madra (Madeira)

deferti (Desertas)

Isole faluaga (Salvages)

Isola alferro (Hierro)

J de palma (Palma)

gomera (Gomera)

J de inferno (Canarie)

J de chanaria (Gran Canaria)

forte ventura (Fuerteventura)

Graciosa

Jaregrança

lanfarot maroxello (Lanzarote)

oriented in a north-south direction. Accompanying these two major islands are the smaller ones of Taumar and Ymana, the latter sometimes called Roillo or Rosellia. Altogether, this cluster of islands around Antillia would make up an Atlantic archipelago, separate and distinct from the Canary, Madeira and Azores archipelagos.

No one has ever resolved the meaning of the seven names in the island's interior. Seemingly, they relate to the seven cities founded by the seven bishops; an unexplained oddity is that five of the seven names, like Antillia itself, begin with *An*: Ansalli, Ansodi, Anhuib, Ansesseli, Ansolli, Aira and Con.

Another striking feature of Antillia and Saluaga is that both are rectangles whose only topographic features are the bays equally spaced around their shores. They, too, are highly stylized, each being tri-lobed and quite unlike anything shown as an inlet on the mainland or on any of the other Atlantic islands. Benincasa's 1470 map shows eight of these indentations on Antillia, but on his 1482 map there are only seven — presumably one for each of the seven cities. Taumar and Roillo, on the other hand, are appropriate in scale and irregular in outline, like any other island.

Finally, Antillia was always placed west of the Azores; no cartographer ever mistook this island for one of the Azores or Canary islands. According to Las Casas, in his *Historia de las Indias*, Christopher Columbus had gathered information in Portugal about Antillia; various people had informed him that "in the sea-charts made in times gone by, were depicted several islands in those seas and parts, especially the island called Antillia, and they placed it a little over 200 leagues west of the Canary Islands and the Azores." Ferdinand Columbus repeats this information in his history and biography of his father. Did these historians borrow from each other? Did they both get their information about Antillia from an earlier source? Or does the 200 leagues (686 nautical miles) simply signify a very great distance?

An important clue about the actual westward distance of Antillia from the Canaries is furnished on the 1436 map of Andrea Bianco. A wide space separates Y^a d'Antillia from the Azores, and in the gap is "*Questo de Mar de Baga*" (Disputed Sea of Baga), the Sargasso Sea. Since this vast sea of floating weeds is bounded on its western edge by the north-flowing Gulf Stream, and Antillia is west of the Sargasso Sea, the island could have represented some part of the New World. When Ferdinand d'Ulmo wrote to the king of Portugal in 1486 that he wished to seek "a great island or islands or *coast of a conti-*

Fig. 8-3.
Grazioso Benincasa map, 1470.

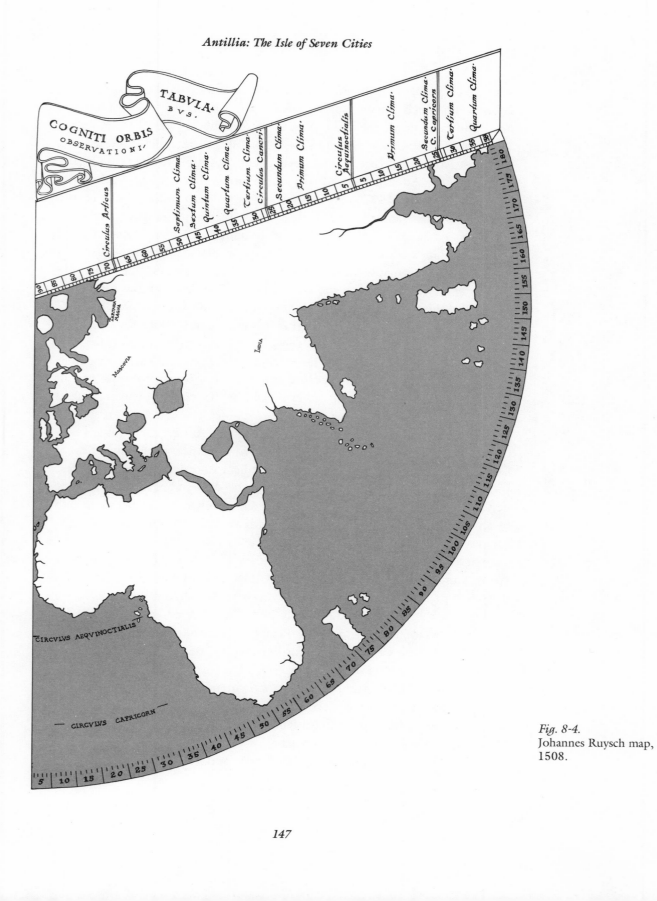

Fig. 8-4.
Johannes Ruysch map,
1508.

nent which probably is the island of the Seven Cities," did he have access to information which has since disappeared? Does the phrase "coast of a continent" indicate knowledge about America before the voyages of Columbus?

In 1493, Peter Martyr d'Anghiera, a Spanish cartographer, historian and humanist, concluded that Bianco's placement of Antillia in the farthest part of the western Atlantic showed that an unknown mariner had reached the West Indies before 1436, that this voyage was lost to history, but that the *tradition* of the islands' existence was maintained until rediscovery finally corroborated its existence. Peter Martyr thought that Cuba, Hispaniola and the other islands adjoining were the Antillae Insulae, the islands of Antillia shown on the old maps. Antonio Galvão, writing fifty years later in his *Discoveries of the World*, echoed the same thought. He declared that "there are some who think that the islands the Portuguese sailors discovered in 1447 when they were driven there by a great storm — islands which they declared were those of Antillia and the Seven Cities — were the Antilles, or New Spain." Those who believe this, he continues, "allege good reasons for their opinion, which here I omit, because they serve not to my purpose. But all their reasons seem to agree, that they should be that country, which is called *Noua Spagna*."[18]

Cartographers as well as historians felt that the Antillia on old maps represented a foreknowledge of the New World. After the discoveries of Columbus, they accordingly transferred Antillia to a new position in the West Indies. Thus, the 1502 map of Cantino calls the West Indies Antilhas del Rey de Castella (Antilles of the King of Spain). On another map of the same date by an anonymous cartographer, these islands are called Antilie. And in 1518, they are still labelled Antilhas de Castela.

Not all cartographers were certain that the Caribbean islands of the New World were really Antillia rediscovered. On his map of 1508, Johannes Ruysch kept Antillia as a large island about six hundred miles west of the Azores, at a latitude of 37°00′ N to 40°00′ N. Below it, a long inscription details the story of the Gothic King Roderick and the legend of the seven bishops, while the Caribbean islands depicted on this map have the names Columbus bestowed on them during his second voyage. But Ruysch was not entirely sure about Hispaniola. Since it was situated in the same position as the Sipangus described by Marco Polo (1500 miles off the coast of Asia), and fit everything written about that island, Ruysch concluded that Hispaniola must be Japan, as Columbus claimed.

So tantalizing is the possibility that Antillia and its sister islands represent a knowledge of the New World perhaps going back as far as the 1300s that historians are still attempting to support the idea. Chief among them is William Babcock, writing extensively for the American Geographical Society Research Series. As testimony that the Antillia archipelago "roughly corresponds to a part of the West Indies and Florida," Babcock thoroughly reviews the most important fifteenth-century maps: Phillips (1424), Beccario (1435), Bianco (1436), Pareto (1455), Roselli (1468) and Benincasa (1482).[19]

Antillia, the largest and most southerly of the islands, Babcock concludes, is Cuba. Saluaga, north of Antillia, is deemed to represent Florida, with the gap between the two islands being the Florida Strait; cartographers, he says, unaware that Florida was the tip of a continent, "severed it from the mainland as the result of guesswork."

Reylla or Roillo, shown on the early maps, is west of Antillia, not unlike the geographic relationship Jamaica bears to Cuba. Though Reylla and Jamaica are approximately matched in relative location and size, there is little else on which to base this identification. Babcock deduces that Taumar, the small island north of Saluaga, "was meant to be symbolic and representative of the sea islands near Florida [Great Abaco and Great Bahamas], rather than any particular one of them."

There is some justification in all these correlations, but they have one major flaw — the question of latitude. Babcock notes that the Antillia group was always shown farther north than the latitude of the Caribbean islands, but he dismisses any objection to the discrepancy by saying that "some dislocation, of course, is to be looked for in mapping exploration in an unscientific period." Cuba, he continues, "is not really directly opposite Portugal but may easily have been believed so." In the eighth or ninth century, Arabian geographers described how to determine latitude from the position of the sun, and by the end of the fifteenth century, mariners could calculate their latitude fairly accurately.

The coastlines of Iberia and North Africa on the Benincasa map can be used to see how well the latitude of the Atlantic islands, including Antillia, were determined. The Madeira archipelago appropriately lies west of Casablanca above Cape Sim, at a latitude roughly 32°30′ N — its true position. The Canaries, as well, are properly shown between the latitudes of 28°00′ N and 29°30′ N, just north of Cape Juby. Even their westward slant, in part forced by the northeast-southwest trend of the West African coast, is correct. In the Azores, the islands of the central group (Fayal, Pico, St. George, and Terceira) are correctly placed due west of Lisbon, Portugal. However, Benincasa strung them all out in a north-south line, so Terceira (labelled Insula de Brazil) is at 37°00′ N instead of its true 38°45′ N latitude — an error of 105 nautical miles. The most northerly (i.e., westerly) island, Flores, and the most southerly, Santa Maria, are off by 95 and 105 nautical miles respectively.

The same technique, comparison with the continental coasts of Africa and Europe, shows the latitude of Antillia at its southern end to be 35°30′ N, and 39°00′ N at its northern end; Saluaga's latitude is between 41°00′ N and 44°30′ N. If Antillia were moved due west while keeping its same latitude, it would extend from Cape Hatteras, North Carolina, to Delaware Bay, and Saluaga would occupy a position from north of Nantucket Island up to Halifax, Nova Scotia. No navigator, even in the fourteenth century, could possibly have made an error of 900 nautical miles in his calculations of the latitude of Antillia, or confuse Florida with Nova Scotia.

This still leaves the mystery of what Antillia and Saluaga represented on the fifteenth-century maps and the hope that some yet undiscovered chronicle or document will answer the question. Meanwhile, though the legend and history of Antillia have been forgotten by most people, the name remains attached to the West Indies of the Caribbean — the Greater Antilles.

The name Sete Cidades (Seven Cities) also still lives. On São Miguel, in the central group of the Azores, two large lakes fill the crater of an extinct volcano. One is bright emerald green in colour, while the other, separated by a narrow causeway, is a crystalline turquoise blue. From the deep valley floor, the evergreen-clad slopes rise precipitously to the volcano's rim. The unruffled waters of the twin lakes reflect the inverted image. Surrounding the shores are seven villages, always called by their collective name: Sete Cidades. Are these few, simple houses of local fishermen and farmers the vestiges of the original colonies of the seven bishops? There are no ruins or other archeological evidence of any settlement that dates back to the eighth century — all that remains is the name. However, it is possible that the refugees from the inequities of King Roderick and the Moorish attacks found a safe haven here on this small bit of land far from the shores of Portugal. Even if this fancy has no basis in fact, a legend could hardly find a more blessed final place of rest than the hidden island valley on São Miguel.

Chapter IX

Hy-Brazil

On the ocean that hollows the rocks where ye dwell,
A shadowy land has appeared, as they tell;
Men thought it a region of sunshine and rest,
And they called it O'Brazil — the isle of the blest.

From year unto year, on the ocean's blue rim,
The beautiful spectre showed lovely and dim;
The golden clouds curtained the deep where it lay,
And it looked like an Eden, away, far away.

(Gerald Griffin)

NO OTHER PHANTOM ISLAND IN THE ATLANTIC is cloaked in so many identities as Hy-Brazil. It was known to lie close to the west coast of Ireland, yet it was seldom seen, for dense fog continuously shrouded it from view. But once every seven years, the veil of fog would lift, and an enchanted sunken island with mountains, verdant pastures filled with sheep, and gleaming cities would rise to become visible. In this Celtic land of enchantment dwelled Faerie Queens, magicians and great healers. Legends and myths of ancient Ireland abound in which heroes, beckoned by the mirage of "gold-roofed towers and domes that glistened from beneath the waves," set out to sea toward the land of magic. Whenever they approached the land, though, it disappeared beneath the water again; only if fire, in some form, was cast upon the land would it become fixed, for "fire is hostile to anything phantasmal."[1]

The island of Hy-Brazil also stood for the pagan Elysium of Greek mythology: a land of ideal happiness "amid the waves' sunset glory," a dwelling-place where neither decay nor sorrow or anything harsh ever befell one, and everlasting sweet song, laughter and the perfume of blossoms held sway. Hy-Brazil was the garden of the Hesperides, west of Ireland, where the sadness of life could be escaped.

Christian writers created from this pagan island a land of truth for those of the Faith. To them, Hy-Brazil was a "Land of the Promise of the Blessed," an earthly paradise, a far-away Eden. This is the island — the Promised Land of the Saints — that Saint Brendan set out to find.

Almost as elusive as the mirage or fog-bank from which Hy-Brazil emerged is the confusion caused by the island's multiplicity of names: Tír fo-Thuin — the Land Under the Wave; Magh Mell — the Land of Truth; Hy na-Beatha — Isle of Life; and Tír na-m-Buadha — the Land of Virtue. In Christian tales, it was known as Tír Tairngiri — the Land of Promise, or Terra Re-promissionis Sanctorum — the Promised Land of the Saints. Most commonly though, it was called Hy-Brazil or some variant, such as Ysole Brazir, Bracir or Hy Breasail; these are its names on fourteenth- and fifteenth-century maps.

Not only did the one island possess a great number of names, but the name Brazil was often applied to several *different* islands, sometimes on the very same chart. On the Pizigani map of 1367, Brazir is clearly applied to a circular island off the southwest coast of Ireland, while one of the islands in the middle group of the Azores is called Insulla de Brazir. On the Solerio map of 1385, two Brazils are marked; one, to the west of Ireland, is Insula de Berzil; the other, in the Azores, is Brazir. The Benincasa map of 1470 and the Bartolomeo Pareto map of 1455 also label the Azorean island (now called Terceira) as Isola de Brazil and Insulla de Brazil.

Four tales about the island go back as far as the sixth century. Bran, son of Febal, went to meet the sea-god Mananann mac Lir in his chariot and visited the magic Island of Laughter. Lochan, Enne and Silvester, the three sons of Conall, as penance for their misdeeds, sailed for forty days to "meet the Lord on the sea." Two men, Snedgus and Mac Riagla, though sentenced to death for murdering King Domnall (AD 639-642), instead were set adrift to explore the outer sea and found many wondrous isles. And, in the *immram* of Màel Dúin, a submarine country was found, with roofed forts, people and cattle, psalm-singing birds, and magic fountains which spouted wine.

Voyages to Hy-Brazil

In the last decades of the fifteenth century, Bristol, England, was a highly prosperous port, engaged in an active trade with Ireland, Spain and Portugal for cloth, wine and wood. Forty years earlier, two ships had sailed from Bristol in an attempt to reach the lands of the Far East and bring back its treasures to increase even further the wealth of their town. Unfortunately, neither of the two ships reached their goal. If the goods of Cathay were denied Bristol merchants, at least there was a chance for profit in the herring and cod fishery off the coast of Iceland. Hy-Brazil, if found, would serve as a convenient base of operations.

It is hard to believe that anyone would actually expect to find an island with such a strong foundation of myth on the face of the earth. But very substantial efforts were made to discover this enchanted island. So strong was the belief in its reality that in 1480 a ship of "80 tons burthern sailed out of Bristol to navigate west of Ireland as far as the island of Brazil."[2] A contemporary account of this expedition by Willelmus Botoner (William of Worcester, 1415-1484), printed in *Itineraria Symonis Simeonis et Willelmi de Worcestre*, explained that, under the direction of John Jay Jr., Thomas Lyde, "the most expert seaman in all of England," set out to navigate as far as the "*insulam de Brasylie.*"[3] But, after sailing the seas for nine months without discovering the islands, they had to abandon their quest on account of storms; they "returned to a port in Ireland to allow the ship and men to rest." The journey was actually shorter than nine months, since they left on July 15 and returned on September 18; in fact, it was about nine weeks.

In spite of this failure, a second expedition was organized the following year, and two vessels, the *Trinity* and the *George*, went "to serche & fynde a certain Isle called the Isle of Brazil." Their holds on the outbound voyage contained a large quantity of salt, a good indication they were headed for the fishing grounds. Nothing came of this expedition, either.

Following the 1480 and 1481 explorations, other mariners continued the search. After John Cabot left Venice in 1490, but before he moved to Valencia, Spain, he lived briefly in London; presumably it was at this time that he supervised the preparations of the ships that left Bristol under his direction in 1491 and 1492 to search for the island of Brazil. These voyages were no more fruitful than the previous ones.

In 1498, Pedro de Ayala, the Spanish envoy to London, reported the scope of the Bristol merchants' efforts to find Brazil and Antillia: two to four ships a year for seven years. When Cabot set off with his five ships and three hundred men in 1498, it was evidently part of his plan to search for the island of Brazil west of Ireland. If he found it, the island could serve as an intermediate station halfway to the Orient. This is exactly what Columbus had thought of doing with Antillia on *his* route to the Far East.

The Cottonian Chronicle of 1498 tells more about Cabot's voyage:

> . . . the King at the besy request and supplicacion of a Straunger Venisian [John Cabot] . . . caused to manne a ship [accompanied by three or four other ships of Bristol] . . . for to serche an Iland whereyn the said Straunger surmysed to be great commodities. The said Straunger, leader of this Flete, wheryn dyuers merchauntes as well of London as Bristowe aventured goodes and sleight merchaundises, which departed from the West Cuntrey in the begynning of Somer, but to this present moneth came nevir Knowlege of their exployt.[4]

John Cabot never returned from this voyage. Somewhere north of Conception Bay, Newfoundland, the ship he was on was lost, but some survivors eventually made their way back to England on another vessel. Although his expedition never reached its goal and did not find the "short northern route to Cathay," Cabot's efforts nevertheless gained much new geographical information, and the world learned about the quantity of fish off the Newfoundland Banks. Tales of "fish swarming so thick they impede the ship" created an extensive Newfoundland fishery for English, French, Spanish and Portuguese fishermen.

Attempts to find the island of Brazil appear to have ended with the Cabot voyages. However, the strength of belief in the island's existence suffered no diminution. In the centuries that followed, there were continual reports of sightings of the enchanted island.

In 1636, a certain Captain Rich reported seeing an island off the west coast of Ireland with "a harbour, and headlands," but when he tried to make a landing, it "vanished in the mist." Another account in 1644 came from Boullage Le Gouz, who claimed that "three miles distant from his ship he saw the phantom island, with trees and cattle." T.J. Westropp, the author of an article on the island of Brazil, said that he personally had seen the island three times. The last sighting occurred during the summer of 1872. It was "a clear evening, with a fine golden sunset, when just as the sun went down, a dark island suddenly appeared far out to sea, but not on the horizon. It had two hills, one wooded; between them, from a low plain, rose towers and curls of smoke." Others with him, including his mother, all "saw it at the same time . . . with such realistic appearance."[5] The brevity of these accounts and their lack of substantiating details help to support them rather than reducing their credibility; at least they contained no faerie-folk or diabolical magicians.

A lengthy letter written in 1675 by William Hamilton of Derry contains one of the most detailed accounts of O'Brazile.[6] Addressed to his cousin living in London, the letter explains why another cousin of theirs, Mathew Calhoon, a "wise man and great scholar," had requested Charles I of England to grant him a patent of ownership for the enchanted island of O'Brazile. Calhoon believed that the "island had been fully discovered . . . and the enchantment broken." Hamilton relates how the island had been found by Captain John Nisbet of Killybegs, in County Donagal, Ireland, in 1674. In September of that year, Nisbet filled several vessels with butter, tallow and hides and sailed to France; on the return trip he brought back French wines. When near the coast of Ireland on the return passage, and just as the sun was rising, "all of a sudden there fell a most terrible thick mist of fog upon the sea, which continued for the space of three hours." Then, just as suddenly, it lifted, and he and his men found themselves close to shore on an unknown coast. These were familiar home waters to the sailors, yet this place was entirely new to them. Since the wind was driving them dangerously close to the land, with rocks not far off, they sounded and anchored in three fathoms of water.

Four of the eight crewmen rowed ashore. After landing, they passed through "a little wood . . . and came upon a most pleasant, green valley filled with many cattle, horses and sheep feeding." They also saw a "strong-like castle" and went there to find out where they were and what to do. But no one responded to their knock upon the door, nor did they hear any sound of any creature — not so much as the barking of a dog. They spent the rest of the day exploring the island, and although they saw many animals, there were no people to enquire of. With night approaching, they returned to shore and built a rousing fire to ward off the cold. Immediately they heard a "terrible, hideous noise" from all over the island, but coming especially from the castle; terrified, they hastened back to their ship. The next morning, as soon as the sun had risen, an ancient, grave gentleman stood with his followers upon the shore of the island. The seamen learned that the elder's ancestors had once been princes of this island, called O'Brazile, but that he and the others had been "tyrannically shut up in the castle by the malicious, diabolical art of a great

Negromancer" who cursed the island, making it unserviceable and invisible to mortals. But now the "spell of enchantment was broken [by fire], and the wicked time expired" — they were free from imprisonment, and the island would forever more be visible.

Captain Nisbet and his men sailed back to Killybegs, with samples of the gold and silver they were given, to spread the news of their remarkable discovery. Three days later a vessel captained by Alexander Johnson went to Brazil to see if the tale was true or not. The island was still there, and Johnson and his crew were nobly entertained by the residents, after which they safely returned to Ireland. But evidently the spell upon the island was not as permanently broken as these men supposed, for once again it sank beneath the surface of the waves, to be shrouded in fog and hidden from view ever after.

True History of the Matter of the Name

Exactly when Terceira, in the Azores, first appeared on maps with the appellation "Brazil" is uncertain. The lettering on the Laurentian portolano of 1351 resembles the word "Brazil," but it is too indistinct to make a positive identification. On the map of the Pizigani Brothers of 1367, though, Terceira is clearly labelled "Jnsola de braçir." The same name is applied to an island ninety to a hundred nautical miles southwest of Ireland as well, and even to a *third* island west of the English Channel. More frequently, this third island was known as Jnsola de Mam (or Man); another phantom island, it quickly disappeared from cartographic records. Terceira continued to be called Braçir, Brazil or a similar name; on the Bartolomeo Pareto map (1455), it is labelled "Insulla de Brazil."

That several islands with the same name appear on one map actually aids identification, for it is not likely that cartographers placed the island of Brazil indiscriminately all over the Atlantic on account of confusion and uncertainty about its location. There really were *two* distinct and different islands, both called Brazil. The name Jnsola de Braçil for Terceira originates in the word "brazil," commonly used during the Middle Ages to mean red dyewood. References to islands where brazil wood may be obtained are found as early as AD 982 in the *Hudúd al-'Álam* (*A Persian Geography: Regions of the World*). And *grana de brasill* (grain of brazil), used for producing dye, is listed as an article of trade in a commercial treaty of 1193 between two Italian city-states. Marco Polo's account of his travels also mentions the brazil crops of Sumatra. None of the records gives an account of exactly how the dye was produced. Most likely the word "brazil" was used generally for any tree or plant from which red dye, a coveted commodity for the flourishing Mediterranean cloth trade in the Middle Ages, could be extracted.

Terceira was obviously an Atlantic source for this precious brazil wood. Later, the island was renamed Ilha de Jesus, then finally Terceira, as it was the third island to be rediscovered by the Portuguese. A remnant of its ancient label still remains: Monte Brazil, one of the volcanic peaks, is on the south coast of the island.

O'Brasil, Hy-Brazil or Breasail, less than a hundred nautical miles off the coast of Ireland, has an entirely different etymology. The most plausible suggestion is that it is from the ancient Gaelic word *breas*, meaning noble, prince or fortunate. It may also be a proper name for a chief or eminent man, in this instance, Saint Bresal (or Breasail).

Saint Bresal (Bressalius de Durthach) was definitely a historical person, not a mythical figure, but beyond this little is known about his life. The son of the first Christian king of Thormond and one of the early Christian missionaries, he was contemporary with Saint Enda of the Aran Islands; Saint Brendan sought him out before setting forth on his voyage. This would place the time Saint Bresal flourished at about 540; however, according to the *Martyrology of Donegal*, in *Lives of the Irish Saints*, Saint Bresal was "the son of Segan, and an Abbot of Iona." If so, he died in 796. Perhaps there were two Saint Bresals; in any case, the saint was venerated and a holy island — the Promised Land of the Saints — was given his name.

An Eden Far Away

From the time Hy-Brazil was first shown on the Angelino de Dalorto map of 1325 until it disappeared from cartographic records in 1865, two aspects of the island remain constant; its location and its physical configuration. Unlike many phantom islands that continually shifted their position on maps during the long period of Atlantic exploration, Hy-Brazil always remained in the

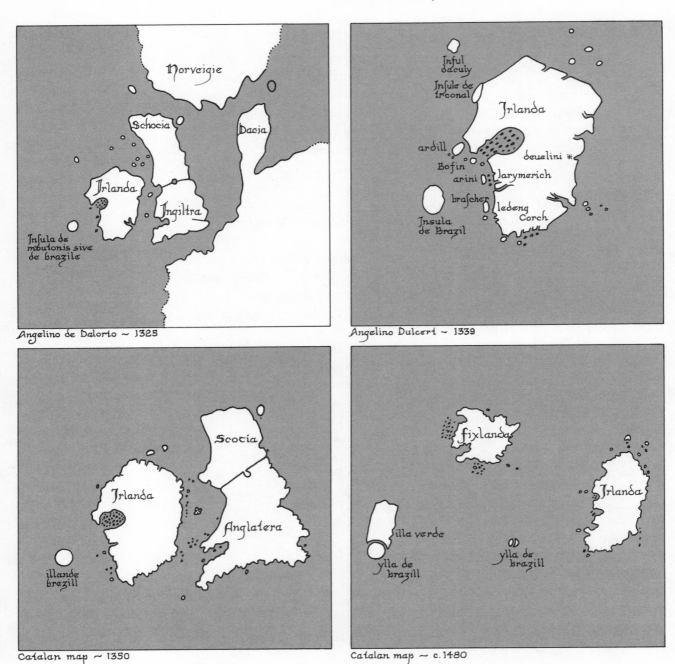

Fig. 9-1.
Four early charts of the North Atlantic in the vicinity of Ireland. The island of Brazil first appears on the Angelino de Dalorto map of 1325. All show Brazil southwest of Galway Bay.

same place. It might be supposed that, once a cartographer had placed Hy-Brazil on his map, other cartographers copied and recopied it on their maps through the centuries, accounting for the constancy of its geographic location.

At some time in the not-too-distant past, could there have actually been an island where none now exists? Could Hy-Brazil have sunk beneath the surface of the waves, not just in a metaphoric sense, but as the result of subsidence of the ocean floor? This has been suggested as an explanation for the disappearance of Buss Island, but there are some important differences between these two islands. Whereas Buss Island was reported to have been seen many hundreds of miles from any known land and in a location now covered by water almost a mile deep, the island of Brazil was shown on maps as being very close to the coast of Ireland and in a region that is still only 600 feet deep. Brazil's subsidence would have been the result of a slow settling of the ocean floor rather than the sudden and violent effect of volcanic action.

In fact, portions of the shallow banks west of Ireland were at one time above water. Shallow-water shells found at Porcupine Bank, just beyond the 100-fathom curve, indicate that at one time it was much closer to the surface, if not actually above it. The same kind of shallow-water shells have been found farther north at Rockall, an inhospitable, solitary peak of granite with vertical cliffs that rise straight out of the water to a height of 63 feet. Rockall used to be larger island than at present, and as recently as the seventeenth century, a nearby shoal was sometimes visible.

There is additional evidence of subsidence in this general region. At one time, the Channel Islands virtually formed a land-bridge between England and France. According to T.J. Westropp, "local histories assert that the Channel Isles were connected with France up to AD 709, and that when Saint Lo visited Jersey on inspection in 565, he could cross onto it by a plank."[7] The Isle of Mam was laid down on the charts where a shoal is now covered with only 6.5 fathoms of water.

According to legend, the island of Hy-Brazil appeared only once every seven years. The number seven had symbolic meaning in both Christian and

Fig. 9-2.
Contemporary chart of the North Atlantic upon which the reported positions of Hy-Brazil and Brazil Rock have been superimposed. The dotted line indicates the 100-fathom curve and the dashed line the 1000-fathom curve.

Celtic lore. But the seven-year duration may mean only that Brazil was *not commonly visible.*

A natural phenomenon could account for the infrequent sightings of Brazil. Mirages, which played a part in the "discovery" of Buss Island, can occur just as well off the coast of Ireland; the thermal inversions which make low-lying islands and even islands beyond the horizon appear as high mountains are not limited to Arctic regions (I myself have experienced the illusion while sailing the mid-coast region of Maine). It is easy to understand how a coast-dweller who one day suddenly sees an island appear above the empty horizon, flickering and undulating before his eyes, would attribute the apparition to magic and enchantment. It would not even be necessary for the island which produced the mirage to be close to shore. To the observer at sea-level, an object that appears to be on the horizon is less than three nautical miles away. But the southwest coast of Ireland and the Aran Islands of Galway Bay rise steeply out of the sea. The 300-foot cliffs of Árainn, the largest of the three Aran Islands, extend one's vision to twenty nautical miles, and the effects of a mirage would enhance the range considerably.

John Cabot never found Brazil, nor did any other mariner after him; nonetheless, the island continued to be shown on nautical charts well into the nineteenth century. Reduced by cartographers from island status, by 1830 it became Brazil Rock, with a position of 51°10′N and 15°30′W. A slightly later chart placed it at 51°10′N and 16°00′W. Brazil Rock remained on the charts until 1865; then, like Buss Island fifteen years earlier, it finally disappeared from the maps altogether.

The other striking characteristic of Hy-Brazil is its shape: perfectly circular, with a clear channel through the middle. No other island except Antillia was shown as a pure geometric shape. In the fifteenth century, cartographers delineated the shores of islands and continental coasts by a uniform, scalloped edge, which indicates their lack of precise geographic information.

However, they always included some features — rivers, general configuration of an island or trend of a coast, or offshore rocks — to show that there was no doubt about the reality of the land. For instance, on the Bartolomeo Pareto map of 1455, the island of Tenerife in the Canaries (labelled "Insulla de Infierno") is obviously a schematic representation, but it is still recognizable and matches the configuration on present-day charts.

The same is true in an even more schematic manner for Insulla d'legname, as shown on many of the early maps. The notch (A) on its southern shore identifies it as the island of Madeira. On shore, a mariner's primary consideration is a secure harbour, one with good holding ground for the anchor and adequate protection from high seas and storm winds. Only two anchorages on Madeira fit these qualifications; both are on the south shore. Whether the solitary notch (A) on Insulla d'legname is meant to represent the harbour at Funchal (B), the island's most im-

portant haven and site of its principal city, or the anchorage in the wide bight below Ponta de São Lourenço (C) is immaterial. A caravel could manoeuvre under sail in either harbour, and both offer surcease from the ever-present northeast trade winds which blow across the island.

On the south side of the island of Terceira, extending three-quarters of a mile seaward, is a long spine of land which terminates at the extinct volcanic

cone of Monte Brasil, rising to a height of 673 feet. This very distinctive landmark forms the western side of the island's major harbour (D). Excellent protection is pro-

vided here in fine, settled weather from June through September. During winter months, however, storms with winds out of the south and east make it dangerous, but perfect protection is provided in the anchorage on the west side of Monte Brasil (E). These two anchorages, one on either side of a mountain, are admirably depicted on the Pizigani map (1367) in a most appropriate graphic symbol. Later, as on the N. de Combitis map of 1400, this form evolved to include the one other possible anchorage on the island's east side at Bahia da Praia da Vitoria (F).

No practical explanation exists for the unique circular shape of the island of Hy-Brazil off the coast of Ireland. But there is a very good reason why it lacks the usual cartographic features: the island did not exist; it already was an abstraction.

An explanation for this island's unusual configuration is found in the *Navigatio* of Saint Brendan, particularly in the descriptions of the Promised Land of the Saints. In the beginning of the story, Saint Barrind narrates a voyage he made to the Promised Land with Mernóc, an anchorite on an island near Slieve League off the west coast of Ireland. They sail westward from this island, Delightful Island, to reach the Promised Land. The fog is so thick they can scarcely see either end of their boat, but then a great light shines around them and the Promised Land is revealed. They land and spend fifteen days walking around, yet they cannot find the end of it. All the plants

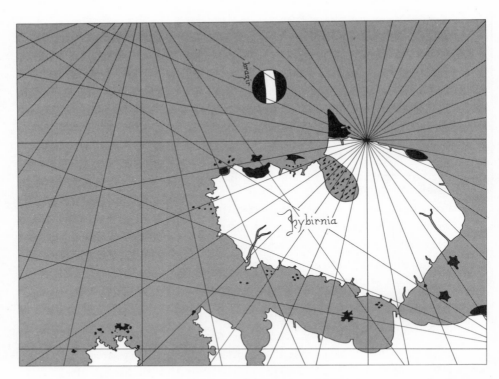

Fig. 9-3.
Detail of the Pizigani
Brothers map, 1367.

have flowers, all the trees bear fruit, and all the stones on the ground are precious. Finally, on the fifteenth day, they find a river, flowing from east to west. They are about to cross it but decide to await advice from God, whereupon an angel appears, saying: "The Lord has revealed to you the land which he will give to his saints. The river there marks the middle of the island." The brothers depart, passing out of the light into the darkness surrounding the island.

Saint Brendan decides to seek this island. After seven years of sailing west, he turns around and sails east for forty days, reaching his goal exactly as an angel had foretold. His experiences on the island are identical to those of Saint Barrind. His pilgrimage at an end, Saint Brendan and his brothers return to the shores of their origin, bringing with them fruits of the land and as many precious stones as their boat can carry.

Many elements of Greek and Celtic origin are found here in the story of Brazil, but none is as strong as the derivation from the *Book of Revelation*. John describes the New Jerusalem as it was revealed to him:

Then the angel showed me the river of life-giving water, sparkling like crystal, flowing from the throne of God and of the Lamb down the middle of its street. On either side of the river grew the tree of life that produces fruit twelve times a year, once each month; the leaves of the trees serve as medicine for the nations. . . . Night will be no more, nor will they need light from lamp or sun, for the Lord God shall give them light, and they shall reign forever and ever. (22:1-5)

The light of the island, experienced by both Saint Barrind and Saint Brendan, is the light of God's grace, and the river that flows through the centre of the Promised Land is "the water of life" as described in the New Jerusalem. John's vision recalls that of Ezekiel:

Then he brought me back to the entrance of the temple, and I saw water flowing out from beneath the threshold of the temple toward the east, for the facade of the temple was toward the east. . . . Then he brought me to the bank of the river. . . . I saw very many trees on both sides. Wherever the river flows, every sort of living creature that can multiply shall live. . . . Along both banks of the river, fruit trees of every kind shall grow; their leaves shall not fade, nor their fruit fail. (47:1, 6-9, 12)

The precious stones lying upon the ground of the Promised Land are mentioned in the description of the New Jerusalem in *Revelation*; elsewhere in the Bible (*Exodus* 28:15-21, *Isaiah* 54:11, 12) they signify the beauty and excellence of God's realm.

Everything thus falls into line: travelling east to reach paradise even though the Island of Delights is located west of Ireland, and incorporation of the Celtic legends of enchanted islands occasionally glimpsed from Ireland's western shores. Naturally, neither Barrind nor Brendan could find an end to the island, even after walking around it for fifteen days, for a circle has no beginning or end. What could be a more fitting symbol for this Promised Land — the New Jerusalem — than a perfect circle bisected by a river?

Chapter X

Saint Ursula & Her Eleven Thousand Virgin Companions

SAINT BARRIND AND SAINT BRENDAN were not the only devout Christians sailing the seas during the Dark Ages in obedience to God's will. Saint Ursula, too, encountered many perils and had many adventures before she reached *her* promised land. However, cartographers never placed Saint Ursula on maps of the Atlantic, even though a specific island was named after her; instead, her legend lives on maps through her eleven thousand companions.

Ursula's courage and virtue made her one of the most venerated saints of medieval times. In Cologne, thousands of pilgrims came to pay homage at the tomb of this virgin martyr and her companions. Throughout the Christian world, churches and religious orders were dedicated in her name and schools and hospitals were established under her patronage.

Throughout the centuries between Ursula's lifetime and the fullest flowering of her legend, many versions of the tale were circulated. In the *Golden Legend*,[1] the most complete and widely accepted version of the tale, Ursula was the daughter of Maurus, a Christian king of Brittany. The fame of her wisdom, beauty and holy life spread across the sea to England. When the English king heard of this admirable woman, he wanted her to be the wife of his only son, and he sent an ambassador to King Maurus requesting the betrothal. Ursula was unwilling to marry a pagan, preferring instead "to devote her life entirely to God's service." Yet she and her father both feared reprisals from the king of England if she did not consent. Justified by a heavenly vision, Ursula agreed to wed, but she asked "to have ten fair and noble companions of a like age to myself be chosen; then to each companion, and for myself, a thousand other virgin maidens assigned. Then, for the eleven thousand, grant us eleven ships. Last, give me three years' time."

Ursula told her father not to worry, for "none can change the Divine goodness which has marked my lot." Even though her father was uncertain of her meaning, he was glad that she agreed. They both hoped that in her absence the English king's son would become a Christian, or, failing that, with the prolonged wait he would simply lose interest. Ursula kept to herself the knowledge she received from an angel: that she would suffer for the sake of the Lord and "win the glorious palm of martyrdom." Ursula, with her companions, made a pilgrimage to Rome. During the three years at sea, Ursula sought heavenly guidance and learned the seaman's craft. In that time, her boat and others in the fleet were scattered by fierce weather, causing Ursula and her companions to be cast among "strange islands, and barbarous peoples."

Then, a great storm blew the maiden fleet to the port of Tiel at the mouth of the Rhine River. From there, they sailed up the river to Cologne. Here an angel came to Ursula as she slept, saying: "Behold, ye shall go to Rome, and thence, when ye all have paid your vows, ye shall return to Cologne in peace. Verily, there is laid up for you a crown of righteousness." The fleet proceeded to Basle, where the maidens disembarked, and they continued on foot over the Alps to Rome.

After they made their vows at the tombs of the apostles, they returned to Cologne, their entourage now including Pope Cyriacus, who had had a heavenly premonition about the impending martyrdom. So many men and women had been converted to Christianity during Ursula's stay in Rome that the emperor feared this new religion would supplant his own. Therefore, he sent messengers to Cologne to ask the prince of the Huns to have his army slaughter the virgins. When the virgins and others in the retinue reached Cologne, the Huns surrounded them and "like wolves raging among the sheep," slew them.

The Huns spared Ursula alone; on account of her great beauty and purity, their chief wanted to marry her. But, full of "virginal intolerance, and Christian dignity," Ursula chose to die rather than betray her faith. The barbarian king of the Huns shot an arrow into her heart and brutally ended her life.

After the passions and fury of the heathens were exhausted, angels appeared, one for each of the martyred virgins, and drove the Huns away. Then the city gates of Cologne were opened, and the bodies were collected and buried in peace. Near their final resting place a small basilica was built as a memorial to the martyred virgins. Through her martyrdom, Ursula achieved the status of sainthood and fulfilled the prophecy of the angel by "becoming the Bride of Heaven in exchange for earthly love and earthly glory."

Historia Fabulae

The legend of Saint Ursula took many centuries to evolve to this form. In a small basilica outside of Cologne, dedicated to some unknown martyred virgins, an inscription in Latin carved into stone states that holy virgins were killed on this site; it records neither the names nor the number of Christian martyrs murdered there. This stone, authenticated and dating to the late fourth or early fifth century, says, "Clematius came from the East; he was terrified by fiery visions, and by the great majesty and the holiness of these virgins"; according to a vow that he made, he rebuilt this basilica at his own expense and on his own land. The inscription ends with a denunciation of the sinners and a threat of divine vengeance. This stone is literally and figuratively the cornerstone of the Saint Ursula legend, establishing the presence of a church dedicated to sacred virgins sometime before 500.

In the late eighth or early ninth century, the story expanded. An unknown author, a native of Cologne, wrote about these sacred maidens in *Sermo in Natali SS. Virginum XI millium*, commonly called *Sermo in Natali*. He mentions the basilica where the saints were martyred and quotes the inscription about how Clematius had it rebuilt in his honour. The writer was of the opinion that the martyred virgins were women who had fled from Britain in order to escape the persecution of the Christians by the Roman emperor Maximian. They freed themselves from the tyranny of one oppressor but were killed by another — the Huns. Not all the victims, the author says, were virgins; some were widows and married people. No date is mentioned, but from the reference to Maximian (Magnus Clemens Maximus), who became master of Britain and Gaul in AD 383, the event must have occurred some time before the stone inscription by Clematius. Neither Ursula's name, nor any others, appear in the account.

Then, in a document dated 922, the number of persons killed takes a dramatic leap from eleven to eleven thousand. This probably happened when an earlier text was copied, and the abbreviation of *XI M.V. (undecim martyres virgines* — eleven martyred virgins) was misunderstood to be *undecim milia virginum* (eleven thousand virgins). Thereafter, the number of eleven thou-

Fig. 10-1.
Facsimile of a late fourth- or early fifth-century stone inscription found in the Church of Saint Ursula, Cologne (broken letters have been filled in).
(Reproduced from *Essays on Religion and Literature*, by Cardinal E.H. Wiseman.)

sand became fixed, and gradually Ursula became the most important figure in the story.

By 1100, the legend reached its fullest development in Germany in *Passio Sanctarum Undecim Millium Virginum*, in which additional details were added, and the story became immensely popular. By the mid-twelfth century, innumerable manuscripts had carried the fame of Saint Ursula and her companions throughout Europe. From Germany, the tale was transported across the sea to Britain, where it was taken up and elaborated upon by Geoffrey of Monmouth, bishop of Aspath, in about 1147. This is the same Geoffrey that brought the world the Arthurian legends and the *Life of Merlin*; the tale of Saint Ursula is found in his *History of the Kings of Britain*, embedded within the framework of the general history of England. By the last quarter of the fifteenth century there were already more than a hundred Latin editions of the tale, plus innumerable translations into vernacular languages of *Lives of the Saints: The Golden Legend*, which Jacobus de Voragine had written near the end of the thirteenth century.

In 1155, an event occurred that greatly strengthened the extravagant story by presenting apparent physical proof of the martyrdom. Excavation of an old Roman town outside of Cologne, Colonia Agrippina, revealed a great number of bones. A young nun named Elizabeth, from a nearby convent in Schönau, proclaimed these to be the bones of the honoured Saint Ursula and her companions. In a series of ecstatic visions, Elizabeth of Schönau not only accounted for all these bodies, but also explained the miraculous presence at the site of the tombs of Pope Cyriacus, an archbishop of Ravenna, several cardinals, and *two* bodies of Clematius. So as to leave no doubt, the tomb of Ursula, neatly labelled "*Ursula Regina,*" was also found.

New revelations were produced in 1183 and 1187 by the canon Bd Joseph Herman. He explained why the bones of children, some as young as two months, had been found there: "Ursula had a fondness for children, which led her to take some little girls with her on her pilgrimage." The bones that had been exhumed, including those of men and children, were what remained from a Roman cemetery. It is difficult now to know whether these two visionaries were perpetrating a fraud, or whether they suffered from self-delusion created by an excess of religious fervour.

The bones satisfied a demand for remains of the martyred virgins. Relic-worship, so strong at the time, led Christians from all over the world to appeal for them; they seemed to be a requirement for every new church dedicated in

Saint Ursula's name. A brisk trade developed in the translation of these relics, which lasted well into the fourteenth century. Entire bodies or fragments went to abbeys throughout Germany, as well as to France, Italy and Spain. Over eleven thousand bodies would seem to have provided an inexhaustible supply, but such was the appetite for these relics that in 1182, in a single move, more than one thousand bodies were transported to the Cistercian abbey of Aldenberg, in the diocese of Cologne.

The veneration of Saint Ursula continued into the sixteenth century, then gradually diminished. The intellectual climate and scientific attitude of the Renaissance rejected the complex symbolism used in the Middle Ages to express theological concepts and human values. Protestants entirely rejected the tradition, and eventually, in 1969, the Catholic Church officially dropped Saint Ursula's feast day from the church calendar.

However, the work of the Ursuline nuns, who are dedicated to educating girls, continues to this day. And the story of Ursula survives in many fine paintings and stained-glass windows. Between the fourteenth and sixteenth centuries more than twenty-five cycles of her life were created, the most notable being the Gothic reliquary shrine painted by the Flemish artist Hans Memling.

Ursula Vindicata

The story of a beautiful princess and eleven thousand virgin companions who made a pilgrimage from Britain to Rome, who undertook this venture by ship, and who eventually all met their end in martyrdom seems preposterous. But, as with other legends, an underlying basis of historical truth can be found.

In the mid-fifth century, just about when the legend started, Europe was being ravaged by Atilla and his Huns, a frightful, cruel and barbarous race of Mongols and Tartars. Authors of the period describe them as savages who deformed their heads and scarified their faces so "they were more hideous than demons." Their only clothing was a shirt that was never changed but worn until it dropped off, covered with a "mantle made entirely of wild rat skins." They were "licentius to a degree." When Atilla came to invade and conquer, his maxim was, "Where Atilla sets his foot, no more grass shall ever grow — nothing but destruction and devastation." Uniquely among the barbarous tribes that invaded the Roman Empire, they fought with bows and arrows; most of the Germanic tribes preferred the sword, lance and pike as their means of killing.

The Huns were ejected from Italy in 450, and an army of 700,000 of them set out to conquer Gaul. But at the battle of Catalaunia in 451 they were defeated by Aëtius, a Roman senator and the governor of Gaul, who had gathered together troops of Goths, Visigoths and Franks. The Huns fled through Belgium; in revenge for their defeat, they destroyed everything in their way, demolishing cities and slaughtering the people. Then they entered Thuringia, the heart of Germany, crossing the Rhine by its only bridge — at Cologne.

While continental Europe was under seige by Mongol tribes, Britain suffered invasions from scattered bands of other warriors. Picts and Scots attacked from the north, and by 367 they had broken through Hadrian's Wall. Starting around 440, the Angles and Saxons swept through Britain, taking possession of the country and exterminating many of its inhabitants. Many Britons left for the continent to escape the assaults coming at them from all directions, fleeing to Batavia and Holland — and to Cologne — to establish colonies. As a safe haven, Cologne had many advantages. Not only was it a capital and a seat of the Roman government, but it was also a Christian city. It was well fortified, and the Rhine River provided an extra defence.

Still on a rampage and thirsty for blood, the Huns arrived at the same time and at the very same place as the Britons appeared. Driven by separate forces, Huns and Britons met in Cologne in 451. Their collision resulted in the massacre that forms the basis of the legend of Saint Ursula and her eleven thousand virgin companions.

It hardly seems possible that as many as eleven thousand could be slaughtered in a single instance. Yet these very same Huns killed 30,000 men in Burgundy in 436. Most likely, though, the number 11,000 should not be taken too literally; it may simply mean an indefinitely large number, much like the medieval military number of 60,000 or the Biblical 1000. Those slain may also have included inhabitants of the city and others from the surrounding countryside who sought safety in the fortified city, as well as the emigrants fleeing attacks by the Angles, Saxons and Picts in England.

Were the eleven thousand all females? Even at an early period in the legend, some accounts affirmed that, although a great majority of the slain were women, men and children were also killed. That *most* were women may be so; men were likely to be killed in battle or fighting elsewhere. Elizabeth of

Schönau was the one responsible for proclaiming that all the unearthed bones were those of the eleven thousand virgins of Saint Ursula.

Could all the females have been virgins? The tradition is that every woman voluntarily laid down her life for Christ rather than sacrifice her virtue to the heathen Huns. By being killed against their will by men inflamed by hatred, revenge and sexual passion, they achieved their martyrdom. Such high value was placed on a woman's virginity that any woman martyr was considered "to be raised to a higher degree of excellence" and given the title of "virgin." By this definition, a married woman, even one with children, would be called a virgin if she was martyred — such was the case of Saint Sabrina. In a like manner, in the Middle Ages the meaning of sainthood was extended to mean any pious Church founder or learned ecclesiastic. In this sense, yes, all the women slain were virgins.

De Nomine Ursulae

But how could a voyage which ostensibly took place between Britain and Germany, in the English Channel and the North Sea, result in islands in the Atlantic being named after Saint Ursula? The story of Saint Ursula became like the seed of a plant carried by ocean currents or a migratory bird and deposited on some distant shore to take root. At the greatest possible distance from her native shore, in the warm, tropical waters of the Caribbean, are islands bearing her legend, a legend carried there by Christopher Columbus.

Columbus sailed on his second voyage to the New World in 1493 with a dual purpose: to colonize the new possessions, and to continue the exploration he started the previous year. He intended to survey islands he had heard about but was unable to explore the first time, as well as to verify his belief that Cuba was not an island but a large promontory of the Asian mainland.

This time Columbus took a more southerly course than on his first voyage, and twenty-one days after leaving Gomera, in the Canaries, he sighted land. Columbus "was as happy as if Heaven had suddenly opened up before them."[2] Since it was Sunday, he named the island Dominica. As it appeared to have no harbour, he and his men crossed over to a second island, which he named Marigalante, after his ship. From there, the fleet sailed to a larger island, now called Guadeloupe, where they found a harbour and anchored.

19°N
18°
17°
16°
15°

68°W 67° 66° 65° 64° 63° 62° 61°

San Juan Bautista (Puerto Rico)

Sta. Ursula y las xi mil Virgines (Virgin Isls.)

Anegada Passage

Santa Cruz

San Cristóbal

San Martin   Antigua

Monserrate

Guadaloupe

Maria-galante

Nov. 3 1493

Dominica

Fig. 10-2.
Caribbean route taken by Christopher Columbus on his second voyage to the New World in 1493. (Adapted from *Columbus*, by F. Fernández-Armesto.)

As Columbus sailed northwest toward Hispaniola, which he had visited on his first voyage, he found and named many islands along the way: Monserrat, Santa Maria de La Redonda, Santa Maria del Antigua, San Martin and Santa Cruz. Continuing his course, Columbus soon sighted a large group of islands, separated by narrow channels, in which the seas beat against rocky coasts. He prudently sent in one of the smaller vessels to explore this new cluster of islands. The report came back that altogether there were as many as fifty islands, which appeared to be inhabited. To the largest of them the Admiral gave the name of Saint Ursula, and the rest he called the Eleven Thousand Virgins. The island which bore Ursula's name never appeared on any map; however, her virgin companions were depicted and have been known ever since as the Virgin Islands.[3]

Obviously, Columbus knew the legend of Saint Ursula. Though the cult of Ursula was strongest in Germany, the Low Countries and northern France, churches dedicated to Saint Ursula and furnished with relics were present during Columbus's time in Italy, Spain and Portugal. He may have been acquainted with one of these churches, or at least exposed to the legend

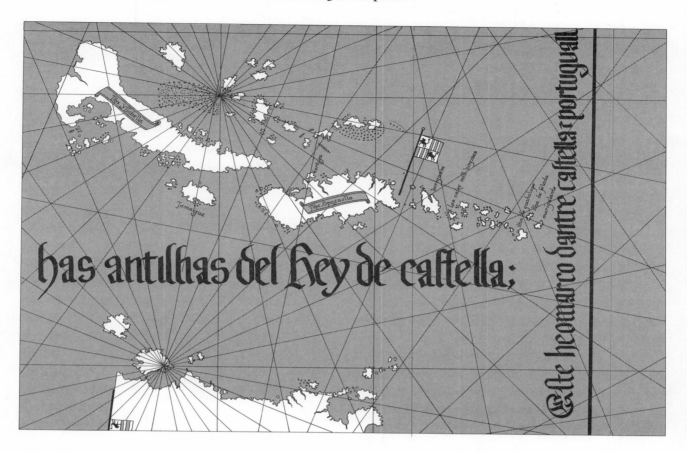

Fig. 10-3.

Cantino world map, 1502. Though none of the maps following Columbus's voyage specifically indicate the single island he named for Saint Ursula, several maps, such as this, denote the Virgin Islands collectively with the label *"Las onize virgines"* — The Eleven Thousand Virgins. The mapmaker has made absolutely certain that the world would recognize that these discoveries made by Columbus belong to Spain. In bold lettering is the label "The Antilles of the King of Castile" and the flag of Castile is planted among the islands. The dominant vertical line shows the demarcation between Castile and Portugal agreed upon in the Treaty of Tordesillas (1494); all the islands west of the line were the property of Spain. Cuba, the queen of the Antilles, is named after Isabella, the other Catholic monarch of Spain, while the second-largest island of the archipelago is called Hispaniola.

through the innumerable cycle paintings of Saint Ursula and her pilgrimage, a subject which found particular favour among the artists of northern Italy.

Columbus has another strong link with the legend. Genoa, the city of his birth and his home until he moved to Lisbon in 1477, was also the abode of Jacobus de Voragine, the author of *The Golden Legend*. He produced a great number of works, but his compilation of the legends of saints was the most popular. As a preacher, his qualities of sanctity, wisdom and gentleness eventually led to his appointment as archbishop of Genoa. During his episcopate, his efforts as a peacemaker in the conflict between the Guelphs and the Ghibellines and his inexhaustible charity in caring for the needy made him a beloved man. When Jacobus died in 1298, he was buried in the church of Saint Dominic in Genoa and venerated as a saint.

Columbus — a man of intense faith who lived in a world where religious experience shaped and directed all thought and action, a man who for a quarter of a century walked the streets of Genoa, steeped in the traditions of its illustrious past — must have known about Jacobus de Voragine and the tale of Saint Ursula recounted in his *Lives of the Saints: The Golden Legend*. And so, ten and a half centuries after the start of the legend, the final link in the history of Saint Ursula and her eleven thousand virgin companions is accounted for.

Chapter XI

The Islands of Saint Brendan

THE ISLANDS OF SAINT BRENDAN ARE LOST in a tangled skein of legend, myth and reality, strewn across the Atlantic from the shores of Africa to the coast of Newfoundland. The tale of Saint Brendan and his fellow monks in their quest for the *terra repromissiones* — the Promised Land — has been variously described as a factual voyage, a visionary fairy tale, a mythical adventure, a monastic pilgrimage, and a delightful fiction; attributions of its date and authorship are as diverse as the many meanings ascribed to the story.

Navigatio Sancti Brendani Abbatis (The Voyage of Saint Brendan the Abbot) did not appear in a written form until about two and a quarter centuries after the death of Saint Brendan (c. 577). The manuscript's precise date is unknown, for the monastic scribes affixed neither a date nor their own names, but style and syntax suggest that it was written either at the very beginning of the ninth century or about the middle of the tenth century.

The *Navigatio* quickly became popular, copied and recopied, translated from Latin to Irish and back to Latin again. In the Middle Ages it was also translated into German, Flemish, Italian, Catalan, French, Norse and Anglo-Norman. This process of transcription, with numerous variations both in content and in form, with some versions in verse and others in prose, continued well into the fifteenth century. To this day, more than 120 manuscripts in Latin alone still survive.

Even the *Navigatio's* place of origin is questionable. It would seem only natural that it was monks in Ireland who wrote about one of their most revered saints. Yet its home may have been the Frankish province of Lotharingia (present-day Lorraine and Belgium). During the early tenth century, Norman invasions of Ireland and Wales prompted many monks to leave their homeland and disperse to the continent, where they established new monasteries. The cities of Verdun, Liége, Cologne and Utrecht greatly benefited from this monastic shift. There, new centres of learning were created, and many literary works were produced by the Irish monks, not just on religious subjects, but on history, geography and philosophy.

The Life and Legend of Saint Brendan

The *life* of Brendan and the *legend* of Brendan are two separate entities, and although it isn't known when the legend began, at least the facts from which it evolved have been documented.

Brendan was not a mythical figure but an esteemed monk, born in southwest Ireland on the Fenit Peninsula, County Kerry, in the last decades of the fifth century — perhaps 483 or 489. He was the son of Findlug, a man "free and of good race, devout and faithful."[1] Saint Brendan's complete heritage is listed in *Lives of the Saints*, from *The Book of Leinster*: "Brenaind [Brendan] son of Findlug, son of Elchu, son of Aelta, of the Ciarralge Luachra of Altraige Caille. At the same time with Oengus, son of Nat-fraich, King of Munster, was he born."[2] Findlug and his wife named the child Mobhí and reared him for the first year of his life. Bishop Eirc baptized Brendan and raised him from his second year onward with the help of a foster-mother, Saint Ita. These two holy persons were responsible for Brendan's early education and religious training. Later, he was taught by Saint Enda, one of the most influential monks in early Irish Christendom.

After his ordination in 512, Brendan attracted a group of disciples and founded a monastery in Ardfert, north of Tralee. As Brendan's reputation and capabilities grew, so did the range of his travels: to the Hebrides Islands and Wales, and allegedly also to Brittany, the Orkney Islands, and even the Färoes. All these island outposts — as far as 520 miles from his native shore of Galway — could be reached only by boat through treacherous, tide-ripped waters. He earned his appellation: "Brendan the Voyager."

Saint Brendan made two trips to the Hebrides, the second one, to the Isle of Iona, undertaken sometime after 563, when Brendan was in his seventies. There he met with the venerable Saint Columba; through his preaching, his holy life, and the establishment of monasteries, including the great monastery on Iona, Saint Columba had converted the whole of northern Scotland to Christianity. Saint Brendan stayed a long while on Iona, and he may even have founded a monastery of his own there.

In Wales, Saint Brendan established the Abbey of Llancarfan, became its abbot, and tutored the Breton Saint Malo. The pious Saint Brendan also founded monasteries throughout Ireland: Ardfert, Inishdadroum in County Clare, and Annadown and Clonfert in County Galway. He began the journey described in the *Navigatio* from Clonfert, and when he died in 578, Clonfert became his burial place.

Sometime after his death, various texts on the lives of saints briefly mention Brendan's having sought the "Land of Promise," visiting many far-off and unusual islands, and seeing varied wonders in the ocean. The *Vita Sancti Brendani* tells more about the *life* of Saint Brendan, whereas the *Navigatio* tells more about his voyage. It is uncertain whether the writing of the *Vita* preceded or followed that of the *Navigatio*; some scholars place the *Vita* in the early ninth century, others date it as late as the twelfth century. Though the *Vita* was not nearly as widely read as the *Navigatio*, there are several versions, among them *Lives of the Saints*, from *The Book of Lismore*, and *Lives of the Saints*, from *The Book of Leinster*. The two works differ somewhat in their accounts of Brendan's journey; by the late Middle Ages, however, the *Vita* and the *Navigatio* became inter-related. Each borrows portions of text from the other; part of the biographical material in the *Vita* is used in either the beginning or at the conclusion of the *Navigatio*, while the *Vita* acquires a more elaborate portrayal of the voyage from the *Navigatio*.

In *Lives of the Saints,* from *The Book of Lismore*, Saint Brendan's birth, a combination of actual and mystical events, appears to have been written and incorporated into the text at a later time than much of the other material. Saint Brendan must already have achieved his fame and become revered, for the text treats his birth as a miraculous event and imbues him with qualities that go even beyond sainthood. Before Brendan was born, his mother had a vision: she "had the full of her bosom of pure gold, and her breasts [were] shining like snow." When she described this vision to Bishop Eirc, he predicted that a marvellous child would be born, "full of the grace of the Holy Spirit." At Brendan's birth, Bishop Eirc also had a vision: the forest around Altraige appeared as though on fire, and the space between Heaven and earth was filled with angels wearing bright white garments. This vision brought the bishop to the place of Brendan's birth, where he knelt in homage before him and then baptized him. After the baptism, a fine mist descended on the region, whereupon the baby was renamed Brendinus — from *broen* (a drop) and *dian* (from above).

In childhood, Saint Brendan was continuously surrounded by innumerable angels in the form of virgins; later, after performing penance for a misdeed, his face shone so brightly that no one could look upon it because of the divine radiance. All the characteristics of the prophets, apostles and disciples are attributed to Saint Brendan in his adult years; he was an evangelist like Matthew, a teacher like Paul, a head of hermits like John the Baptist, and so forth.

Saint Brendan was not the only religious figure to establish monasteries in Ireland, nor was he alone in setting out on journeys to distant lands. During the fifth and sixth centuries, Christian culture, recently introduced to Ireland, rapidly developed and expanded. Clerics and scholars left the continent to settle in a land less convulsed with wars. In the remote and unpopulated areas of Ireland they created a monastic way of life that allowed them not only to fulfil their missionary duties but to establish centres of learning, art and culture based on the accumulated knowledge of past centuries. They were the best-educated men of western Europe, well read in all the classical Greek and Roman works, and they had an excellent grasp of the physical nature of the world from Arab geographers and Ptolemy of Alexandria. Undisturbed by invasion, they kept this fund of information alive and handed it down in a manuscript tradition from generation to generation for nearly five centuries.

From the sixth century onwards, some Irish abbots and their disciples ventured forth in their curraghs from island to island in search of remote, isolated places to which, like Eastern anchorites, they could withdraw into a private "desert." Separated from home and friends, these hermits renounced their worldly goods to serve God in lonely solitude and prayer. A missionary motive prompted other monks to travel from Ireland to all the nearby island groups. In their evangelical zeal, Irish monks went far beyond the shores of Scotland, Wales and Brittany. They reached the Orkneys by 579, the Shetlands before 620, and, later, the Färoes. Eventually they reached Iceland (called Thule) in the year 770.

Some wanderers returned to the continent, where they spread the faith in every Christian and semi-Christian country. These Irish monks established centres of religion and scholarship from Luxeuil and Fontaine in the Vosges mountains of France to Bobbio in the Apennines of northern Italy. Expeditions in the sixth and seventh centuries led to the founding of monasteries by

Saint Gall in Switzerland, Saint Catald in the south of Italy, Saint Colman in Austria, and Saint Kilins in Franconia. These became the centres of intellectual, philosophical and cultural activity in the Middle Ages; even kings and emperors went there for advice. One Frankish observer said, "It's as though almost all of Ireland had emigrated with a flock of philosophers to our shores."

Not only are the date and place of origin of the *Navigatio* problematic; it is certain that a great many authors had a hand in its development. What may have started out as a simple and direct account of the travels and deeds of one much-revered saint slowly accrued components from the travels of other wandering clerics and became embellished with general information on the geography of the Atlantic.

The components of each version of the *Navigatio* came to depend less on what *Brendan* did than on what the *author* did. Each author, whether involved in translating, transcribing, or creating a new narrative, brought to it his own knowledge and gave it his own special emphasis, fashioning it to best capture the interest of his particular audience. The voyage of Saint Brendan became a literary theme flexibile enough to use as an almost wholly secular tale, filled with the most fantastic marvels and adventures, or as a simple allegory of Christian piety. It could also incorporate a great deal of Celtic tradition, which peaceably co-existed with the new faith. In addition, myths from classical antiquity — Homer's *Adventures of Odysseus* (Ulysses) and Virgil's *Adventures of Aeneus* — faintly reverberate throughout. All versions of the *Navigatio*, however, share the basic story of a long sea-voyage in search of the blissful Otherworld, with visits to many islands and encounters with miracles and monsters. Not until the tenth century did the *Navigatio* achieve a fairly standard structure and content. The tale's adaptability, with its syntheses of such disparate traditions, is one of the keys to its popularity and longevity.

Navigatio of Saint Brendan

The version of the *Navigatio* written in Ireland around the year 800, and translated from Latin into English by John J. O'Meara, makes a useful text.[3] Not only is it an accurate translation of a version early enough to be relatively free of the personal flourishes of later transcriptions, but it also has the decided advantage of being easily available to anyone who wishes to read the complete tale.

In this version, Saint Brendan, famous for his mighty works and spiritual father of nearly three thousand monks, receives a visit from another holy man, Saint Barrind, who describes a journey undertaken with his disciple, Mernóc, to a nearby island called the Promised Land of the Saints. Saint Brendan resolves to go in search of this island himself. The other monks encourage him, but before he leaves, he seeks the will of God. After fasting for forty days, Brendan, and fourteen brothers from his monastery, sail west to the island of Saint Enda. They receive his blessing and return to the mainland, where they build a curragh of timber and ox-hides and equip it with sail and oars, as well as supplies for forty days. Before they leave, three additional brothers from Brendan's monastery ask to be included in the pilgrimage.

After Saint Brendan and his monks sail for fifteen days, the wind drops, and they continue to row until their strength fails. Forty days pass, and they become hungry and thirsty. Guided by God, the monks reach a high, rocky island, but three more days pass before they can find a suitable place to land their boat. Ashore, they discover an uninhabited town with a great hall, where, laid out on a table, food and drink await them. Brendan admonishes the brothers not to let Satan tempt them to steal any of the vessels or fixtures hanging from the walls. But one of the latecomer monks ignores this warning and leaves with a silver bridle given him by the devil. Prayer is too late to save

Fig. 11-1.
A woodcut by Anton Sorg (Augsburg, 1476) showing Saint Brendan and his brethren landing, not upon an island as they had supposed, but upon a fish — "the foremost of all that swim in the ocean" — named Jasconius; *jasconiase* is the Irish word for fish.

the repentant monk. Brendan buries his body on the spot, but not before his soul, in the form of a small Ethiopian child, departs the body "to be received by the angels of light."

A messenger from God provides the travellers with fresh provisions, which last them almost a year; then they arrive at an island containing flocks of sheep bigger than cattle, all of them pure white in colour. The day being Maundy Thursday, Saint Brendan proposes a sacrifice of one of the spotless lambs to God. On Good Friday, while preparing for the service, a messenger tells them that they will celebrate Holy Saturday here, but that God wants them to celebrate the Masses and Vigils of the Resurrection on another nearby island; afterwards, they will sail to a third island, called the Paradise of the Birds, and remain there until the octave of

Pentecost. When the monks arrive at the island to which they had been directed to celebrate Easter Sunday, they build a fire with driftwood to cook their meal. As the pot begins to boil, their island suddenly swims out from under them. Frightened, they all rush to their boat and sail away. Brendan calms them by explaining that they had landed on the back of the greatest of all fish — a whale.

On the next island, the monks find a tree covered with so many white birds that they can see neither its leaves nor its branches. One bird flies down to Brendan and tells him that he has spent one year on his journey, but that six years remain until he finds the Promised Land of the Saints. The bird adds that each year Brendan and his brothers will return to celebrate Easter here. Furthermore, after eight months they will arrive at an island called the Community of Ailbe, where they will spend Christmas Day. As predicted, they arrive at that island, and a man of God leads them to his monastery. Divine Providence has sustained him and his twenty-four brothers for the past eighty years. On the octave of Epiphany, when the feast days are over, Brendan and his followers row and sail to an island where they land and drink from a clear well. Ignoring Saint Brendan's warning, some of the monks drink too heavily from the well and are overcome by a sleep which lasts for three days and three nights. Fleeing this danger, they set sail, only to be becalmed in a coagulated sea.

By now, another year has passed, and once again Brendan and his monks celebrate Easter on the triad of islands — the Island of Sheep, Jasconius the Whale and the Paradise of Birds. Then, after sailing for another forty days, the venerable Father and his companions are attacked by an immense beast intent on devouring them. But when they pray for deliverance, a mighty monster emitting fire from its mouth cuts the wretched beast into three parts. Another day, the monks disembark on an island where they see the tail end of the slain monster. They collect roots and plants, stow water in containers, and salt the flesh of the slain beast to provision the journey.

On a flat island level with the sea, three choirs greet them: one of boys, another of youths, and a third of elders. The second latecomer to the pilgrimage remains here to spend his life as an anchorite. No trees relieve the monotony of this land, yet it is covered with large white and purple fruit, which yield a pound of juice each, enough to feed the brothers for the next twelve days. When they embark again, a bird drops into their boat a branch bearing a cluster of grapes of extraordinary redness and as big as apples, which feeds them for another three days. Then they come to an island densely covered with trees laden with the same crop of grapes, and the "perfume of pomegranates" pervades the air. Brendan and his followers stay for forty days. After they set sail again, a gryphon attacks them, but, as before, God defends them — a bird tears out the gryphon's eyes, pursues it high into the sky and kills it. Not many days afterward, the monks return to the Island of the Community of Ailbe to celebrate Christmas. Later, when they celebrate the feast of Saint Peter (June 29) in the boat, the sea is so clear they can see all the fish lying underneath them.

One day, Saint Brendan and his brothers come upon a "pillar of bright crystal" the colour of silver but harder than marble. They examine its foundation and the wide-meshed net which surrounds it. Brendan measures each of the pillar's four sides and finds them all to be exactly the same in length, about seven hundred yards. After spending four days inspecting the four angles of the pillar, the monks find a chalice of the same colour and material as the pillar lying in a window. They take the crystal chalice with them and resume their voyage. After eight days they catch sight of the Island of Smiths, and Brendan entreats his brethren to row away as quickly as possible; they can hear the blows of hammers on iron and anvils, and smoke arises from the sea, which boils as though a volcano is erupting. They flee, only to come upon a mountain the colour of coal, with smoke and flames rising from its summit. Here, a multitude of demons carry off the third latecomer, condemned to a shameful death in hell.

Saint Brendan sails south for seven days and comes upon a man, shaggy and unsightly, sitting on a rock. This is the unhappy Judas, "the most evil trader ever," who describes his terrible punishment: torment by an infinite number of demons. The venerable Father next encounters the Island of Paul, a hermit who has lived here for ninety of his 140 years while awaiting the day of his judgement; he survives on fish brought by a friendly otter and drinks from a trickle of water which appears each Sunday. This man of God gives Brendan his blessing, and the monks sail south.

As foretold, Brendan and his monks revisit the triad of islands to celebrate Easter as they had done for the last six years. Now their seven-year voyage is near an end, and after forty days of sailing toward the east they pass through a dense fog and arrive at the island that has been the object of their pilgrimage. A youth, embracing them, tells them that this is the land they had so long been seeking. They could not find it immediately, he says, because "God wanted to show his varied secrets in the great ocean." Their stay is brief, for they must return to the land of their birth. Saint Brendan and his brothers gather samples of the ripe fruit and a variety of precious stones, and they leave for the Island of Delights near Slieve League. There, they avail themselves of Mernóc's hospitality for three days, and he blesses them. Saint Brendan returns home and recounts to all the other brothers of his monastery "the marvellous wonders God deigned to show him." The holy abbot eventually dies, and the story of his exemplary life is passed on from generation to generation to the honour and glory of the Lord.

Structure of the Navigatio

The *Navigatio* is a carefully structured tale in which a dramatic and beguiling narrative swiftly unfolds. The journey lasts seven years, but within this period, time is condensed, stretched or suspended. The direction of Saint Brendan's travels is extraordinary, not determined by him but preordained by God, and communicated by holy men, or angels. God miraculously provides food and water.

The time of the year is usually expressed, not by the passage of seasons bringing scorching sun or freezing cold and snow, but by the liturgical calendar. But at the very beginning of the story, Saint Brendan sets sail and steers "westwards into the summer solstice" — that is, he embarks on his voyage on June 21, when the sun reaches its northernmost declination at the tropic of Cancer. This celestial reference is part of the Celtic tradition, which so diligently and accurately kept track of the movements of the planets and stars with megalithic monuments.

Superimposed on the calendar is a repetitive pattern of days, the significance of which is symbolic rather than numerical. The boat is carried along for forty days; the monks remain on an island for forty days; after fasting for forty days they set out again. This forty-day period is common in the Bible, especially in the Old Testament, but also notably in the accounts of Christ's temptation in the wilderness.

The seven years that it took for Saint Brendan to arrive at the heavenly paradise is also significant. In the Old and New Testaments, the number seven suggests fullness and completeness. As the symbol of perfection, it stands for Christ's universal power. This is particularly strong in the Apocalypse, or the *Book of Revelation*, from which much of the symbolism of the *Navigatio* comes: John receives a prophetic message to give to the seven churches of Asia; God's voice announces judgement and doom in seven thunders; there are seven messages, seven seals, seven plagues and seven bowls of God's wrath; and seven trumpets announce seven symbolic disasters.[4] The seventh angel blowing the last trumpet announces God's reign and his victory over diabolical powers. The number seven is also important in Celtic legends, in which islands of enchantment appear off the coast of Ireland only once in seven years. Celtic gods and fairy-folk, mermaids and mermen, all inhabit these islands. Drawing upon these two great traditions, Christian and Celtic, Saint Brendan's voyage had to have lasted exactly seven years.

The number three also recurs in the *Navigatio*. Three islands are visited repeatedly, and periods of fasting, rowing, investigation or celebration are of three days' duration. Clearly, the number three relates to the Holy Trinity — Father, Son and Holy Spirit; but it can as well signify the three parts of the universe — Heaven, Earth and Sea. In the *Book of Revelation*, "Three angels proclaim eminent judgement on the world, calling all peoples to worship God the creator" (14:6-13).[5] The concept of threeness is equally strong in the Irish and Welsh native tradition, where characters or events are frequently grouped in threes. Often, three persons represent a single individual; the unity in triplication intensifies the dramatic effect and conveys an image of totality.

Time and space are stylized in other ways. The narrative starts with Saint Barrind visiting his disciple Mernóc on the Delightful Island, a three-day journey from the mainland. From there, Barrind and Mernóc embark to the Promised Land of the Saints. After Saint Brendan and his fellow monks reach their goal, the Promised Land, they stop at the Island of Delights for three days and receive a blessing. The story is circular, the sequence of the islands visited at the end of the *Navigatio* a mirror image of those visited at the beginning.

It seems strange that the *climax* of the story, the arrival of Saint Barrind at the Promised Land, should be given at the very start — only to be repeated by Saint Brendan at the end. Though this symmetry has a certain pleasing aesthetic quality, it has a more important function as a carefully devised symbolic logic. The *purpose* of the tale is to propagate the Christian religion; therefore, Brendan's revelation to his readers is the same as John's in the *Book of Revelation*:

> [God] made [the revelation of Jesus Christ] known by sending his angel to his servant John, who gives witness to the word of God and to the testimony of Jesus Christ by repeating what he saw. (1:1-2)

In the *Navigatio*, Saint Barrind is the angel messenger, Saint Brendan is the counterpart of John, and the Promised Land of the Saints is the Temple of the New Jerusalem. In the *Book of Revelation*, God gives John and the seven churches of Asia his greetings, and says: "I am the Alpha and the Omega . . . the one who is and who was and who is to come, the almighty" (1:18) — God is the first and the last, the beginning and the end. By starting and ending the *Navigatio* with a description of the Promised Land, Brendan's author acknowledges the triumph of God in the same manner as in the *Book of Revelation*.

Why should Saint Brendan have had to sail west for seven years before he could turn and sail east to find the Promised Land of the Saints? He knew from Saint Barrind that the Promised Land was close to the Delightful Island (near Slieve League). Why didn't he sail directly there? One reason for the roundabout journey is that the source of light (literally the "rising of the sun") is in the east, and so is the place of paradise, according to the *Book of Genesis*. If Saint Brendan immediately headed east to start his search, he would have sailed across the Irish Sea to a land he knew quite well — England — which certainly was not the Promised Land. For proper construction of the story, he first had to sail westward, which enabled him to sail east to reach his goal.

The journey had to last for seven years, according to one of God's messengers, because "God wanted to show you [Brendan] his varied secrets in the great ocean." Since the entire journey is a metaphor, the holy conflict between the forces of good and evil had to be fought and the battle won to the everlasting glory of God; only then could Saint Brendan reach the Promised Land of the Saints.

Content of the Navigatio

Symbolic language gives the *Navigatio* its directness and deceptive simplicity, while at the same time enhancing it with a rich and complex imagery. On the Island of the Paradise of Birds, Saint Brendan wonders why such a multitude of birds should congregate in one spot. He asks God to reveal his secret, and, when one of the birds flies down to the boat, stretches its wings "as it were a sign of joy, and look[s] with a peaceful mien" at Brendan, he surmises that the birds are messengers of God. His visitor confirms this; they are the angels cast out of paradise with Satan. Since they themselves committed no sin, God did not banish them to hell but allows them "to wander through the various regions of the air and the firmament and the earth, just like the other spirits that travel on their missions." On holy days and Sundays they are given bodies so that they may praise their creator.

In both the Old and New Testaments, ample evidence is provided for belief in angels. Superior to humans in power and intelligence, they act as intermediaries, transmitting messages from God. Throughout the *Navigatio*, angels (birds) perform two functions: as in Heaven, they sing the praises of God, and they let God's will be known to Saint Brendan to guide him on his way. They also represent a happy combination of Christian and Celtic traditions. Supernatural animals and birds abound in Irish mythology. Bright-plumaged birds, making enchanting music, soothingly sweet, appear in practically all the tales of the Happy Otherworld. The transmigration of souls into the bodies of birds is a constant theme in Irish literature. Birds accompany gods and goddesses, or deities transform themselves (entirely or partially) into birds.

Saint Brendan and his brothers call upon the Lord three times to defend them from an enormous beast that spouts foam from its nostrils and threatens to eat them. God sends a fire-breathing monster which attacks the wicked beast and cuts it into three parts. Brendan exclaims, "Look, my sons, at the great deeds of our Saviour! See how the beasts obey their creator." Finding the end portion of the slain beast, Saint Brendan declares, "See what wished to devour you! You now shall devour it!" The Bible calls this aquatic villain Leviathan, or Rahab; it is Satan, the great enemy of God. In Christian iconography, the various ocean monsters represent the forces of evil, and God's vanquishing them imposes order on primeval chaos. "On that day, the Lord will punish with his sword that is cruel, great, and strong, Leviathan the fleeing serpent, Leviathan the coiled serpent; and he will slay the dragon that is in the sea" (*Isaiah* 27:1). In the Brendan tale, destruction of the wretched beast demonstrates God's "dominion over the sea, and over all rebellious creatures."

Shortly after Saint Brendan's encounter with the sea monster, a second beast tries to devour Brendan and his followers. This one, rather than a denizen of the deep, is a sky-dweller. God sends the bird which had earlier brought them a branch of grapes to kill it . In this case, the evil symbolized by the beast is far more explicit: the attacker is a gryphon — an animal having the body and hind-quarters of a lion and the head and wings of an eagle. In the fables of India, gryphons guard the gold in northern deserts. In Greek mythology, gryphons protect the gold of Zeus — "the hounds of Zeus that never bark"; for Dionysus, God of the vine and, like Brendan, a seafarer, the gryphon guards the ever-flowing bowl of wine; and Apollo, god of light and truth, has gryphons to protect the treasures he keeps in the region beyond the North Wind — the Land of Hyperboreans.

But the gryphon in the *Navigatio* is most like the one found in the *Book of Revelation*. Because of its conglomerate parts, the gryphon symbolized strength and swiftness; it was such a common motif in Babylonian art that it had come to represent that empire itself. To John, Babylonia personifies the pagan Roman Empire, the persecutor of the Church; the gryphon represents the "bestial power hostile to God," and its destruction, God's wrath at sin. These are also the meanings Brendan's author attaches to the struggle between the gryphon and the bird. Brendan's rescuer tears out the gryphon's eyes, robbing it of reason and wisdom (which the eyes symbolized), thus weakening it for the kill. The bird is not identified specifically in the *Navigatio*; all that is said is that it "flew so high up into the sky that the brothers could scarcely see it." From this description alone, the bird could have been a hawk or a lark; since it was a "magic" bird it could conceivably even have been a pelican. But taken in the context of the Brendan story and its extensive Christian iconography, the bird symbolized could only be an eagle. The eagle's greatness in size and strength and its ability to "soar upwards toward heaven and gaze directly at the sun" made it the emblem of spiritual power.

The theme of conflict between forces of good and evil is common in Arabic as well as Christian tales. The tenth-century Arab geographer and historian, Mas'ûdî, tells the story of a sea monster very like Brendan's:

> Other people think that *tinnîn* is a monster who was born out of the depths of the ocean. Once he became strong he made war with other animals of the sea. Then God sent angels, inside of clouds, who took this monster, whose shape was that of a brilliant and sparkling black snake, out of the abyss. His thrashing tail leveled the most solid edifices and the highest trees, even the mountains; his very breath pulled trees with the strongest roots and trunks out of the ground. Then the angels in the clouds threw him in the land of Gog and Magog (Yâdjudj wa-Mâdjudj), and the cloud emitted hail down upon the monster and killed him. After, his flesh became food for the people of Gog and Magog. Here, you have a belief attributed to Ibn'Abbâs.[6]

Here, the sea monster *tinnîn* is equivalent to the wicked beast that tried to destroy Brendan and his followers; the angels that destroy it by hail represent God's victory over evil and the restoration of order. As in the Brendan tale, the slain monster in the Arabic tale becomes food for its intended victims. In the Bible, the lands of Gog and Magog were a symbol of all pagan nations (*Revelation* 20:8); to the Hebrews, they were the symbolic name for the northernmost known countries. In medieval times there was an interchange of information between the Arab world and the countries of northern Europe. But as with so much of the literature surrounding the tale of the *Navigatio*, it is impossible to determine who borrowed from whom, and at what time.

If the *Navigatio* was solely an allegorical story, without reality in time and space, it could not have carried its message with such intensity or sustained the reader's interest for long. The author skilfully blended elements of reality with his highly stylized, abstract form and traditional symbolic language. He introduced historical persons, places and events into the tale and thereby increased its credibility and reinforced the power of its message.

Before embarking on his voyage, Saint Brendan travelled to an island off the west coast of Ireland to ask the blessing of Saint Enda. This holy father, who lived to the fourth decade of the sixth century, is said to have been a disciple of Saint Patrick. Saint Enda founded monasteries in the Boyne Valley of east-central Ireland and later moved to Inishmore, the largest of the three main Aran Islands, where he set up his principal monastery. There he instructed numerous disciples, including Brendan. It was not only physically possible but quite natural for Brendan to travel to Inishmore to seek his mentor's permission for the voyage. Actually, according to the *Lives of the Irish Saints and Martyrs*, Saint Brendan also remained with Saint Enda at Aran for three days during the last year of Saint Enda's life.[7]

The Delightful Island, where Saint Barrind's disciple, Mernóc, lived the life of a hermit, has been identified as Fair Island, near Slieve League in County Donegal, off the northwest coast of Ireland. Saint Barrind and Mernóc set out from the Delightful (Fair) Island to find the Promised Land, and Saint Brendan lands on this same island at the end of *his* journey.

Saint Ailbe, of the Community of Ailbe (where Saint Brendan celebrates Christmas), was a contemporary of Saint Enda. However, his biography contains a confused mixture of realistic deeds, contradictory traditions and strange fables, ranging from stories about his being suckled and raised from birth by a she-wolf to a narrative of his travels to Rome where he was consecrated bishop. Saint Ailbe was reputedly one of the four holy men who preached the Gospel in Ireland before the time of Saint Patrick, and he helped Saint Enda receive the necessary grant to found his monastery on Inishmore. *The Book of Lismore* says that Saint Ailbe sailed in search of the Land of Promise, but it does not say in what direction he sailed or whether he reached his goal. The *Navigatio* suggests that he founded a monastery on one of the islands on which he landed.

Daily monastic rituals, with the observance of canonical hours, prayers and vigils, vespers, masses, feastings and fastings, are all described in detail throughout the *Navigatio*. For these, the author obviously used his own experiences. He adds to the portrayal of monastic life explicit descriptions of the physical character of the islands the monks visit, with their rocky cliffs, high mountains, various kinds of vegetation, and shorelines that took many days to circumnavigate. He presents a graphic image of the Isle of Smiths, where burning slag hurls down, the sea boils, and smoke rises from the sea; the Fiery Mountain, which pushes its smoking peak through the clouds; and cliffs, perpendicular as a wall and coal-black, "so high [the monks] could scarcely see the top." The Island of Sheep, on the other hand, is a picture of beneficence. Large spring-fed streams teem with fish, and the huge white sheep grazing in lush pastures are free from the strain of winter. These realistic details bring the flights of fancy, the miraculous events and all the symbols and images to a halt. The commonplace keeps the story within the realm of an earthly experience and thereby strengthens the reader's faith in the extraordinary.

Islands of Fancy, Islands of Reality

So successful was the author of the *Navigatio* in integrating a feeling of realism with a fantastic tale that more than one historian has been tempted to ascribe a known geographic location for each of the islands he describes. The Island of Smiths and the Fiery Mountain can be recognized as Mount Hekla and the frequent volcanic activity ringing the shores of Iceland, and the Island of Sheep is the Färoes. Other identifications are more difficult, and historians attempting to provide a correlative for every island visited by Saint Brendan have had to make his voyage range widely over the Atlantic — all the way from Jan Mayen Island in the Arctic (the Fiery Mountain) to the Bahamas (the Island of the Three Choirs) and to Jamaica (the Island of Grapes).

The correlation of these islands also means an acceptance that the voyage actually was made by Saint Brendan, that it was not fiction pieced together from diverse sources. Tim Severin, author, historian and sailor, took a very practical approach to the problem of authenticating Saint Brendan's voyage.[8] He built a curragh, a boat consisting of a hide-covered shell on a wicker frame, as much like Brendan's as physically possible, to see if it could be sailed to North America. In 1976, he and his crew sailed westward from the same point in Ireland as did Brendan and his monks. They followed the traditional "stepping-stone" route used by Irish travellers from the sixth century onward — Ireland to the Hebrides, thence to the Färoe Islands, Iceland, Greenland, and finally Newfoundland — to recreate the saga. On June 26, 1977, they landed in Newfoundland. This remarkable achievement ended all controversy over whether such a voyage was possible. Using the prevailing wind and current patterns of northern latitudes, Severin found a "logical progression" of landfalls, one conceivably the same as Saint Brendan's; the islands he visited and the events he encountered closely paralleled those of the ancient legend.

Unfortunately, proof that it *could* be done is not the same as proof that it *was* done. Tim Severin's expedition does not rule out the possibility that the *Navigatio* was constructed from the voyages of a number of Irish monks, amalgamated for the sake of unity into a single epic. Even if all the islands in the *Navigatio* could be identified, it would still not be a simple task to trace the path of Saint Brendan's voyage. Frequently, two or more widely separated islands can be found to match an island described in the *Navigatio*. Moreover, did Saint Brendan take a northerly route, or one to the south? This question can be convincingly answered either way.

Mount Hekla (or Mounts Eyjafjallajokul and Katla) on Iceland, with a centuries-long history of volcanic activity, fits perfectly with the Fiery Mountain and with Brendan's description of an erupting volcano rising from the ocean floor. The 320-foot vertical black cliffs of Dyrholaey and those of Reykjanes Peninsula both match Brendan's cliffs.

Brendan's crystal pillar would seem to be none other than a rather fanciful report of an iceberg. That the pillar first appeared to Brendan to be "not far distant" yet he took three days to reach it may be accounted for by two facts: an iceberg's great size and its unusual colour make it stand out clearly against the horizon; and, in the Arctic and sub-Arctic regions during the summertime, whenever a mass of warm air is trapped over the cold water, islands or icebergs can be visible and seem nearby even though they are actually beyond the horizon. The "net" surrounding the pillar could have been loose pack-ice with enough channels to allow Brendan's curragh to pass through and reach the iceberg. But there is one disquieting element in correlating the crystal column with an iceberg: though Saint Brendan and his fellow monks spend a great deal of time examining the crystal pillar and reported their findings at great length, they never mention that it is cold, nor that it is made of, or in the midst of, or even like, ice.

Saint Brendan may have encountered pack-ice elsewhere in the sea. At one point in the *Navigatio*, the wind drops and the "sea coagulated, as it were — it was so smooth." Tim Severin points out that Brendan "may have reached an area of frazil ice, one of the first stages of pack-ice development, where spicules of ice hang in the water in total calm, and then coalesce into lumps which resemble the curds floating on the surface of coagulating milk."[9] The region of Greenland on fifteenth-century maps often carries the inscription, "*Mare quod Frequenter Congelata*" (Here the Sea is Frequently Congealed).

With such convincing evidence for a route in northern latitudes, how could anyone imagine a southerly passage for Saint Brendan? The Azores were created by subaquatic eruptions along the Mid-Atlantic Ridge; they, along with the Canaries and Madeiras, are all volcanic in origin. The Fiery Mountain in Brendan's travels could have been Pico de Teide, the 3460-metre (12,198-foot) peak on the island of Tenerife in the Canaries. No longer active, and now snow-capped throughout the year, Pico de Teide was eruptive in the not-too-distant past; the label Ysola del Inferno on all important maps of the fourteenth and fifteenth centuries provides evidence. Volcanic activity in this region of the Atlantic, though minimal over the past centuries, may well have been greater in Saint Brendan's time. As for the Island of Smiths, remnants of volcanos which rose from the seabed and then subsided are found not only near Iceland and Greenland, but occur off the coast of Terceira in the Azores. Even now, on the island of São Miguel in the Azores, steam rises into the air from numerous vents and fissures connecting with the core of the earth.

The Coagulated Sea which kept Saint Brendan's curragh trapped for twenty days takes on a distinctly southerly cast if the imprisonment is attributed to seaweed, rather than ice. The text, though ambiguous, gives the impression that the wind remained calm for twenty days, and it was not until a favourable wind arose that the monks were able to be on their way again. In northern latitudes, where the prevailing westerlies dominate the weather pattern, periods of calm are distinctly rare; when they do occur, which may be less than once in a month, they seldom last for more than a few hours.

But to the south and west of the Azores, in the middle of the Atlantic

Ocean basin, the weather is dominated by a huge high pressure cell called the Azores-Bermuda High. Winds are predominately light and variable in direction, with frequent and prolonged calms. Sargasso weed floats freely on the surface, packed into dense masses and confined by the general clockwise circulation of the ocean's currents. Nothing in O'Meara's translation of the *Navigatio* indicates that the "coagulated sea" was made up of seaweed, but other versions of the tale use the words "thick curdled mass" and "marsh," terms suggestive of the Sargasso Sea.

Equally uncertain is the location of the pair of islands where Saint Brendan and his fellow monks celebrated Easter — the Isle of Sheep and the Island of the Birds, separated only by a narrow channel. These could be two of the Färoe Islands. Situated roughly two hundred miles north of Scotland, the Färoes were visited in the sixth and seventh centuries by Irish seamen, who settled there and imported the sheep which to this day are a major part of the islands' economy. At the beginning of the ninth century, Norsemen explored and colonized these islands; the very name "Färoe" is derived from the Danish word *faar*, meaning sheep. An extraordinary population of birds lives on all the islands of this archipelago. Members of the Alcidae family — guillemots, puffins and (in Saint Brendan's time) auks — stay year-round, and their numbers in the summer are swelled by migratory plovers, gulls, skuas, arctic terns and kittiwakes.

The Färoe Islands closely match the account of the Isle of Sheep and Island of the Birds on three counts: the physical characteristics of the islands and their closeness to one another; the character and quantity of animal and bird life found there; and the natural progression of a northerly route from the northernmost islands of the Hebrides. Alexander von Humboldt, the noted nineteenth-century historian and scientist, was so convinced of this that, in his *Examen Critique de l'Historie de la Geographie du Nouveau Continent*, he never considers any but a northerly route for Saint Brendan.

Even so, there is reason to believe that the Isle of Sheep and Island of Birds indicate a *southerly* passage. Dominick Daly, writing in the *Celtic Review* (1909), believed that the island of Tenerife, the largest and most fertile of the Canary Islands, was Saint Brendan's Isle of Sheep. He based his conclusion on a much earlier work written by the Spanish friar Alonso de Espinosa between 1580 and 1590 while he resided on Tenerife.[10] In *The Guanches of Tenerife: The Holy Image of Our Lady of Candelaria and the Spanish Conquest and Settlement*, Espinosa recounts how the northern side of Tenerife was populated by "fleece-robed inhabitants who lived mainly by their flocks." Espinosa says that the Guanches, whose traditions go back 1520 years, believe that "sixty people came to their island," they knew not from where, and formed a settlement. These first comers were "the sons and brothers of the great one, from Heaven." The notion, Espinosa continues, that the "Apostles sent a bishop [Saint Brendan] to preach the faith" is supported by a quotation from a Roman calendar in the time of the Emperor Justinian, whose reign (527-565) falls within the lifetime of Saint Brendan.[11]

Espinosa also says, "In [the Fortunate Islands] there was a man of great abstinence, a native of Scotia [i.e., Ireland], father and shepherd of 3000 monks for the space of seven years"; during this time, the "father and shepherd" resuscitated a dead giant and baptized him.

In the *Navigatio*, the beast of the sea which attempts to devour Saint Brendan is sparingly described: it is of immense size and spouts foam from its nostrils. But the *Vita Sancti Brendani* from *The Book of Lismore* gives it a more specific identity: it is as a great sea-cat, "bigger than an ox or a three-year-old horse, overgrown by feeding on fish of the sea; bigger than a brazen cauldron was each of his eyes; a boar's tusk had he; furzy hair upon him; and he had a maw of a leopard with the strength of a lion, and the voracity of a hound." In short, the monster is a walrus. The second monster that came to do battle with this devouring beast is specifically called a huge sea-whale. The walrus is a creature of Arctic seas, and although it once ranged farther south than it does now, appearing in the Gulf of St. Lawrence and around Nova Scotia, it certainly was never found anywhere near the Canary or Madeira islands.

The information given in the *Navigatio* is simply too vague or contradictory to match the various islands visited by Saint Brendan with a physical counterpart in the Atlantic. Equally fruitless is to look to the voyage of Saint Brendan as "proof" that the Irish reached America some time in the Middle Ages before the Vikings. That this problem should exist at all is due to a confusion between the form of the story and its content. By viewing the voyage as a structural device for the tale, rather than as an actual expedition undertaken by Saint Brendan, one comes much closer to understanding its meaning. The form of narrative in which gods or heroes travel over the sea in their quest for the Happy Otherworld has served well since the time of the ancient Greeks and Romans. It is also found in the voyage-stories and poems of the Irish *immrama*. Here, in the Christian tale of Saint Brendan and his fellow monks, it illustrates moral and spiritual truth.

Within the framework of the voyage, allegory and metaphor convey the author's message, the same message proclaimed by John in the *Book of Reve-*

lation. As in other apocalyptic writing, the *Book of Revelation* is filled with symbolic language, and colours, numbers and various creatures have special meaning — indeed, this is one of the chief characteristics of such writing. These descriptions are not meant to be taken literally or pictured realistically; instead, a second meaning is intended to be read into them. Symbolic language abounds in the *Navigatio*, not only because it suits the purpose so well in presenting the struggle of Christ's representative — Brendan — against Satan and his ultimate victory, but because much of it comes directly from *Revelation.*

But metaphors and allegories are difficult to accept, especially when there are a great number of them in one story. However, tied within the framework of a voyage taken by a well-known, much-revered saint such as Saint Brendan, and with added realistic descriptions of islands and everyday monastic life, the allegory takes on the *appearance* of reality and thus is more easily understood. Recognizing this artistic device not only helps to explain the popularity of the *Navigatio* throughout Europe, but also accounts for why some authors have been misled into searching for an identifiable counterpart to each of the islands in the story.

Nothing in Saint Brendan's narrative is accidental or arbitrary; every element is necessary, and carries with it a second, symbolic meaning. A few examples show that Brendan's voyage was really intended as a metaphor.

First, Saint Brendan chooses "fourteen brothers out of the whole community" (monastery) to accompany him to the Promised Land. Fourteen is not a capriciously selected number. Saint Matthew's narrative of the lineage of Jesus forms a prologue to the coming of Christ, and in the *Navigatio* the fourteen brothers perform the same function: they represent the fourteen generations from Abraham to David the King, the fourteen generations from David to Jechoniah and his brothers at the time of the Babylonian exile, and the fourteen generations from the Babylonian exile to the birth of Jesus — the Messiah.[12]

The crystal pillar, which appears so clearly to be a fanciful description of an iceberg, assumes an entirely new meaning in the context of a metaphoric voyage. Icebergs may have an infinite variety of shapes, but the one presented to us in the *Navagatio* is the least likely of all. This iceberg-pillar is perfectly square and so large that Brendan took four days to sail around it. The pillar in this version of the *Navigatio* is of bright crystal, but the Anglo-Norman version of the *Navigatio* depicts it more elaborately; it is "of jacinth [a blue gem] set in the middle of the ocean and surmounted by an altar of emerald under a golden, jewelled canopy." It is neither cold nor icy. What Saint Brendan describes is not an iceberg at all, but the vision of the New Jerusalem in the *Book of Revelation*:

> He took me in spirit to a great, high mountain and showed me the holy city of Jerusalem coming down out of heaven from God. Its radiance was like that of a precious stone, like jasper, clear as crystal. It gleamed with the splendour of God. . . . The city was square, its length the same as its width. He measured the city with the rod and found it 12,000 stades in length, width and height. He also measured its wall: 144 cubits (21:10-11, 16-17).

The chalice and paten Saint Brendan takes from a window on one side of the pillar are a gift from Jesus Christ so "that the wonder be manifested to many in order that they may believe" — an appropriate token to take home from the New Jerusalem. Setting the crystal pillar, representing the New Jerusalem, against the Island of Smiths and the Fiery Mountain seems natural. These islands, spewing molten lava and incandescent chunks of pumice into the air and sea, are the netherworld of fire and sulphur — the realm of Satan. Once again, the *Navigatio* reveals the struggle between the forces of good and evil.

The monastery and church on the Island of Saint Ailbe, where Brendan spent Christmas, is described in such scrupulous detail, with all the customs and practices of monastic life, that one hardly notices the skilful blending of realism and symbolism. The community of Ailbe represents the New Heaven and the New Earth as revealed by John — another manifestation of the New Jerusalem. And the church in the monastery on the island is the Temple of the New Jerusalem.

In the monastery live twenty-four brothers, and within the church are twenty-four seats arranged in a circle, with an extra seat for the abbot between the two choirs of twelve men. In *Revelation*, the twenty-four elders represent the twelve tribes of Israel and the twelve apostles, the leaders of the New Israel. John derived his description of the Temple of the New Jerusalem in part from Ezekiel's vision of a utopian New Temple (the New Israel), and in part from the great letter written by the Apostle Paul to the Christians in Ephesus. Paul says:

[Y]ou are fellow citizens with the holy ones and members of the household of God, built upon the foundation of the apostles and prophets, with Christ Jesus himself as the capstone. Through him the whole structure is held together and grows to a temple sacred to the Lord. (*Ephesians* 2:19-21)

In the *Navigatio*, then, the abbot of the monastery personifies Christ as the "capstone" of the Temple.

Brendan finds the church has three altars inside: three lights burn before the middle one and two lights before the altar to either side, making seven lights in all. The heavenly temple described by John has only one altar, symbolizing the New Israel, but it, too, has seven lights. The three altars of Ailbe are made of crystal cut in a square, and the chalice, paten and cruet are also of crystal, a much-enhanced reminder of the crystal pillar. To the modern reader this duplication of symbols might seem redundant, but in the Middle Ages such repetition was frequently used to strengthen and reinforce the message.

That the *Navigatio* should be so much like the *Book of Revelation* in allegorical content, metaphor and all other symbolic language is not surprising when one stops to consider the *function* of the story, who it was written for, and what the intended message was. The *Book of Revelation* was written toward the end of the first century AD, a period of Roman domination and fierce persecution of Christians in Asia Minor. The work is a plea for the individual Christian to hold fast in his faith and not let the pagan forces destroy him — in the end, God will triumph. The prediction for the destiny of the Churches is that, although afflicted, "they shall be redeemed, saved, and glorified."

During the period when the *Navigatio* was written, the Irish Church also was under attack. In 795 the Vikings first appeared in Eire and they continued to raid it until 920, when they took Limerick. From their settlements in Dublin and Waterford, the Norse spread to form other colonies throughout Ireland. Not until the battle of Clontarf, near Dublin, in 1014 did the threat of Norse conquest end. Then, the Norman invasions in the tenth and eleventh centuries drove monks and scholars from Ireland to the continent. During this three-hundred-year period, there was no prospect of a normal life in Ireland, especially in the religious communities. The *Navigatio* achieved its full expression in response to forces like those which impelled the *Book of Revelation*. Both books tell the story of the "decisive struggle of Christ and his followers against Satan." The voyage of Saint Brendan is a metaphoric voyage — a journey of the soul to the Promised Land. It is the story of each person's search for salvation, a maintaining of faith in Christianity in the face of hardships and struggles. At the same time, it tells of the testing of the Church itself and its institutions against paganism.

The Word and the Line Conflated

To determine the geographic location of the Islands of Saint Brendan, cartographers of the Middle Ages seized upon the many references to classical mythology found in the *Navigatio* rather than upon its Christian iconography. To them, the apples or pomegranates (the two were often used interchangeably) were the golden apples of Greek mythology that Gaea gave to Hera at her marriage to Zeus. The three daughters of Zeus — the Hesperides: Aegle (Brightness), Erythia (Scarlet) and Hesperarethusa (Sunset Glow) — lived on an island in the far ocean, west of Mount Atlas; there, with the help of a dragon, they guarded the orchard where the golden apples grew.

Apples are also associated with paradise in the Bible, especially in the garden of Eden, and the association also recurs constantly in Celtic lore. In the tale of Bran, a late seventh-century Irish antecedent to Saint Brendan's travels, Bran learns of the Celtic Elysium from a female visitant who brings a "magic apple-bough covered with white blossoms into his hall, and sings to him of a joyous land":

> There is a distant isle,
> Around which sea-horses glisten:
> A fair course against the white-swelling surge . . .
> A delight of the eyes, a glorious range,
> Is the plain on which the hosts hold games . . .
> Lovely land through the world's age,
> On which the many blossoms drop.
> An ancient tree there is with blossoms,
> On which birds call to the hours . . .
> Splendours of every colour glisten
> Throughout the gentle-voiced plains . . .

Unknown is wailing or treachery
In the familiar cultivated land,
There is nothing rough or hard,
But sweet music striking on the ear,
Without grief, without sorrow, without death.[13]

Manannán mac Lir, an Irish deity whose name literally means "son of the sea," had as his realm not only the sea but a supernatural island as well — Emhain Ablach — Emhain of the apple trees. Across the Irish Sea in England, the legendary King Arthur was conveyed for the healing of his wounds after his final battle to Avalon — the Island of Apples, called Fortunate.

An otherworldly island paradise is indicated in the *Navigatio* by the presence of apples and apple-like fruit. Saint Brendan and his followers find on the Island of Strong Men fruit of great size, each "like a large ball," which, when squeezed, yield a pound of juice. The three choirs on the island recall the three Hesperides sisters, who "sang in chorus near springs which spurted forth ambrosia." The cluster of grapes Saint Brendan receives from the great bird are of extraordinary redness, and each grape is as big as an apple. A nearby island is so fertile that all the trees bend down to the ground with this same fruit. The island has "a perfume like that of a house filled with pomegranates."

Cartographers of the Middle Ages had to decide where they should place on their maps these gardens of paradise lying at the aqueous bounds of the world. They inherited a vague tradition, maintained throughout the centuries, of the existence of *real* islands in the Atlantic off the coast of Africa. But the information about Atlantic islands was often confused and interwoven with legends.

By the first century BC, three island groups in the Atlantic, west of Africa were already distinguished: Insulae Fortunatae, Insulae Hesperidum and the Purpurariae. Strabo (65 BC) spoke of "the golden apples of the Hesperides, the Islands of the Blessed . . . opposite Gades [Cadiz]." In his *Life of Sertorius*, Plutarch relates the plight of this Roman captain when he had to flee from his own countrymen who had displaced him (about 50 BC). At Cadiz, Sertorius met sailors who had just returned from islands in the Atlantic called Buenaventuradas. So pleasing was their description of this island's many wonderful qualities and its salubrius climate that Sertorius "desired to go there and live in quiet, without the care of living wars." In the time of Sertorius sailors not only knew that the two Canary Islands of Lancerote and Fuerteventura

Fig. 11-2.
Ebstorf world map, c. 1235.
(Reproduced courtesy of the
Newberry Library.)

existed and what they were like, but their position as well. Plutarch declares, "it is generally believed these are the Elysian Fields of which Homer sings."

In the second century, Ptolemy showed two of the Canary Islands on his famous world map. He called them Insulae Fortunatae because they were blessed with a beneficent climate and generous fertility. Five centuries later, Saint Isidore of Seville said about these islands, "*Fortunatae Insulae faelices et abeatae fructum ubertate . . . poma sylvarum parturient, fortuitus vitibus juga collium vestiuntur*" (The Fortunate Islands are pleasing and blessed with the richness of fruits of the land. . . . They are filled with apple trees, and, by good fortune, covered with edible [grape] vines).[14]

The earliest map on which the Island of Saint Brendan appears is the Ebstorf world map of 1235. Discovered in Ebstorf, Germany, it was used as an altarpiece in a Benedictine monastery. Gervase of Tilbury, an English teacher of

199

law and provost in Ebstorf in the mid-thirteenth century, wrote a compendium on cosmology and geography, *Otia Imperialia*, in which he recorded both known facts and legends; Gervase is the presumed maker of the Ebstorf map as well.

The map is circular in shape and superimposed on the figure of a crucified Christ. The head of Christ, at the top of the map, is east, and the arms point north and south. Since the map was used for ecclesiastical purposes, it it only natural that Jerusalem, the most holy of Christian cities, occupies the centre of the map. In *Otia Imperialia*, Gervase also reasons that, since the Emperor Augustus started his survey of the empire in Judea, it had to be the "heart of the earth." Furthermore, he declares, Jerusalem is halfway between the north and the south, and therefore it must follow that there is as much land to the east as there is to the west; thus, Jerusalem "occupie[s] the centre of the known world."

The entire surface of Gervase's map is covered with an unordered, bewildering profusion of features. Within the interstices of a complex maze of rivers, lakes and seas are cities, animals, plants, Biblical scenes and mythical races of humans, many of a fantastic appearance. All are labelled, in many cases with extensive captions. But when one strips away all the detail, leaving only the waterways and major landmasses, and rotates the map to the more familiar orientation, with north at the top, it becomes apparent that the Ebstorf map is merely a highly elaborated version of the T-O type map from classical times. On the Roman T-O maps, the rivers Tanais (Don) and Nile and the Black and Aegean seas separate Asia from the continents of Europe and Africa, which are divided from one another by the Mediterranean Sea. In the Ebstorf map, though, Africa is somewhat extended to accommodate more recent geographical knowledge. A continuous, circulating ocean confines all in a disc-shaped world.

In this ocean on the Ebstorf map, at the farthest bounds of the known world, is an island bearing the caption: "*Insula p[er]dita hanc invenit S[an]c[tu]s Brandanus a qua cum navigasset a nullo hominum a postea a inventa*" (The Lost Island [Perdita]; this is the island found by Saint Brendan, and after he sailed away it was never again seen by any man). Even without geographic coordinates of latitude and longitude, this is clearly one of the

Fig. 11-3.
Simplification of the Ebstorf map, with all pictorial content removed, leaving only the landmasses and waterways. Both the Ebstorf map and the inset, a typical T-O map, have been rotated 90° to place north at the top.

Fortunate Isles, for it is shown (as on other medieval maps) where the Atlas mountains meet the sea.

Among the sources Gervase used in his *Otia Imperialia* was *De Imagine Mundi* by Honorius of Atun, one of the important geographic encyclopedias of the period (about 1100). In *De Imagine Mundi*, Honorius discusses the Isle of the Gorgons, the Hesperides, and the Island of Perdita (Lost Island). According to legend, he says, the Island of Perdita is known to exist, but can be found only by chance encounter and not by deliberate search; hence its name. This paradise "exceeded all the surrounding countries in the delightfulness and fertility of all things to be found therein." Since the Fortunate Islands — the Canaries — were noted for all these qualities, it seemed only natural that they must have been the islands encountered by Saint Brendan in his navigations. Thus a geography of legend was linked with a geography of reality, and a site was created for the Islands of Saint Brendan.

Gervase's uniting of Perdita/Hesperides/Fortunate Islands with the Islands of Saint Brendan was no mere caprice of a single cartographer; the same thing is found on another, slightly later map. The Hereford map (c. 1290), found in the Hereford Cathedral of Norman France, shares many characteristics of the Ebstorf map; of the Roman T-O type, it is filled with a multitude of scenes and captions and used as an altarpiece. Like its counterpart, it shows an island in the location of the Canary Islands which bears the inscription: *Fortunatae Insulae sex sunt Insulae Sct Brandani.* There is no doubt about who made this map, for an inscription reads: "Let all men who own, hear, read or see this story pray to Jesus for mercy for Richard of Haldingham and Lafford, who conceived and created it, that he may have joy in Heaven."[15]

By the beginning of the fourteenth century, Atlantic islands of long-standing tradition began to give way to a new geography of reality. On the Angelinus Dulcert map of 1339, the Hesperides and the Fortunate Islands of Ptolemy are replaced by three islands of the Canary archipelago: Vegi Mari (Lobos), Insula de Lanzarotus Marocelus (Lanzarote) and La Forte Ventura (Fuerteventura). A new constellation of islands also appears. North of the Canaries, and somewhat farther offshore, are three islands: Canaria, Insula de Caprara and Coruimaris. They are definitely the Madeira Islands, for they are correctly placed relative to the Canary Islands and to the African coast. Collectively, though, they are labelled "*Insulle Sct Brandani siue puelarum.*"

The designation "Islands of St. Brendan" has become dislodged from the

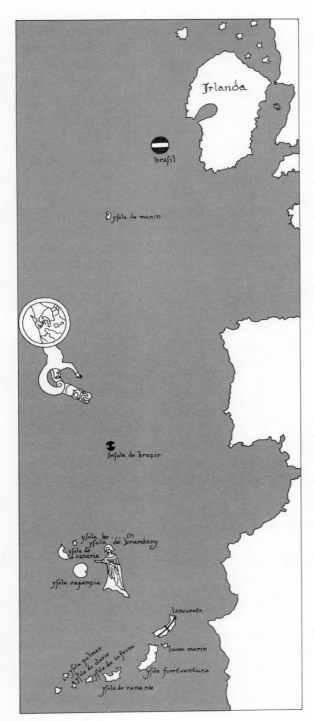

Fortunate Islands and drifted slightly to the north. The appropriation of the title for this new group is equally valid, for they, too, have all those qualities of the Isles of the Blest — balmy climate, abundant fruit and natural beauty. Once the Canary Islands became well known, depicted on maps and colonized, they could no longer also accommodate the legends of the past. The Pizigani map of 1367, only a few years later, reasserts this new location of the Islands of Saint Brendan. But now, instead of three, there are one unnamed and seven named Canary Islands.[16] The Madeira Islands are little changed from the Dulcert map, and, as on the Dulcert map, all of the Madeiras on the Pizigani map are collectively labelled "Islands of St. Brendan." An adjacent drawing of the figure of a kneeling monk reinforces the identification.

As might be expected, the discoveries, or rather re-discoveries, which brought the Azores into the realm of reality once again required a new location for the Islands of Saint Brendan. On the Bartolomeo Pareto map of 1455, almost all the blank spaces are filled in. The Madeira and Canary islands are completely and accurately depicted, most already carrying the names by which they are known today. Stretching in a straight line north of these archipelagos are eight of the nine Azores islands: Louo (Santa Maria), Capraria (São Miguel), Insulla de Brazil (Terceira), Insulla de Uentura (Fayal), Collonbi (Pico), San Zorzo (St. George), Li Conieri (Flores) and Corvui Marini (Corvo).

On the Pareto map, as on all others of the period, the three island chains — the Azores, Madeiras and Canaries — are strung in a north-south line, as though they are all in the same longitude. This should not be interpreted to mean that geographers and cartographers did not know the dispersion and true position of these archipelagos. There was still no way to measure longitude, and distances could only be given in terms of so many days'

Fig. 11-4.
Pizigani map, 1367. Saint Brendan is kneeling by his islands.

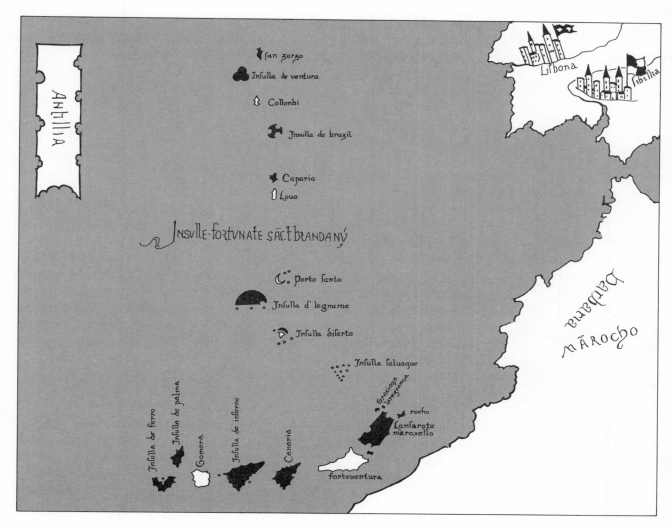

Anthlia

fan zorzo

Infulla de ventura

Collonbi

Infulla de brazil

Caparia

Louo

Insvlle·fortvnate·sāct·brandaný

Porto Santo

Infulla d'legname

Infulla diferte

Infulla faluaque

Graciosa
linterzgranca

rocho

Lanfarote
maroxello

Infulla de ferro

Infulla de palma

Gomera

Infulla de inferno

Canaria

forteuentura

Lifbona

Sibrilia

Barbaria

mãrocho

voyage from a starting point. Nor was there any real need for accuracy, since these maps were not intended for navigational purposes. Within each group there is a logic to the placement of the individual islands, and mariners knew, in the most general terms, how much farther west they needed to sail in order to reach each group. Keeping the islands all in the same apparent longitude was only a cartographic convention — one that best made use of the available space.

What does matter is the continual shifting of the "Fortunate" islands of Saint Brendan to a new position at the extreme limits of the known world. Once the Azores became settled, with thriving centres of agriculture, fishing

Fig. 11-5.
Bartolomeo Pareto map (1455) showing the Atlantic archipelagos.

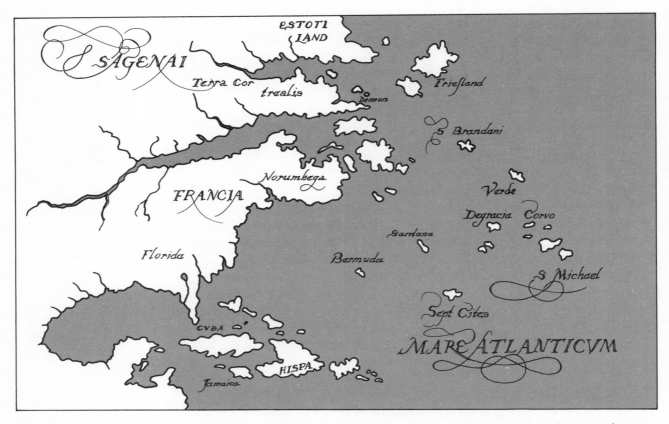

Fig. 11-6.
Early seventeenth-century
map of the New World by
R. Petri. The island of Saint
Brendan, in its ever-westward
migration, has come to rest
off the coast of Newfoundland.

and trade, they, like the Madeira and Canary Islands before them, no longer seemed possible as the site of the legendary paradise. Explorations to the west showed that the Atlantic Ocean did not terminate on the shores of Asia as had previously been thought, but upon North America. After the second voyage of Giovanni Verrazzano in 1526, it became apparent that the coast of North and South America was one continuous, unbroken line, unsevered by any river or strait leading to the Orient. Knowledge of the topography of these lands extended beyond the shores, as shown on maps by the representation of mountains, rivers and cities.

All this newly acquired information did not cause the Islands of Saint Brendan to cease to exist. Wrenched from the traditional locus off the west coast of Africa, they took refuge in the farthest western reaches of the Atlantic — in waters that were the last frontier of exploration. With this move another change occurs; now, instead of the multiple islands of Saint Brendan, there is only a single island that bears his name. On the Abraham Ortelius map of 1570, which displays a rapidly expanding and accurate knowledge of the New World, the Island of Saint Brendan (S. Brandani) is 650 miles north of the Azores, not far off the coast of Newfoundland and Labrador, keeping company with the other mythical islands of Frisland, Demonias and Verde. There it remained on the seventeenth-century map by Petri, in spite of the great contradiction that by these shores, at a latitude north of 50°, no one could ever consider it a balmy paradise, redolent with all the fruits of nature. Legends do not die easily.

Eventually, the Island of Saint Brendan came to rest in the middle of a group of islands deep within Newfoundland's Bonavista Bay. Whether this Island of Saint Brendan was named by the English who came to Bonavista Bay as migratory fishermen at the end of the seventeenth century, or later, by Irish immigrants who settled there in the 1840s, is uncertain. But the answer is of slight importance, for shortly thereafter, in 1884, it was renamed Cottel Island, the name it bears today. Thus the constant search for the permanent home of the Islands of Saint Brendan — a search which encompassed thirteen centuries of travel, each time inexorably farther west and north — finally reached its utmost limits, then faded altogether from cartographic history.

Of all the Atlantic islands that never existed, the Islands of Saint Brendan were the ultimate phantom islands, for they were not the product of an empirical knowledge of geography but were an imaginary realm created to understand the cosmos and man's place within it; they were attempts to comprehend the unknown and bring order out of confusion. The Islands of Saint Brendan embodied an essentially universal theme: they were the happy, peaceful Otherworld — the Elysian fields of Greece, "the abode of peace and harmony with its soft green meadows, lovely groves, sunlight that glows purple, and delicious life-giving air"; they were the Christian Kingdom of Heaven, wherein "the river of life-giving water, sparkling like crystal, flows from the throne of God . . . and the tree of life produces fruit twelve times a year . . . and nothing accursed will be found"; and they were the Celtic island across the sea that "transcends the limitations of human time, a multicoloured land of surpassing beauty, where only sweet music strikes the ear, where sweet water streams flow through the land, and purple is the surface of every plain."

In deciding where to place these islands, cartographers used the same approach as they did for all the other phantom islands. They took fragments of information which were often vague, confused and intertwined with myth and legend, and united them with a geography of tradition. As new information was brought back by mariners venturing out into the Atlantic, pushing back its boundaries, the geography of legend and tradition gradually gave way to a geography of reality.

Although the phantom islands are no longer shown on maps, the legends that created them remain windows into the human spirit and an important part of the legacy of exploration into the Great Green Sea of Gloom — the North Atlantic Ocean.

Notes

CHAPTER I
Mapping the Unknown Seas

1 Justin Windsor, ed., *Narrative and Critical History of America* (Boston: Houghton, Mifflin, 1889), 14.

2 Strabo, *Geographia* i:4,6; in Felipe Fernández-Armesto, *Columbus* (Oxford: Oxford University Press, 1992), 28.

3 Washington Irving, *Columbus: His Life and Voyages* (New York: Putnam, 1920), 18.

4 Plato related the tale of the lost island of Atlantis 2300 years ago. He said that an island larger than Africa and Asia together, lying in the Atlantic opposite the Pillars of Hercules, had disappeared beneath the surface of the waves 9000 years earlier. I have not included Atlantis as one of the phantom islands of the Atlantic, partly because so much has already been written about it, including accounts which attempt to substantiate its actual existence, that one more recapitulation of the story hardly seems necessary; and partly because in the Middle Ages it did not appear on the maps. Cartographers seem to have relegated the story of Atlantis to the status of a purely imaginary tale from ancient Greece, never transposing it into an island of reality as they did other islands of legend.

5 C.H. Oldfather, trans., *Diodorus Siculus* (Cambridge: Harvard University Press, 1970), 3:145.

6 Avienus, *Ora Maritima*, in Geoffrey Ashe, *Land to the West: St. Brendan's Voyage to America* (New York: Viking, 1962), 136.

7 Ashe 136.

8 Some historians believe it was not Thule that Pytheas was describing, but the coast of Norway, which has the same latitude and astronomical conditions given in the account.

9 Lactantius, *Institutiones divinae* III:24. In Adolf Erik Nordenskiöld, *Facsimile-Atlas to the Early History of Cartography, with Reproductions of the Most Important Maps Printed in the XV and XVI Centuries* (Stockholm, 1889. Rpt. New York: Dover, 1973), 72. Translation obtained through the courtesy of the Department of Linguistics, University of Guadalajara, Guadalajara, Mexico.

10 Dicuil, "*Liber de Mensura Orbis Terrae.*" Edited by J.J. Tierney. *Scriptores Latini Hiberniae* VI (Dublin: Dublin Institute for Advanced Studies, 1967), 73.

CHAPTER II
Geographical Knowledge of the Muslims

1 Mas'ûdî, *Murûj al-Dahab*, 1:8 "Description of the Land and the Seas," in Taris Khalidi, *Islamic Historiography: The Histories of Mas'ûdî* (Albany: State University of New York Press, 1975), 179.

2 V. Minorsky, trans., *Hudûd al-'Âlam (The Regions of the World: A Persian Geography)* (London: Luzac, 1970), 49.

3 Minorsky III:58.

4 Clark B. Firestone, *The Coasts of Illusion: A Study of Travel Tales* (New York: Harper, 1924), 270.

5 R. Manny, "Navigations Arabes Anonymes aux Canaries au XIIIe Siecle," *Notes Africaines* (1960), 61.

6 F. Rosenthal, trans., *The Muqaddimah*, Bollingen Series 43 (Princeton: Princeton University Press, 1958), 1:116.

7 Place names removed from Ibn Khaldûn's map: Lamlam Country; Maghzâwah Country; Kanem; Zaghây; Gawgaw; Bornu; Nubia; at-Tâjuwîn; Abyssinia; Ghânah; Lamtah; as-Sûs; Morocco; Tangier; Sinhâjah; Dartah; Ifrîqiyah; Desert of Berenice; Inner Oases; Fezzan; Jarid; Kawâr; Beja; Hijâz; Syria; Yemen; Yamâmah (Alamâniyah); Mukran; al-Basrah; Irâq; ash-Shihr; Oman; Kirmân; Fârs; al-Bahlûs; Azerbaijan; Desert; Khuwârizm; Khurâsân; Eastern India; Tashkent; Soghd; Tughuzghuz; Gascogne; Calabria; Venice; Germany; Macedonia; Bohemia; Jathûliyah; Jarmâniyah; al-Baylaqân; Armenia; Tabaristân; Alans; Bashqirs; Bulgars; Pechenegs; Stinking Land; Waste Country; Ghuzz; Turgish; Adhkish; Khallukh; Kimäk.

CHAPTER III
Filling in the Empty Spaces

1 The English mile equals 1609.3 metres or 5310 feet. Originally it was the Roman linear measurement of 1000 paces, about 1618 yards (4854 feet). Today, in the United Kingdom, some parts of the Commonwealth, and the United States, the statute mile (used for land measurement) has been standardized at 1609 metres (5280 feet). The nautical mile is 1852 metres (6076 feet), which equals one minute of arc of the circumference of the earth.

2 With a modern instrument, the sextant, these results would be refined by various correction values. Also, declination is added *algebraically*; therefore, if the observation is taken in the northern hemisphere but the sun is in its southern

declination, the number representing the sun's declination assumes a negative value.

3 There are two kinds of compass errors; *variation*, which is the result of changes in the earth's magnetic field over the surface of the globe, and *deviation*, produced by ferrous metals in close proximity to the compass.

4 Sir Richard Hawkins, *The Observations of Sir Richard Hawkins* (London: Argonaut, 1933), XV: 38.

5 Hawkins XV:39. Hawkins was also astute enough to notice the curative effect of citrus fruit on scurvy, a disease caused by lack of Vitamin C (ascorbic acid) and known about since the time of Hippocrates. In 1590, a fleet of English ships was becalmed for almost six months. Hawkins described the scurvy outbreak and its symptoms and noted that the disease is most common among English sailors unused to heat and unwholesome airs, which have a deleterious effect on the digestion. Hawkins says: "That which I have seene most fruitfull for this sicknesse, is sower Oranges and Lemmons." However, for his own protection against scurvy Hawkins relied upon a patent medicine, "Doctor *Stevens*, his water." Unfortunately, Hawkins took his observation no further and concluded that "the principall of all, is the ayres of the Land; for, the Sea is naturall for fishes, and the Land for men" (*Observations* XVI 42). James Lind, a Scottish naval surgeon, established in a series of shipboard experiments 164 years later that oranges and lemons cured scurvy; he published his findings in *A Treatise on the Scurvy* (1753). Still, it took an additional forty-two years for this knowledge to be put to practical use, when Sir Gilbert Blaine recommended that lime juice be issued to all British naval vessels.

CHAPTER IV
Rediscovery of the Atlantic Archipelagos

1 Cathay, the medieval name popularized by Marco Polo for all of China, related specifically only to that part of China north of the Yangste River.

2 Max Justo Guedes and Gerald Lombardi, eds. *Portugal/Brazil: The Age of Atlantic Discoveries* (New York: New York Public Library, 1990), 1.

CHAPTER V
Isle of Demons

1 Horace Beck, *Folklore and the Sea* (Middletown, CT: Wesleyan University Press, 1973), 275.

2 Chris Leahy, *The Birdwatcher's Companion* (New York: McGraw-Hill, 1982), 39, 102, 103.

3 W.F. Ganong, *Crucial Maps in the Early Cartography and Place-Nomenclature of the Atlantic Coast of Canada* (Toronto: University of Toronto Press, 1964), 281.

CHAPTER VI
Frisland

1 Richard Hakluyt, *The Third and Last Volume of the Voyages, Navigations, Traffiques, and Discoueries of the English Nation* (London: Bishop, Newberie and Barker, 1600). I have transcribed the text as it was published in 1600, but with some modernized usage and spelling to make it more readable. Portions of the work not relevant to the subject of Frisland are presented here:

In the year of our Lord 1200, there was in the city of Venice a famous gentleman named Messer *Marino Zeno*, who, for his great virtue and singular wisdom, was called and elected governor in certain commonwealths of *Italy*: in the administration whereof he bore himself so discretely, that he was beloved by all men, and his name greatly revered by those that never knew or saw his person. And among his sundry worthy works, this is recorded of him, that he pacified certain grievous rival dissentions that arose among the citizens of *Verona*: Whereas otherwise, if by his grave advise and great diligence they had not been presented, the matter was likely to break out into hot quarrels of war. He was the first *Podesta*, or *Ruler*, that the Commonwealth of *Venice* appointed in Constantinople in the year 1205 when our state was ruled by the French Barons. This Gentleman had a son named Messer *Pietro,* who was the father of the Duke *Rinieri*, which Duke, dying without a son, made his heir M. *Andrea*, the son of M. *Marco* his brother. This M. *Andrea* was Captain General and Procurator, a man of great reputation for the many rare qualities he possessed. He had a son M. *Rinieri*, a worthy Senator and prudent consellor: of whom descended M. *Pietro*, Captain General of the league of the Christians against the Turks, who was called *Dragon*, for in his shield, instead of a *Mansrone* which was his arms at first, he bore a *Dragon*. He was father to. . . .

But the fisherman who with his fellows showed them the manner of taking fish with nets, saved their lives: and would go every day to fish in the sea and in fresh rivers, and take a great abundance of fish and give it to the chief men of the country, whereby he was so favoured, that he was very well beloved and honoured by everyone.

The fame of this man being spread abroad in the country, there was a Lord thereby, that was very desirous to have him with him, and to see how he used his miraculous art of catching fish, in so much that he made war with the other Lord with whom he was before, and in the end prevailing, since he was mightier and a better warrier, the fisherman was sent to him with the rest of his company. And for the space of thirteen years that he dwelt in those parts, he says, he was sent in this order to more than 25 Lords, for they had continual war among themselves, this Lord with that Lord, and he with another, only to have him to dwell with them: so that wandering up and down the country without any certain abode in one place, he knew almost all those parts. He says, that it is a very great country and as it were a new world: the people are very rude and void of all goodness, they go all naked so that they are unbearably vexed with cold, neither do they have the wit to cover their bodies with the skins of beasts which they take in hunting, they have no kind of metal, they live by hunting, they carry certain lances of wood sharpend at the point, they have bows, and strings whereof are made of beasts skins: they are very fierce people, they make cruel wars with one another, and eat one another, they have governors and certain laws very diverse among themselves. But the farther Southwards, the more civility there is, the air being somewhat temperate, so that there they have cities and temples to idols, wherein they sacrifice men and afterwards eat them, they have there some knowledge and use of gold and silver. . . .

And he is thoroughly credited because of the mariners, who approve many strange things, that he reports to be true. Wherefore this Lord is resolved to send me forth with a fleet towards those parts, and there are so many that desire to go on that voyage, for the novelty and strangeness of the thing, that I think we shall be very strongly appointed, without any public expense at all. And this is the tenor of the letter mentioned before, which I have here set down to give intelligence of another voyage that M. *Antonio* made, being set out with many barks, and men, notwithstanding he was not captain, as he had thought at first he should be: for *Zichmni* went in his own person: and concerning that matter I have a letter in the following form.

One great preparation for the voyage of Estotiland was begun in an unlucky hour: for three days before our departure the fisherman that should have been our guide died: notwithstanding that Lord would not give over the enterprise, but instead of the fisherman took certain mariners that returned from the Island with him: and so making our Navigation to the Westwards, we discovered certain Islands subject to *Frisland*, and having passed certain shelves we stayed at *Ledouo* for seven days to refresh ourselves, and to furnish the fleet with necessary provision. Departing from there we arrived the first of July at the Isle of *Ilose*: and on account of the unfavourable wind, we did not stay there, but passed forth, and being upon the main sea, there immediately arose a cruel tempest, when for eight days time we were miserably vexed, not knowing where we were, and a great part of the barks were lost, afterward the weather becoming fair, we gathered up the broken pieces of the barks that were lost, and sailing with a prosperous wind we discovered land to the West. Wherefore keeping our course directly upon it, we arrived in a good and safe harbour, where we saw an infinite company of people ready in arms, come running very furiously to the waterside, as it were for defence of the Iland. Wherefore *Zichmni* causing his men to make figures of peace unto them, they sent ten men unto us that could speak ten languages, but we could understand none of them, except one that was of *Island*. He being brought before our prince and asked, what was the name of the Island, and what people inhabited it, and who governed it, answered, that the Island was called *Icaria* and that all the kings that reigned there, were called *Icari*, after the the name of the first king of that place, which as they say was the son of *Dedalus* king of *Scotland*, who conquered that Island, left his son there for king, and left them those laws that they retain to this present day, and after this, desiring to sail farther, in a great tempest that arose, was drowned, wherefore for a memorial of his death, they call those seas yet, the *Icarian* Sea, and the kings of the Island *Icari*, and for that they were contented with that state, which God had given them, neither would they alter one iota of their laws and customs, they would not receive any stranger: wherefore they requested of our prince that he would not seek to violate their laws, which they had received from that king of worthy memory and observed very duly to the present: which if he did attempt, it would result in his manifest destruction, they being all resolutely bent rather to leave their life, than to lose in any respect the use of their laws. Notwithstanding, that we should not think they did altogether refute conversation and traffic with other men, they told us in conclusion that they would willingly receive one of our men, and prefer him to be one of the chief among them, only to learn my language the Italian tongue, and to be informed of our manners and customs, as they had already received those other ten of ten various other nations, that came to their Island. To these things our Prince answered nothing at all, but ordering his men to seek some good harbour, he made figures as though he would depart, and sailing round about the Island, he saw at last a harbour on the East side of the Island, where he put in with all his Fleet: the mariners went on land to take in wood and water, which they did with as great speed as they could, not doubting that they would be assaulted by the inhabitants, as indeed happened, for those that dwelt thereabouts, making figures unto the other with fire and smoke, put themselves presently in arms and the other coming to them, they came all running down to the seaside upon our men, with bows and arrows, and other weapons, so that many were slain and various others badly wounded. And we made signs of peace to them, but it was to no purpose, for their rage increased more and more, as though they had fought for land and living. Wherefore we were forced to depart, and to sail along in a great circuit about the Island, being always accompanied upon the hill tops and the seacoasts with an infinite number of armed men: and so doubling the Cape of the Island towards the North, we found many great shoals, among which for the space of ten days we were in continual danger of losing our whole fleet, but that it pleased God all that while to send us fair weather.

Wherefore proceeding on till we came to the East cape, we saw the inhabitants still on the hilltops and by the seacoast keep with us, and in making great outcries and shooting at us from afar, they uttered their old spiteful affection towards us. Wherefore we determined to stay in some safe harbour, and see if we might speak once again with the *Islander*, but our determination was frustrated: for the people more like beasts then men, stood continually in arms with intent to beat us back, if we should come onto land. Wherefore *Zichmni* seeing he could not prevail, and thinking if he should have preferred and followed obstinately his purpose, their victuals would have failed them, he departed with a fair wind and sailed five days to the Westwards, but the wind changing to the Southwest, and the sea becoming rough, we sailed four days with the wind astern, and at length discovering land, were afraid to approach near it, the sea having grown, and our not knowing what land it was: but God provided for us, and with the wind ceasing there came a great calm. Wherefore some of our company rowing to land with oars, returned and brought us news to our great comfort, that they had found a very good country and a better harbour: upon which news we towed our ships and final barks to land, and entering into a harbour, we saw far off a great mountain, that cast forth smoke, which gave us good hope that we should find some inhabitants in the Island, neither would *Zichmni* rest, although it were a great way off, but sent one hundred soldiers to search the country and bring report what people they were that inhabited it, and in the meantime they took in wood and water for the provision of the fleet, and catch a great number of fish and sea fowl and found such abundance of birds eggs, that our men that were half famished, were filled therewithal. While we were riding [at anchor] here, the month of June began, at which time the air in the Island was so temperate and pleasant as is impossible to express: but when we could see no people at all, we suspected greatly that this pleasant place was desolate and uninhabited. We gave name to the haven calling it Trin, and the point that stretched out into the sea, we called *Capo de Trin*. The one hundred soldiers that were sent out, returned after eight days, and brought word that they had been through the Island and at the mountain, and that the smoke was a natural thing proceeding from a great fire that was in the bottom of the hill, and that there was a spring from which issued a certain water like pitch which ran into the sea, and that thereabouts dwelt great multitudes of people half wild, hiding themselves in caves in the ground, of small stature, and very fearfull; for as soon as they saw the soldiers they fled into their holes, and that there was a great river and a very good and safe harbour. *Zichmni* being thus informed, and seeing that it had a wholesome and pure air, and a very fruitful soil and fair rivers, with various commodities, fell into such a liking for the place, that he determined to inhabit it, and built a city there. But his people being weary and faint with long and tedious travel began to murmer, saying that they would return to their country, for winter was at hand, and if they entered into the harbour, they should not be able to come out again before the next Summer. . . .

All these letters were written by M. *Antonio* to Messer *Carlo* his brother; and it grieves me that the books and various other writings concerning these purposes are miserably lost: for being but a child when they came to my hands, and not knowing what they were, (as the manner of children is) I tore them, and rent them in pieces, which now I cannot remember but to my exceeding great grief. Notwithstanding, so that the memory of so many good things should not be left, whatsoever I could get of this matter, I have disposed and put in order in the former discourse, to the end that this age might be partly satisfied, to which we are more beholden for the great discoveries made in those parts than to any other of the time past, being most studious of the new relations and discoveries of strange countries made by the great minds and industry of our ancestors.

2 It wasn't until the Arctic explorer Robert Peary reached the North Pole in 1909 that Greenland was finally proven to be an island, unattached to any continental landmass.

3 Samuel Purchas, *Purchas his Pilgrimes* (London, 1626), 807; also in F.W. Lucas, *Annals of the Voyages of the Brothers Antonio and Nicolo Zeno* (London: Hakluyt Society, 1873), 37.

4 Lucas 30. Dr. Dee was actively involved in England's search for the Northwest Passage. As an astrologer and mathematician, he advised some of Britain's most distinguished navigators, such as Martin Frobisher and John Davis, in their exploration of the New World. Dr. Dee, like Robert Thorne, fifty years earlier, and other intellectuals and geographers of the day, believed that when explorers approached the North Pole they would find the weather warm and the seas free of ice. The writings of these men prompted the voyage of Henry Hudson in 1607, when he attempted to sail from England directly over the North Pole to Cathay.

5 Major identifies these islands as: Talas (Yelli), Broas (East and West Barras), Iscant (Unst), Trans (St. Ronan's Isle), Mimant (Mainland), Dambere (Hamna) and Bres (Bressay).

CHAPTER VII
Buss Island

1 Samuel Eliot Morison, *The Great Explorers: The European Discovery of America* (New York: Oxford University Press, 1978), 278.

2 Miller Christy, *Expeditions to Greenland, 1605-1612* (London: Hakluyt Society, 1896), 166.

3 Christy 167.

4 Alice Johnson, "The Mythical Land of Buss," *The Beaver* (Dec. 1942), 44.

5 Samuel Purchas, *Purchas his Pilgrimes* (1625) III: 582.

6 Christy 173.

7 Christy 177.

8 E.E. Rich, ed. *Minutes of the Hudson's Bay Company, 1671-1674* (Toronto: Champlain Society, 1942), B:151.

9 Johnson 44.

10 The name first selected for this island was Saint Brendan, which would have been a most appropriate counterpart to the Island of Smiths described in Brendan's *Navigatio*. Instead, the name Surtsey was derived from Surt, leader of the five giants in Norse mythology. In the story of *Ragnarok* (Doom of the Gods), Surt rode over the Bridge of Bifrost (Rainbow Bridge, or Milky Way) which leads from this world to the realm of Asgard. There, he defeated Odin, hero of their warriers, captured Asgard, and consumed by fire the great hall of Valhalla.

11 Christy 181.

12 Christy 183

13 Henry S. Poole, "The Sunken Land of Bus (lat. 35 west, long. 53 north)." *Proceedings and Transactions of the Nova Scotia Institute of Science* 11 (April 1904), 193.

14 Poole 193.

15 Christy 202.

16 Christy 179.

17 Johnson 47.

18 Hudson's Bay Company Archives, Provincial Archives of Manitoba, RG20/4/29 "Buss Island," Memorandum, 21 June 1934, Leveson Gower to the Secretary [HBC], 3 and 4.

19 Hudson's Bay Company Archives, Memorandum, 21 June, 1934, 3.

CHAPTER VIII
Antillia

1 Kenneth Baxter Wolf, trans. "Chronicle of Alfonso III," *Conquerors and Chroniclers of Early Medieval Spain*. Translated Texts for Historians, Vol. 9 (Liverpool: Liverpool University Press, 1990), 50.

2 Wolf 36.

3 William H. Babcock, *Legendary Islands of the Atlantic: A Study in Medieval Geography* (Plainview, NY: Books for Libraries, 1972), 11.

4 Armando Cortesão, *A Study in the History of Early Navigation and Cartography* (Coimbra, Portugal: University of Coimbra Press, 1954), 72.

5 From *Tratado dos Diversos e Desuayrados Caminhos*, Lisboa, 1563, 8:22, in Henry Harrisse, *The Discovery of North America: A Critical, Documentary and Historic Investigation* (London: Henry Stevens, 1892), 3:51.

6 Samuel Eliot Morison, *Portuguese Voyages to America in the Fifteenth Century* (Cambridge: Harvard University Press, 1940), 21.

7 Jaime Cortesão, *A Viagem de Diogo de Teive e Pero Vasquez de la Frontera ao Banco da Terra Nova em 1452 (The Journey of Diogo de Teive and Pero Vasquez [Teive's pilot] to the Frontier of the Terra Nova [Newfoundland] Banks in 1452)*, in Harrisse, *The Discovery of North America*, 655.

8 Thomas Johnson Westropp, "Brasil and the Legendary Islands of the North Atlantic: Their History and Fable. A Contribution to the Atlantic Problem," *Proceedings of the Royal Irish Academy* 30:C:8 (Dublin: Hodges, Figgis, 1912), 248.

9 From *Alguns Documentos da Torre do Tombo*, 41, in Armando Cortesão, 70.

10 Armando Cortesão 70.

11 *The Journal of Christopher Columbus . . . and Documents Relating to the Voyages of John Cabot and Gaspar Corte Real* (London: Hakluyt Society, 1893), 9.

12 A complete discussion of the Toscanelli letter is in Felipe Fernández-Armesto, *Columbus*, and a transcription of the letter is in *The Journal of Christopher Columbus . . . and Documents relating to the Voyages of John Cabot and Gaspar Corte Real*, 9. The date of this letter to Martins was June 24, 1474, but Toscanelli's copy of it to Columbus was undated. From its content it appears to have been written in July of that same year. The map which accompanied it became the property of Las Casas after the death of Christopher Columbus and his son Ferdinand. Subsequently, it was lost. As for the original letter in Latin from Toscanelli to Martins, there remains only a copy of it written by Columbus himself. Invariably, any mention of this famous Toscanelli letter is accompanied by the phrase "of doubtful authenticity," yet the case for its validity is much stronger than any put forth for doubting it.

13 Henry Percival Biggar, *The Precursors of Jacques Cartier, 1497-1543: A Collection of Documents Relating to the Early History of the Dominion of Canada* (Ottawa: Canadian Archives, 1911).

14 *Archivo di Stato*, Milan, Venetian Transcripts, No. 195, in H.P. Biggar, *Precursors of Cartier*, 15.

15 Harrisse, *Cabot*, 328.

16 Fridtjof Nansen, *In Northern Mists: Arctic Exploration in Early Times* (New York: Stokes, 1911), 325.

17 Whether these two men were merely repeating what they had heard from Cabot about the distance (400 leagues) or converted the distance to leagues of their own country is unknown.

18 Armando Cortesão 72.

19 Babcock 149-63.

CHAPTER IX
Hy-Brazil

1 As with so many of these tales, an Islamic counterpart can be found. A tenth-century anonymous Arab author tells about an island in the west:

In the great ocean is an island which is visible at sea at some distance, but if one tries to approach it, it withdraws and disappears. If one returns to the place one started from, it is seen again as before. In this tale, it is not fire that fixes the island and prevents its concealment, but a little fish called *shakil* that must be carried by the sailor if he is to discover the island. Upon this island is a tree that sprouts at sunrise, grows and strengthens as the sun ascends in the sky, and disappears at sunset — then starts the cycle over again the next day: the sun-tree of Indian legends.

2 Harrisse, *Discovery of North America*, 659.

3 Harrisse, *Discovery of North America*, 659.

4 *Journal of Christopher Columbus . . . and Documents Relating to the Voyages of John Cabot and Gaspar Corte Real*, 210.

5 Westropp 257. If only one of Westropp's group had not exclaimed that he "could see New York," the story would be a bit more credible.

6 This letter is found in its entirety in George C. Carey, "Enchanted-Island Traditions of the Sixteenth and Seventeenth Centuries," *Atlantic Neptune* 29: 2 (Oct. 1969), 275-281.

7 Westropp 246, 247.

CHAPTER X
Saint Ursula

1 Jacobus de Voragine, *Lives of the Saints: The Golden Legend* (London: Longmans, Green, 1941). The synopsis of the tale of Saint Ursula and the quotations are taken from this book.

2 Bartolomé de Las Casas, *Historia de las Indias* (New York: Harper & Row, 1971), 44.

3 It is difficult to tell which of the Virgin Islands Columbus had in view when he named the largest one Saint Ursula; St. Thomas, St. John and Tortula are roughly the same size. Probably his angle of approach to these islands caused one of them to appear larger than the others.

CHAPTER XI
Saint Brendan

1 Whitley Stokes, ed. and trans., *Lives of Saints from the Book of Lismore (The Book of Mac Carthy Reagh)* (Oxford: Clarendon Press 1890), 248.

2 Stokes 349.

3 John O'Meara, *The Voyage of Saint Brendan: Journey to the Promised Land* (Dublin: Dolmen Press, 1978).

4 Asia is the name of the Roman province in western Asia Minor at the time of John

(the end of first century AD) and geographically corresponds with present-day Turkey. The seven churches are: Ephesus, Smyrna, Sardis, Pergamum, Thyatira, Philadelphia and Laodicen. It may be taken from this that God, through John, is giving a message to the *whole* Church.

5 The Bible used for this and all subsequent quotations is *The New American Bible: Saint Joseph Edition* (New York: Catholic Book Publishing Co., 1970).

6 Mas'ûdî, *The Book of Wonders*, Ch. 8, "Description of the Land and Seas," p. 110, ¶ 286.

7 Saint Enda died c. 540 and was buried at Tighlagheany on Inishmore in the Aran Islands, where some remains of the school he founded are still to be seen.

8 Tim Severin, *The Brendan Voyage* (New York: McGraw-Hill, 1978).

9 Severin 246.

10 Friar Alonso de Espinosa, *The Guanches of Tenerife: The Holy Image of Our Lady of Candelaria, and the Spanish Conquest and Settlement* (Nendeln, Liechtenstein: Kraus Reprint, 1972).

11 Espinosa 29.

12 Before Saint Brendan sets forth, three additional brothers from his monastery join the pilgrimage, but none of the three remains to the end of the voyage. They are a divisive force and must be disposed of before the voyage can come to a successful conclusion. The source of the three additional monks is uncertain. If the secular Irish *immram* of Máel Dúin was known before the *Navigatio* became a written text, as some authors suggest, the three latecomers could have been derived from this source; indeed, Máel Dúin visits twenty-nine islands and encounters many wondrous events, some of which are almost identical to those of Saint Brendan's voyage. Or the three latecomers may be an amalgamation of the voyage of Saint Brendan with another legend from Brendan's life. The Book of Lismore contains a story of three young Irish clerics who went to sea on a pilgrimage. Two of them died, but the third lived on an island "until he was aged and withered, and till Brenainn [Brendan] came from the sea; and Brenainn blessed him and gave his communion and sacrifice, and so he went to heaven; and a watch of angels is always over them in their island."

13 Ashe 56.

14 Saint Isidore of Seville, *Etymologiae,* Book 14, Ch. 6, in Dicuil *"Liber de Mensura Orbis Terrae*, 115.

15 Leo Bagrow, *History of Cartography* (Cambridge: Harvard University Press, 1964), 50.

16 The seven named Canary Islands are: Louno Marin (Lobos), Lancaroto (Lanzarote), Ysola Forte Ventura (Fuerteventura), Ysola de Canarie (Gran Canaria), Ysola del Inferno (Tenerife), Ysola de Clarie (Gomera) and Ysola de Palmer (Palma). Lobos, a small islet at the northeast extremity of Fuerteventura, is not considered one of the seven principal Canary Islands. The remaining unnamed island is Hierro.

Bibliography

Aristotle. *Meteorologica*. Translated by H.D.P. Lee. Cambridge: Harvard University Press, 1962.

Ashe, Geoffrey. *Land to the West: St. Brendan's Voyage to America*. New York: Viking, 1962.

Baarslag, Karl. *Islands of Adventure*. New York: Farrar & Rinehart, 1940.

Babcock, William H. *Early Norse Visits to North America*. Smithsonian Miscellaneous Collections 59:19. Washington: Smithsonian, 1913.

Babcock, William H. *Legendary Islands of the Atlantic: A Study in Medieval Geography*. American Geographical Society Research Series 8. Greenwich, CT: Condé Nast, 1922. Rpt. Plainview, NY: Books for Libraries, 1972.

Bagrow, Leo. *History of Cartography*. Revised and enlarged by R.A. Skelton. 2nd ed. Cambridge: Harvard University Press, 1964.

Baxter, James Phinney. *A Memoir of Jacques Cartier, Sieur de Limoilou: His Voyages to the St. Lawrence*. New York: Dodd, Mead, 1906.

Beazley, Raymond C. *The Dawn of Modern Geography*. Vols. 1, 2. London: John Murray, 1897. Rpt. Oxford: Clarendon, 1949.

Beck, Horace. *Folklore and the Sea*. Middletown, CT: Wesleyan University Press and Marine Historical Assoc., 1973.

Biggar, Henry Percival, ed. *The Precursors of Jacques Cartier, 1497-1534: A Collection of Documents Relating to the Early History of the Dominion of Canada*. Publication of the Public Archives of Canada, No. 5. Ottawa: Government Printing Bureau, 1911.

Biggar, Henry Percival, ed. *A Collection of Documents Relating to Jacques Cartier and the Sieur de Roberval*. Publication of the Public Archives of Canada, No. 14. Ottawa: n.p., 1930.

Book of the Knowledge of all the Kingdoms, Lands, and Lordships that are in the World, and the Arms and Devices of each Land and Lordship, or of the Kings and Lords who Possess Them (1340). Translated and edited by Clements R. Markham. Notes by Marcos Jimenez de la Espada (1877). London: Hakluyt Society, 1912. Rpt. Nendeln, Liechtenstein: Kraus Reprint, 1967.

Bricker, Charles. *Landmarks of Mapmaking: An Illustrated Survey of Maps and Map-makers.* Amsterdam: Elsevier, 1968.

Carey, George G. "Enchanted-island Traditions of the Sixteenth and Seventeenth Centuries." *Atlantic Neptune* 29: 2 (October, 1969).

Christy, Miller. *Expeditions to Greenland, 1605-1612.* London: Hakluyt Society, 1896.

Conyngham, David Power. *Lives of the Irish Saints and Martyrs.* New York: D. & J. Sadlier, 1885.

Cortesão, Armando. *A Study in the History of Early Navigation and Cartography.* Coimbra, Portugal: University of Coimbra Press, 1954.

Cruden, Alexander. *Cruden's Useful Concordance of the Holy Scriptures.* Old Tappan, NJ: Revell, 1977.

Dicuil. "*Liber de Mensura Orbis Terrae.*" Edited by J.J. Tierney. *Scriptores Latini Hiberniae* VI. Dublin: Dublin Institute for Advanced Studies, 1967.

Dunbabin, Thomas. "The Elusive Island of Busse." *Canadian Geographical Journal* 55:3 (Sept. 1957).

Espinosa, Alonso de. *The Guanches of Tenerife: The Holy Image of Our Lady of Candelaria, and the Spanish Conquest and Settlement.* Translated and edited by Clements R. Markham. Nendeln, Liechtenstein: Kraus Reprint, 1972

Farmer, David Hugh, ed. *Oxford Dictionary of Saints.* 2nd ed. Oxford: Oxford University Press, 1987.

Fernández-Armesto, Felipe. *Columbus.* Oxford: Oxford University Press, 1992.

Firestone, Clark B. *The Coasts of Illusion: A Study of Travel Tales.* New York: Harper, 1924.

Francillon, R.E., and F.H. Cowen. *Saint Ursula: Sacred Cantata.* London: Metzler, 1937.

Ganong, W.F. *Crucial Maps in the Early Cartography and Place-Nomenclature of the Atlantic Coast of Canada.* Toronto: University of Toronto Press with the Royal Society of Canada, 1964.

Geoffrey of Monmouth. *The History of the Kings of Britain.* Translated by Lewis Thorpe. Baltimore: Penguin, 1966.

Grenfell, Wilfred T. *Labrador: The Country and the People.* New York: Macmillan, 1912.

Guedes, Max Justo, and Gerald Lombardi, eds. *Portugal/Brazil: The Age of Atlantic Discoveries.* Exhibition catalogue. New York: New York Public Library, 1990.

Guillaume, M. *The Shrine of Saint Ursula.* Paris: Marion Press, 1939.

Hakluyt, Richard. *The Third and Last Volume of the Voyages, Navigations, Traffiques, and Discoueries of the English Nation.* London: George Bishop, Ralfe Newberie and Robert Barker, 1600.

Hammond, N.G.L., and H.H. Scullard, eds. *Oxford Classical Dictionary.* 2nd ed. Oxford: Clarendon Press, 1970.

Harrisse, Henry. *The Discovery of North America: A Critical, Documentary and Historic Investigation.* London: Henry Stevens, 1792.

_____. *Decouverte et Evolution Cartographique de Terre-Neuve.* Paris and London: Stevens and Styles, 1900.

Harris, R. Cole, ed. *Historical Atlas of Canada, Vol. 1: From the Beginning to 1800.* Toronto: University of Toronto Press, 1987.

Hawkins, Richard. *The Observations of Sir Richard Hawkins.* London: Argonaut, 1933.

Hermannsson, Halldór. *The Cartography of Iceland.* Ithaca, NY: Cornell University Library, 1931.

Hogarth, Donald D. "The *Emmanuel* of Bridgewater and Discovery of Martin Frobisher's 'Black Ore' in Ireland." *Neptune* (Journal of the Peabody Museum), 1991.

Hudson's Bay Company Archives, Provincial Archives of Manitoba, RG20/4/29 "Buss Island."

Hudûd al-'Âlam (The Regions of the World: A Persian Geography). Translated by V. Minorsky. Edited by C.E. Bosworth. London: Luzac, 1970.

Irving, Washington. *Columbus: His Life and Voyages.* New York: Putnam, 1920.

Johnson, Alice M. "The Mythical Land of Buss." *The Beaver* (Journal of the Hudson's Bay Company) (December, 1942).

The Journal of Christopher Columbus (during his first voyage 1492-1493) and Documents Relating to the Voyages of John Cabot and Gaspar Corte Real. Translated by Clements R. Markham. Hakluyt Society Publication No. 86. London: Hakluyt Society, 1843.

Kerr, D.G.G. *Historical Atlas of Canada.* 3rd ed. Toronto: Nelson, 1975.

Khaldûn, Ibn. *Muqaddimah* (An Introduction to History). Translated by Franz Rosenthal. Bollingen Series 43. Princeton: Princeton University Press, 1958.

Khalidi, Taris. *Islamic Historiography: The Histories of Mas'ûdî.* Albany, NY: State University of New York Press, 1975.

Khan, M.S. "Al-Mas'ûdî and the Geography of India." *Zeitschrift der Deutschen Morgenländischen Gesellschaft* 131:1. Wiesbaden: Kommissionsverlag Franz Steiner, 1981.

Las Casas, Bartolomè de. *Historia de las Indias.* Translated and edited by Andrèe Collard. New York: Harper, 1971.

Leahy, Chris. *The Bird Watcher's Companion.* New York: McGraw Hill, 1982.

Lee, H.D.P. *Aristotle's Meteorologica.* Cambridge: Harvard University Press, 1962.

Lescarbot, Marc. *The History of New France.* 3 vols. Toronto: Champlain Society, 1907.

Lucas, Frederick W. *The Annals of the Voyages of the Brothers Nicolò and Antonio Zeno in the North Atlantic About the End of the Fourteenth Century and the Claim Founded Thereon to a Venetian Discovery of America.* London: Stevens and Stiles, 1898.

MacCana, Proinsias. *Celtic Mythology*. London: Hamlyn, 1970.

Mackenzie, W.G. "Disappearing Islands and Other Arctic Phenomena." *North/Nord* 19:4 (July-August 1972).

Major, Richard Henry. *The Voyages of the Venetian Brothers Nicolò and Antonio Zeno, to the Northern Seas, in the XIVth Century, Comprising the Latest Known Accounts of the Lost Colony of Greenland; and of the Northmen in America Before Columbus*. London: Hakluyt Society, 1873.

Marcus, G.J. *The Conquest of the North Atlantic*. New York: Oxford University Press, 1981.

Manny, R. "Navigations Arabes Anonymes aux Canaries au XIIIe Siecle," *Notes Africaines*, 1960.

Morison, Samuel Eliot *The Great Explorers: The European Discovery of America*. New York: Oxford University Press, 1978.

Morison, Samuel Eliot. *Portuguese Voyages to America in the Fifteenth Century*. Cambridge: Harvard University Press, 1940.

Nansen, Fridtjof. *In Northern Mists: Arctic Exploration in Early Times*. Translated by Arthur G. Chater. New York: Stokes, 1911.

Navarre, Marguerite de. *The Heptameron*. Translated and introduced by P.A. Chilton. Aylesbury, England: Penguin, 1984.

The New American Bible, Saint Joseph Edition. New York: Catholic Book Publishing, 1970.

Nordenskiöld, Adolf Erik. *Facsimile-Atlas to the Early History of Cartography, with Reproductions of the Most Important Maps Printed in the XV and XVI Centuries*. Stockholm, 1889. Rpt. New York: Dover, 1973.

O'Hanlon, John. *Lives of the Irish Saints . . . Compiled from Calendars, Martyrologies, and Various Sources Relating to the Ancient Church History of Ireland*. Vol. 5. Dublin: Duffy, 1875.

Oldfather, C.H., trans. *Diodorus Siculus*. Vol. 3. Cambridge: Harvard University Press, 1970.

O'Meara, John, trans. *The Voyage of Saint Brendan: Journey to the Promised Land (Navigatio Sancti Brendani Abbatis)*. Atlantic Highlands, NJ: Dolmen Press and Dublin Humanities Press, 1978.

Parkman, Francis. *Pioneers of France in the New World*. 25th ed. Boston: Little, Brown, 1894.

Plummer, Carolus. *Miscellanea Hagiographica Hibernica: Vitae Adhuc Ineditae Sanctorum Mac Creiche Naile Cranat*. Brussels: Société des Bollandistes, 1925.

Pohl, Frederick. *Atlantic Crossings Before Columbus*. New York: Norton, 1961.

Poole, Henry S. "The Sunken Land of Bus (lat. 35 west, long. 53 north)." *Proceedings and Transactions of the Nova Scotia Institute of Science* 11 (April 1904).

Purchas, Samuel. *Purchas his Pilgrimes, In Five Books, The Third Part, Voyages and Discoveries of the North Parts of the World [etc]*. London, 1625, 1626.

Ramsay, Raymond H. *No Longer on the Map: Discovering Places that Never Were*. New York: Viking, 1972.

Rich, E.E., ed. *Minutes of the Hudson's Bay Company, 1671-1674*. Toronto: Champlain Society, for The Hudson's Bay Record Society, 1942.

Rosenthal, F., trans. *The Muqaddimah*. Bollingen Series 43. Princeton: Princeton University Press, 1958.

Selmer, Carl, ed. *Navigatio Sancti Brendani Abbatis: from Early Latin Manuscripts*. Dublin: Four Courts, 1989.

Severin, Tim. *The Brendan Voyage*. New York, McGraw-Hill, 1978.

Short, Ian, and Brian Merrilees, eds. *The Anglo-Norman Voyage of St. Brendan/Benedeit*. Manchester: Manchester University Press, 1979.

Smallwood, Joseph P., ed. *The Book of Newfoundland*. Vols. 3, 4. St. John's: Newfoundland Book Publishers, 1967.

Stokes, Whitley, ed. and trans. *Lives of the Saints from the Book of Lismore (The Book of Mac Carthy Reagh)*. Oxford: Clarendon Press 1890.

Thurston, Herbert, and Donald Attwater, eds. *Butler's Lives of the Saints*. Vol. 4 (October, November, December) Palm Publishers, Great Britain, 1956.

Tooley, R.V. *Maps and Mapmakers*. London: Batsford, 1949.

Tout, Mary. *Historical Essays: The Legend of Saint Ursula*. Edited by Thomas Frederic Tout and James Tate. London: University of Manchester Press, 1907.

Voragine, Jacobus de. *Lives of the Saints: The Golden Legend*. Translated and adapted by Granger Ryan and Helmut Ripperger. London: Longmans, Green, 1941.

Westropp, Thomas Johnson. "Brasil and the Legendary Islands of the North Atlantic: Their History and Fable. A Contribution to the Atlantic Problem." *Proceedings of the Royal Irish Academy* 30:C:8. Dublin: Hodges, Figgis, 1912.

Winsor, Justin, ed. *Narrative and Critical History of America*. Boston: Houghton, Mifflin, 1889.

Wiseman, E.H., Cardinal. "The Truth of Supposed Legends and Fables," in *Essays on Religion and Literature*. Edited by H.E. Manning. London: Longman, Green, 1865.

Wolf, Kenneth Baxter, trans. *Conquerors and Chroniclers of Early Medieval Spain*. Translated Texts for Historians, Vol. 9. Liverpool: Liverpool University Press, 1990.

Wright, John Kirtland. *The Geographical Lore of the Time of the Crusades: A Study in the History of Medieval Science and Tradition in Western Europe*. New York: American Geographical Society, 1925. Rpt. New York: Dover, 1965.

List of Illustrations

Index